Pops

Popscript:
Graduate Research in Popular Music Studies

Edited by Simone Krüger and Ron Moy
Liverpool John Moores University, UK

Lulu Press

For our students

Table of Contents

List of Illustrations

About the Editors

Simone Krüger is a Programme Leader in Popular Music Studies at Liverpool John Moores University, UK, with research interests in ethnomusicology and world music pedagogy, music education (ethnography education and employability), popular music and cultural studies, globalization, and the music of Paraguay. She is the author of *Experiencing Ethnomusicology: Teaching and Learning in European Universities* (Ashgate 2009) and *Popular Musics in World Perspective* (Polity forthcoming), co-editor of *The Globalization of Musics in Transit: Music Migration and Tourism* (Routledge 2013), guest editor of *Ethnomusicology in the Academy: International Perspectives* (The World of Music 2009), and editor of the *Journal of World Popular Music* (Equinox). Correspondence to: Liverpool John Moores University, School of Art and Design, 2 Duckinfield Road, Liverpool L3 5RY, s.kruger@ljmu.ac.uk.

Ron Moy has lectured in the field of Popular Music Studies since 1992. Amongst his publications are *An Analysis of the Position and Status of Sound Ratio in Contemporary Society* (Edwin Mellen 2000); *Popular Music Genres: An Introduction* (with Stuart Borthwick, Edinburgh UP 2004); *Kate Bush and Hounds of Love* (Ashgate 2007) and the forthcoming *Authorship Roles in Popular Music: Issues and Debates* (Routledge [expected] 2015). He has recently made a scholarly contribution to the Liverpool Tate exhibition 'Glam: the Performance of Style'. Correspondence to: Liverpool John Moores University, School of Art and Design, 2 Duckinfield Road, Liverpool L3 5RY, R.D.Moy@ljmu.ac.uk.

Introduction

Simone Krüger and Ron Moy

Thank you for picking up this book, which we entitled *Popscript* to describe the content presented here, namely writings about popular music. The idea underpinning the book emerged during discussions in our office at Liverpool John Moores University about the sad fact that most undergraduate research and writing is usually read by a mere handful of people, but it often deserves a much wider readership, given its quality and rigour, and the passion and commitment invested by students in their research and writing. We therefore thought it would be wonderful to reward students by bringing their best work into the public domain, and we found that the incentive of being published in a book edited by their tutors provided an extra level of stimulus and encouragement to produce work of the highest quality.

Inside this book, you will find several examples of written work produced by our final year students on the BA Popular Music Studies at Liverpool John Moores University who completed their degree in 2014. We hope this selection of their work will demonstrate something of the talent and diversity of interests that we nurture as part of this degree. The work has been chosen on merit, with only the very best pieces being chosen from the assignments submitted by the whole cohort, but we must also give credit to all the final year students, who have recently contributed to making the degree so successful and fulfilling for staff and students. Most of these essays were written as part of the study module, which was led by Ron and allowed students the freedom to choose their own research topic and methodology. Although students were given tutorial guidance, the resulting studys are very much their own and all the more impressive as a result.

We hope you enjoy *Popscript* and recommend it to friends, tutors, peers and others who study popular music or have an interest in research and writing about popular music. No profit is being made from the book, which is available for free in hardcopy and e-book format. Just a brief note on copyright: Any copyrighted material reproduced in this book, such as literary (written), dramatic (theatrical), musical, artistic work (art, photographs etc) is used here for the sole purpose of non-commercial research and private study and is supported by a sufficient acknowledgment (see http://www.ipo.gov.uk/types/copy/c-other/c-exception/c-exception-research.htm, accessed 5 May 2014).

CHAPTER 1

David Sylvian, Personae and Authenticity

Sarah O'Hara

David Sylvian's transition from Japan frontman to solo and collaborative artist has always been of immense interest to me. The Japan album *Gentlemen take Polaroids* (Sylvian 1980) has provided hours of listening pleasure due to its atonal melodies and experiments with sound. However, the change in visual and musical aesthetics between Japan's inception in 1976 and Sylvian's solo career leads one to question Sylvian as an ever-changing performer through analysis of genre and personae. Thus this raised the question – why did Sylvian use personae such as the one presented on the *Gentlemen take Polaroids* album, and why was there a sudden shift towards changing both his sound and image?

The first section will focus on the Nightporter persona constructed on the *Gentlemen take Polaroids* album, examining its main characteristics and visual attributes. This will include an analysis of the album's cover art work that features Sylvian alone and as the sole focus of the band Japan. Additionally songs such as 'The Nightporter', 'Gentlemen take Polaroids' and 'Taking Islands in Africa' (Sylvian 1980) will be analysed for themes that relate to the character's construction that market Sylvian in a particular way to audiences. However by applying theories of authenticity and persona, the Nightporter will be deconstructed to reveal how creating a character to reinforce a musician's status as 'authentic' actually contradicts it.

The second section will focus again on Sylvian's Nightporter persona, but instead the analyses will shift to the concept of authorship. Firstly through an analysis of the synth-pop genre in relation to the songs on *Gentlemen take Polaroids*, in particular 'Burning Bridges', it will be discussed how Sylvian's authoring of the bands uncommercial and avant-garde sound reinforced his own ideological position as 'authentic'. However by applying theories of authorship to Sylvian's persona, it will then be discussed how regardless of any authorial or ideological intentions Sylvian may have had in the utilisation of this persona, authored meaning does not lie with the creator but with the audience who receive the image and the media who market it.

Both sections will serve to prove my hypostudy: That the utilisation of personae and genre by Sylvian represents his desire to author himself as an 'authentic' performer, although the use of persona and the way it was interpreted by audiences and the media problematises the notion of Sylvian as 'authentic'.

Methodology & Literature Review

Having chosen David Sylvian as the subject of research, it had to be decided what concepts in particular would be the basis of the analysis within the following study. Having read the biography *David Sylvian: The Last Romantic* (Power 2004) it had come to my attention that Sylvian had undergone a series of transformations from glam rock adolescent, to synth-pop pioneer and avant-garde composer within his musical career. However alongside these changes in musical genre were changes in image, with Power stating that upon embarking on a solo career David Sylvian:

> Also chose to abandon the heavily stylised image that had brought him success in the first place in favour of a nondescript appearance and positively spectral public profile. (2004:9)

This raised significant questions about why he would choose to change his famous feminised public appearance alongside a change in genre from synth-pop to avant-garde. Thus it was decided to focus on the persona utilised on the *Gentlemen take Polaroids* album (Virgin 1980), as I was curious to analyse what problems arose from this persona that would possibly be the catalyst for Sylvian changing both his image and sound. However upon reading accounts from former Japan manager Simon Napier Bell in the book *Black Vinyl: White Powder* (2002) a hypostudy began to form:

> He was sixties Jagger crossed with teenage Bardot; young Elvis with adolescent Fonda; instantly provocative, pouting and sultry. He wasn't camp, nor even slightly effeminate, he was self-creation, an obviously unique species created from months of hard work in a front of a bedroom mirror. (2001:221)

This notion of self-creation suggested that Sylvian intentionally sculpted and authored a specific public image, in order to market himself in a particular manner to audiences. Napier-Bell's comment that 'If anyone came into the studio and said what Japan were recording sounded like a hit, David stopped working on it. He was afraid of producing anything that sounded crassly commercial' (in Reynolds 2013:79) also suggested a broader question in regards to authenticity. Was Sylvian intentionally authoring specific personae that would market himself as an 'authentic' musician to audiences? Thus the first part of one's study for this study, as stated in the introduction, was formed.

Although both *David Sylvian: The Last Romantic* and *Black Vinyl, White Powder* were useful in initially informing my understanding of Sylvian's career, in addition to my own knowledge of his musical works, relevant literature was vital in providing theories on which I could base my own analysis of the use of personae and notions of authenticity and authorship within Sylvian's career. The literature reviewed raised three significant themes, which will be subsequently discussed below.

Persona

Literature relevant to this theme includes *Persona and Performance: The meaning of role in Drama, Therapy and Everyday Life* (Landy 1993) and *Faking it: The Quest for authenticity in Popular Music* (Barker & Taylor 2007). Landy defines persona in relation to theatre as being able to 'communicate a feeling or idea through a character' (1993:73), suggesting that personae are constructions rather than reflections of the actual performer. This immediately began to contradict notions of authenticity in relation to Sylvian, as it helped me to understand how persona are not actually a reflection of the musician. This was a useful starting point for my own analyses of the Nightporter persona. However whereas Landy situates personae in a theatrical context, Barker and Taylor situate the discussion of personae in relation to popular music, providing a more direct link to one's study in relation to persona, authenticity and music.

Whereas Landy's theories are useful in understanding some the roles of personae within performance, Barker and Taylor further this discussion by placing the discussion in relation to the concept of authenticity. As authenticity is a main theme in both sections when discussing persona and authenticity, this text was exceedingly useful in helping one to understand the ways that musicians use persona to reinforce their own desires to be seen as 'authentic'. They argue that there are two ways a performer can address the concept of authenticity: either by glorifying the difference between your persona and the 'real' musician, or by fusing the two. The first way was particularly relevant to the discussion of Sylvian's representation on the *Gentlemen take Polaroids* album, as it helped me to understand that theatricality and authenticity are usually not associated with one another in popular music through examples of performers such as Madonna. This linked to the analysis of Sylvian's image in particular. Thus as authenticity and personae were two of the focuses within the study, both these books would serve to aid my understanding and support my own analyses of Sylvian's personae. Having found a base text for discussions around authenticity, I decided to source other texts that would define authenticity in relation to popular music and aid my own understanding of how authenticity is constructed.

Authenticity

Literature relevant to this theme includes *The Popular Music Studies Reader* (Bennett, Shank, & Toynbee, ed. 2006), which includes discussions of authenticity in relation popular music and performance. Barry Shank argued that authenticity was 'not simply a matter of romantic self-expression or a faithful devotion to a strict interpretation of tradition, but rather is a result of a thoughtful self-reflection on one's own conditions of possibility' (2006:56). This suggested that authenticity is not a reflection of fantasy, but rather should define the musician in relation to reality, thus creating the idea that musicians who use characters as a public image rather than their own image are not 'authentic'. This was useful in reinforcing the previous theories of authenticity reviewed in Barker and Taylor's book, and began building my own idea of what authenticity was in relation to popular music performers. Additionally *The Popular Music Studies Reader*, unlike *Faking it: The Quest for Authenticity in Popular Music*, was published on an academic label (Routledge) signifying its scholarly underpinning. This was useful as the texts describing Sylvian. *David Sylvian: The Last Romantic* and *Black Vinyl: White Powder* were primarily reflections or journalistic interpretations of his career. Thus reviewing academic literature in relation to concepts such as authenticity helped to provide an objective analysis of Sylvian's image and sound rather than a subjective opinion of it. In considering that Sylvian authored a particular image to be perceived an 'authentic' by audiences, further literature in regards to authorship were reviewed.

Authorship

Literature relevant to this theme includes *Judith Butler: Live theory* (Kirby 2006) and the Roland Barthes essay 'The Death of the Author' (1968). Both raise a similar issue in relation to authorship – that the creator a text is not the author but that the author is actually the reader who interprets meaning from a text, or the institution who actively seeks to present an artist associated with them in a certain way. For example Barthes suggests that 'the birth of the reader must be at the cost of the death of the author' (Barthes 1968; Grant 2008:100). Additionally Judith Butler's theories of post-structuralism were useful in understand authorship as a problematic notion in regards to the artist, suggesting that institutions of power result in the text (in the case of this study– Sylvian's public persona) being 'formed in submission' (Butler; Kirby 2006:109).

Through reviewing authorship theory by academic scholars and theorists, this aiding my understanding in regards to how although a musician may wish to be perceived in a certain way to the audience, there are other cultural factors such as the media that contradict any creative and authorial intention. Thus this helped to form the second part of this study's study – that the marketing of Sylvian's personae problematizes his status as an 'authentic' musician.

Having reviewed academic and non-academic literature in relation to the three concepts of persona, authenticity and authorship, I was able to start planning out the two sections included within this study. By firstly discussing the creation of persona, I was able to analyse how firstly Sylvian's own use of persona contradicted any ideological position in regards to authenticity. However this discussion then raised the question of whether Sylvian had any control over how he was perceived by audiences and within the media, thus leading into the second section's discussion in relation to authorship.

Once I had understood theories in relation to these concepts, they were applied to analyses of the Nightporter persona. This was through an analysis of the songs on the album, and how they characterised this persona lyrically through signified meaning. Additionally as a majority of marketing was focused heavily on Sylvian's image within the press, analyses of the album cover for *Gentlemen take Polaroids* were undertaken in relation to the theories in the texts reviewed. This analysis of image also led to reviewing teen press magazines in the 1980's, particularly *Smash Hits* magazine that in 1980 used the album cover as a selling point for one of their issues. These covers were analysed from the *Smash Hits* compilation book - *The Best of Smash Hits: The 80's* (Frith, ed. 2006).

Through this methodology and subsequent literature review, the following studywas formed.

'Nightporters come; Nightporters go…Nightporters slip away':

David Sylvian and personae

The following section discusses theories of authenticity in relation to personae and the musical texts of David Sylvian. The discussion of personae will relate directly to the album *Gentlemen take Polaroids* (Virgin Records 1980). In considering theories of authenticity and personae, this section will serve to support the hypostudy that the way Sylvian represents himself on this album problemastises his status as an 'authentic' musician.

Sylvian is accredited as the primary songwriter on not only his own solo albums, but also on a majority of Japan albums including *Gentlemen take Polaroids* and has commented on his control over the band's musical direction: 'I tend to be too much of a perfectionist. It caused a lot of problems in the studio' (Sylvian in Reynolds 2013:80), adding that 'The feeling between members wasn't too good because I was putting limitations on them' (Ibid.:82). This signifies Sylvian's desire to be seen as an auteur and the main creative force within the group, which is supported by Shuker's definition that Auteur theory 'identify popular music auteurs as producers of 'art', extending the cultural form and, in the process, challenging the listeners' (Shuker 2012:20). Considering Shuker's definition it can be argued that Sylvian's creative control over his solo compositions and Japan's music reflected his desire to create non-mainstream music. For example in 'Burning Bridges' (Sylvian 1980), the song does not follow the strict linear song writing pattern of intro, verse, chorus, verse, chorus, middle eight, chorus, out-tro. Instead the largely instrumental track combines synstudyer and saxophone melodies until the final minute when Sylvian's vocals enter – 'It's all behind me now, the world is done'. This lyric suggests Sylvian searching for a new direction for his music after the largely glam-rock ethos of past albums *Adolescent Sex* (Hansa Ariola 1977) and *Obscure Alternatives* (Hansa Ariola 1978), whilst the irregular song structure and length of the track (5 minutes 20 seconds) signifies a desire to produce uncommercial, challenging music. This choice to consciously create challenging music therefore certifies his wish to be seen as an auteur, and an 'authentic' musician, which is supported by Roy Shuker's statement that 'applying auteur theory to popular music means distinguishing it from mass or popular culture'. However this raises a broader issue – although a musician such as Sylvian wishes to be represented as 'authentic', how do they ensure that they are represented in such a way?

Hugh Barker and Yuval Taylor theorise that there are two ways that a performer can choose to represent themselves to an audience:

1) The first is to glorify the degree to which you are faking it – to theatrically celebrate your ability to perform a role and to take on a persona or series that is clearly not meant to reflect the real you. (2007:244)

2) The second approach to this problem is for the performer to try minimise the gap between person and persona. To do this you must try to project the authentic person and also live up to the persona that you project. (2007:245)

Both ways contemplate the idea of using a persona within popular music to communicate a desired representation to the audience. Personae have been widely discussed in academic literature, particularly in relation to theatre. Drama theorist Landy suggests that 'A primary function of the performer role is to communicate a feeling or idea through a character' (1993:73). This definition of performers as characters, a representation of a personae rather than a reflection of the person themselves, problemastises authenticity in relation performance when applied to popular music. For example, Hugh Barker and Yuval Taylor argue that 'theatricality and authenticity tend to remain at opposite musical poles' (2007:244), whilst Roy Shuker further supplements this by suggesting that:

> Authenticity assumes that the producers of musical texts undertook the 'creative work' themselves; that there is an element of originality or creativity present, along with connotations of seriousness, sincerity and uniqueness. (2012:22).

It can therefore be suggested that although the musician may write their own lyrics or contribute musically to a composition, by adopting a persona within popular music the performer's own self-identity can be questioned. This is because the persona is a theatrical tool that does not reflect their own personality, and more so a cultivation of the way they want to be perceived by audiences.

However, in considering Sylvian's representation on the *Gentlemen take Polaroids* album, it be considered that this personae was consciously constructed to reflect and communicate a particular set of ideologies through the music (the first method suggested by Barker and Taylor). However through an analysis of his 'Nightporter' persona this will serve to support the hypostudy that this representation problematises notions of authenticity within Sylvian's musical texts.

It can be considered that Sylvian's 'Nightporter' persona on the *Gentlemen take Polaroids* album is a constructed character that problemastises Sylvian's authenticity because of issues surrounding the abandonment of personal identity. When theorising the concept of personal identity, Jonathan Rée suggests that:

> The problem of personal identity, one may say, arises from play-acting and the adoption of artificial voices; the origins of distinct personalities, in acts of personation and impersonation. The accomplishment of a storyteller, rather than the attribute of a character…the concept of narrative, in other words, is not so much a justification of the idea of personal identity, as an elucidation of its structure as an inescapable piece of make-believe. (Rée in Frith 1996:273).

Rée's theory appears to suggest that personal identity is problematised when a performer adopts what he calls an 'artificial voice' (Ibid). This voice can thus be interpreted as a persona. In doing so it can be argued that the performer becomes a storyteller with a distinct set of ideologies attributed to that particular persona that are communicated through a narrative, which in the case of popular music is told through lyrics. This is supported by drama theorist Landy who describes the performer's creative process as 'one of projection, imposing their visions and images upon fictional characters who are both similar to and different from the artists' (1993:161). Additionally the idea of projecting images was reinforced by Sylvian in a *Smash Hits* interview – 'Our albums are based on imagery and building up a certain atmosphere which the listener can lose himself in', (Sylvian 1982:86), signifying that the lyrics on the Japan albums were not necessarily a reflection of Sylvian himself but an embodiment of Ree's 'artificial voice'.

Although biographer Martin Power suggests that on the *Gentlemen take Polaroids* album, 'Nightporter marked the first real example of Sylvian using first person narrative to convey a sense of longing and regret to his audience', it can be argued upon closer analysis of the lyrics they exemplify the idea of Ree's 'artificial voice'. For example the lyrics on 'Nightporter' (Sylvian 1980) raise three significant themes for the duration of the song. At the beginning Sylvian sings 'Could I ever explain, this feeling of love it just lingers on. The fear in my heart that keeps telling me which way to turn', connoting romance and longing for another person. The chorus 'Here I am alone again, a quiet town where life gives in' signifies escapism, and combined with the themes raised by the verse creates the ideology that romance can provide this escape.

Whereas the use of the pronoun 'I' could be interpreted by audiences as being a reference to Sylvian himself, these three themes are recurrent throughout the entirety of the album as shown in the examples below:

Song	Example lyrics	Themes
'Gentlemen take Polaroids' (Sylvian, 1980)	'There's a girl about town I'd like to go, I'd like to slip away with you. If you said you loved me, how could I mind'	Love, longing & escapism
'My new career' (Sylvian, 1980)	'I never wanted to be on my own, I could be wrong but I just slipped away from	Longing & escapism

	home'	
'Taking Islands in Africa' (Sylvian, 1980)	'Taking islands in Africa, watch the slow boat hit and run. Outside there's a world waiting, I'll take it all by storm'	Romance, longing & escapism

The repeated use of these themes throughout the album appears to build up a picture of Sylvian's persona as an escapist and romantic figure who travels frequently. Landy has suggested that 'society and culture, taken together, are powerful determinants of how, when, and why we take on and play out our roles' (1993:149), suggesting that personae such as the Nightporter are reactions to the social and cultural experiences musicians encounter in their lives. Sylvian has commented on his life growing up, stating in one interview that 'I have been teaching myself all my life, trying to correct the impressions forced upon me in childhood. I felt trapped when I was eight. I've always hated authority' (Sylvian in Eggar 1982:15). Sylvian's creation of a romantic and constantly travelling persona can therefore be considered an embodiment of the psychoanalytical Ego, which has been defined as 'mastering the threats of trauma' (Kohut and Levarie 1957:406). It can be argued that Sylvian is therefore living out these romantic and escapist ideologies through the Nightporter character, and thus mastering his trauma of having certain ideologies thrust upon him growing up.

It has been suggested that 'music produces in us a state that operates somewhat like a dream in the psychoanalytical sense' (Tailor & Paperte in Shepherd & Wicke 1997:60), whilst Shepherd & Wicke further this to argue that 'if a dream memory is easily forgotten…in a work of art the unconscious symbolism stands permanently embodied…we cannot forget it or destroy it thus' (1997:61). These statements create the ideology that music can communicate the unconscious or repressed desires of a performer, which in the case of the Nightporter persona seem to reflect Sylvian's repressed desires to escape his formative years. Whilst lyrically the character represented reflects how Sylvian wishes to live (thus abandoning any sense of personal identity), his physical representation on the *Gentlemen take Polaroids* album cover further challenges of authenticity in relation to Sylvian's personae.

It has been considered that 'authenticity is rarely an issue with music for which the performer intentionally adopts a theatrical approach' (Barker & Taylor 2007:244). However upon analysis of the cover of the *Gentlemen take Polaroids* album it can be considered that a theatrical approach was adopted by Sylvian in regards to his appearance, thus opposing a representation of the 'real' and 'authentic' Sylvian. For example he is featured alone on the cover, wearing heavy make-up and dressed all in black. The make-up can be interpreted as a mask, which creates the ideology that the representation of Sylvian on the cover as the Nightporter is an assumed identity of which to hide behind, again reinforcing the theme of escapism explored in the lyrics. This is supported by Landy's theory that:

> Underneath the persona is a lost person, a stranger. In quality the performer role is like a narcotic – addictive and capable of blocking out the pull and responsibilities of other roles. It offers a momentary fix, but leaves an emptiness behind, a desire for more. The performer role helps one distance from the reality of the everyday. (1993:72).

Landy's suggestion that the persona 'helps one distance from the reality of the everyday' is reinforced by the binary opposites of the black clothing worn by Sylvian on the front cover, and the rain that surrounds him. Black connotes death whereas rain connotes water and new life, creating the ideology that through this persona, Sylvian is portraying a desire to be reborn into a new existence through a new identity.

However in regards to identity and authenticity, Barry Shank argues that: 'Authenticity is not simply a matter of romantic self-expression or a faithful devotion to a strict interpretation of tradition, but rather is a result of a thoughtful self-reflection on one's own conditions of possibility' (2006:56). This suggests that creating a persona in order to express repressed feelings, such as Sylvian's communications of escapism, do not present musicians as 'authentic'. Instead a musician can be considered 'authentic' when they contemplate their own existence and the person that they are, rather than the person that they desire to be. Thus this opposes problemastises the notion of Sylvian as an 'authentic' musician in regards to his use of persona, as on the album cover he can be seen to express a desired identity rather than questioning the identity that has been cultivated by his social and cultural upbringing.

This section has discussed the Nightporter persona in relation to the songs on *Gentlemen take Polaroids* and Sylvian's visual appearance on the album cover. Whereas it has been suggested that the use of a persona contradicts Sylvian's desired status as an authentic musician, it must be questioned to what extent forces outside of Sylvian's control utilised this persona to market him in a particular way to audiences. Judith Butler suggests that:

> Culture is capable of producing ontological (ways of being) and epistemological (ways of knowing) frames of reference. (Kirby 2006:23).

This suggests that culture and cultural forms such as the media can cultivate representations of identity. Thus it can be questioned: Was Sylvian's authorship of the Nightporter persona solely responsible for contradicted his own assumed authenticity throughout his career in Japan, or were the audiences receiving the text and the media marketing Sylvian authoring their own interpretations of this persona that opposed him as an 'authentic' musician? This will be discussed in the subsequent section: David Sylvian, authenticity and authorship.

'Gentlemen take Polaroids...they fall in love, they fall in love': David Sylvian, Authenticity and Authorship

The following section discusses theories of authenticity and authorship in relation to the marketing of David Sylvian in the media during the 'Nightporter' period, particularly in the teen press of the early 1980's. Through an analysis of David Sylvian's musical works and the subsequent marketing of Sylvian as a teen idol, this section will serve to support the original hypostudy of this study: That Sylvian's adopted personae and the subsequent marketing of these personae problematise the concept of him authoring his own sound and image and Sylvian's status as an 'authentic' musician.

When considering authenticity in relation to a performer's public image, Hugh Barker and Yuval Taylor state that:

> The process of becoming a well-known musician always involves thinking about how to project yourself onto others. There is a gap

between the person you think you are and the persona that others perceive. As a musician in the public view, you are forced to contemplate how big a gap this is, and to think about how you want to be perceived. (2007:244).

This suggests that once a musician is in the public view, they must consider the way that they want to be perceived by audiences and how to author their chosen public image. However this suggests that musicians have total creative freedom over their self-authored image, which raises a critical issue – does the musician author their own image or is their public image imposed upon them by particular cultural institutions, and what ramifications does this have in regards to authenticity? Simon Frith argues that once a musician adopts characteristics of a certain popular music genre within their musical works, they are subject to marketing expectations that target particular audience demographics:

> Once signed, once labelled, musicians will thereafter be expected to act and play and look in certain ways; decisions about recording sessions, promotional photos, record jackets, press interviews, video styles and so on, will all be taken with genre rules in mind. (1996:76).

This view is reinforced by the post-structualist theory that as subjects we are 'formed in submission' (Butler; Kirby 2006:109). Thus it can be considered that although David Sylvian may have wanted to be perceived as an 'authentic' musician, his public image was constructed and authored not by himself, but the media who marketed him and the audience these texts were marketed towards. This supported by Roland Barthes' authorship theory that 'the author is a modern figure, a product of our society' (Barthes 1968; Grant 2008:97).

The genre conventions evident on the Japan album *Gentlemen take Polaroids* (Virgin Records 1981), from which his Nightporter persona is evident (as discussed in the previous section) are indicative of synth-pop, a genre that by the early 1980's had become part of the mainstream chart after the release of number one records such as Gary Numan and Tubeway Army's 'Are friends electric' (Numan 1979). For example Japan's 'Methods of Dance' (Sylvian 1980) has high in the mix synstudyers and maintains a rigid 4:4 rhythm, which according to Borthwick and Moy 'fuelled most synthpop tracks' (Borthwick & Moy 2004:123). Former Japan guitarist Rob Dean described *Gentlemen take*

Polaroids as 'a rather cold, albeit more sophisticated album' (Dean in Reynolds 2013:79), stating that their sound on the album was 'moving more towards electronic music, with YMO, Eno and Kraftwerk being the strongest influences, and a distorted guitar started to feel more intrusive rather than complementary' (2013:80). The word 'cold' has connotations of starkness and alienation, which were also identifiable characteristics of early synth-pop music. This is supported by the idea that within synth-pop 'the rock aesthetic was replaced by synthetic textures often redolent of alienation, 'European-ness' and a robotic rigidity that was as much to do with the limitations of new technology as any formulated artistic credo' (Borthwick & Moy 2004:121).

Although synth-pop would later become a staple of the mainstream chart, it can be suggested that David Sylvian did not intend on producing commercial pop music, with former Japan manager Simon Napier-Bell stating that:

> He was terrified of being condemned for being commercial. He could live with being condemned as esoteric or peculiar, but he couldn't live with [being called] commercial. The only thing that he could hold onto was that his music was weird, or beyond understanding. (Power 2004:48)

Indeed upon analysis of the song 'Burning Bridges' (Sylvian 1980) from *Gentlemen take Polaroids*, the structure of the song does not signify traits of commerciality. Whereas chart pop has been defined as having 'a general accessibility, commercial orientation, an emphasis on memorable hooks, or choruses, and a lyrical preoccupation with romantic love as a theme' (Shuker 2012:259), the structure of 'Burning Bridges' breaks the expected pop song expectation. For example it does not follow the usual pop song structure of introduction, verse, chorus, verse, chorus, middle eight, chorus and out-tro. Also the song has been composed entirely with synstudyers (with the exception of a single saxophone melody), with only three lines of sung vocals. As such this signifies that there are no identifiable hooks or melodies that the audience can sing along with, creating the ideology that the song would be inaccessible or 'difficult' for a mainstream chart audience. This is supported by the theory that 'difficulty becomes part of the ideological position of avant-garde composers, where the prestige of a composition or a composer proceeds from the challenges the music presents, and where popularity might be considered as an index of failure' (McClary 1989; 2012:348). In considering both McClary's statement and the notion that chart 'bubblegum' pop was historically considered 'fake, without depth, or manufactured for public consumption' (Barker & Taylor, 2007:160), it can be argued that the uncommercial structure and musical characteristics of 'Burning Bridges' were a reflection of David Sylvian's ideology to be presented as an 'authentic' musician, rather than producing standardised music for a mass audience for profit.

Whereas each member of Japan contributed musically to *Gentlemen take Polaroids*, Reynolds suggests that David Sylvian 'had very definite ideas about how Japan should be presented, visually and sonically, and his new-found focus would alienate him from his bandmates' (2013:80). This suggests Sylvian in the position of the auteur, who 'transforms the material into an expression of his own personality' (Buscombe 1973; Caughie 1981:23). Although songs such as 'Swing' (Sylvian 1980) demonstrate trademark sounds of other Japan members, including Mick Karn's fretless bass slides that gave him the accorded status of a 'world-class bassist' (Power 2004:63), Reynolds' statement creates the ideology of Sylvian as the leader and primary author of the group's sound and image regardless of the other musician's inputs. This is further reinforced by the album sleeve notes for *Gentlemen take Polaroids*, which credit Sylvian as both the lyrical and musical composer of each song – 'All tracks composed by D. Sylvian' (Virgin Records 1980).

However although Sylvian exorcised authorial influence over the sound of Japan, he can be considered as influencing the band's feminised image:

> Wearing make-up on the train from Lewisham to London caused him [David Sylvian] to be watched – it was exciting – it put him immediately on-stage. Before long, on David's instructions, Mick and Steve followed suit, and more reluctantly, Richard too. (Napier-Bell 2001:227).

On the cover of the *Gentlemen take Polaroids* album, there is a close-up of Sylvian's face covered heavily with make-up. The white base make-up connotes other-world-ness, whilst the pink lipstick, blue eye shadow and highlighted cheek bones signify androgyny. Roland Barthes argues that:

> a text is made of multiple writings, drawn from many cultures and
> entering into mutual relations of dialogue, parody, contestation, but
> there is one place where this multiplicity is focused and that place is
> the reader, not, as was hitherto said, the author. (1968; Grant
> 2008:100).

This suggests that a text can be authored by many cultural influences,
which in the case of Sylvian, it can be considered that the feminised
aesthetic of the band was drawn from his musical influences growing
up – 'a definite 'Glam Rock' influence began to rear its head, with the
latest singles by David Bowie, The Sweet and Roxy music all
purchased, duly dissected and musically attempted' (Power 2004:16). In
comparing Sylvian's image on the *Gentlemen take Polaroids* album cover
and David Bowie's visual appearance on his infamous 'Starman' *Top of
the Pops* appearance in 1972 (BBC Worldwide 2004), the similarities
between the two are evident. In particular the use of pale white make-
up and blue eye shadow during Bowie's 'Starman' performance as
Ziggy Stardust were characteristic of his alien persona, creating the
ideology of Bowie performing in a guise rather than as him. Thus the
use of heavily stylised make-up on the *Gentlemen take Polaroids* album
cover suggests Sylvian emulating Bowie and adopting a separate
persona on which to market himself to an audience, through both
sound and image (This particular persona having been discussed in the
previous section).

However Barthes' theory that a text's authored influences are focused
upon by the reader and not by the author suggests that although
Sylvian initially chose to wear make-up as part of this particular
persona, it is the reader of this image that interprets it for meaning.
Thus the audience author a musician's public image and not the
musician themselves, which links to Barthes' ultimate statement that
'the birth of the reader must be at the cost of the death of the author'
(Barthes 1968; Grant 2008:100). This then raises the question – how
was Sylvian's desired perception as an 'authentic' musician
problematised by the audience's interpretation of his image and the
marketing of Sylvian within the teen press?

According to Simon Napier-Bell, a majority of Japan's marketing was
based upon Sylvian's image:

In *The News of the World* there was a photo of David with the caption: 'The Most Beautiful Man in the World!'...a week later it was in all the Japanese teen magazines and soon after that it was in the British monthlies. Then copycat hairstyles began to be seen around London's trendy clubs, like Blitz'. (2001:254).

Indeed upon analysis of the three *Smash Hits* magazine covers featuring Japan as the cover between 1980 and 1982 (as sourced from Frith 2006:175-179), two of the covers feature a close-up of Sylvian's face whilst the third places Sylvian within the middle of the band, signifying him as the focal point of the group. According to Lathrop magazine editors:

> Know exactly who their readers are, because they share many of the same interests. Knowing precisely the kinds of information their readers seek, they shape the magazine to suit the reader's preferences (which in turn, generates greater sales). (2003:44).

It has been stated that 'by 1981, a host of acts connected to synthpop had tasted chart success, including Depeche Mode, Visage, Orchestral Manoevres in the Dark, Ultravox and the 'market leaders' Spandau Ballet and Duran Duran' (Borthwick & Moy, 2004:121). In considering Lathrop's argument that magazine editors know the content their readers seek, it can be considered that *Smash Hits* magazine targeted the youth sub-culture known as the New Romantics in their marketing of Sylvian due to the scenes association with the development of the synth-pop genre. Thus by targeting this audience, this would generate a higher readership for the magazine by audiences who want to know more about the pop-stars whose music they are placing into the charts through record sales. However it can be argued that this problemastises Sylvian as an 'authentic' musician when marketed as a musician associated with the New Romantic movement.

According to Simon Reynolds 'the Blitz scene was the vanguard of a general shift in pop culture back to fantasy and escapism' (2005:326), with visual identities playing with notions of 'gender-bending, cross-dressing and the wearing of make-up for men' (Borthwick & Moy 2004:132). Upon analysis of the two *Smash Hits* covers featuring Sylvian alone on the covers in 1980 and 1982, both display traits of the New Romantic visual and ideological aesthetic. Both images are a close-up of Sylvian, with the pink lipstick worn connoting romance and again, the concept of androgyny. The pale white make-up makes the pink lipstick and cheekbones (made noticeable by the use of blusher) a focal point, highlighting these particular facial features to the reader. This links Sylvian's appearance to the New Romantic visual aesthetic, as they present Sylvian as an effeminate musician who could appeal to both a male and female audience. Andrew Branch suggests that 'hard, physical, emotionally restrained was the predominant form of masculine identity valued in working class cultures during this period [1970's]' (2012:25). If emotionally restrained and tough had been the traits of masculine identity in the 1970's, then the marketing of musicians such as Sylvian allowed audiences to escape this expectation through the imagery presented to them in magazines. For example Sylvian stares directly forward in both the images, creating the idea that he is looking back at the reader. The emphasis placed on his lips invites the audience into a moment of intimacy with Sylvian, allowing readers both male and female to express their supressed feelings of desire through this metaphorical moment of intimacy with the image of Sylvian. Thus this expresses the New Romantic ideology of escapism through the audience's authored meaning of the image, emphasised by Sheila Whiteley's theory that 'while it would be easy to suggest that identification relates strongly to their androgynous images, it is nevertheless evident that they provide multiple possibilities of what it means to be male in our culture' (2006:249-250).

Therefore although Sylvian has distanced himself from the New Romantic movement, 'It's fancy dress. Dressing up to be something, to play a part, just for one night. That's something we've never done' (Power 2004:54), it can be argued that the marketing of Sylvian by the teen press in association with the New Romantic movement has shifted the authored meaning of his public image and persona to the reader and the institutions who marketed him, rather than himself as author. This links to Judith Butler's theory that 'subjection is a kind of power that not only unilaterally acts on a given individual as a form of domination, but also activates or forms the subject' (1997:84; Kirby 2006:114). However to what extent does this authored association with the New Romantic subculture question David Sylvian as an 'authentic' musician?

According to Dave Rimmer 'after the monochrome blacks and greys of punk/new wave, synthpop was promoted by a youth media interested in people who wanted to be pop stars' (1985:19; Borthwick & Moy

2004:124), suggesting that musicians associated with synth-pop and the New Romantic scene embraced capitalism and commerciality. This opposes Hugh Barker and Yuval Taylor's definition of 'the authentic musical experience, with its rejection of music that is labelled contrived, pretentious, artificial, or overly commercial' (2007:ix). Thus through association with a commercial genre Sylvian can be seen to be instantly labelled inauthentic, as an association creates the ideology that Sylvian is producing music for commodity rather than for creative and artistic satisfaction. This is supported by Roy Shuker's statement that 'authenticity continues to serve an important ideological function, helping differentiate particular forms of musical cultural capital' (2012:23).

This section has explored the music of *Gentlemen take Polaroids* in addition and the problems arising from the marketing of Sylvian within the media. However whilst it has been discussed that Sylvian's authenticity and authorial status were problematised through the media's association between him and the New Romantic sub-culture, Sylvian has previously stated that:

> The music was a mask as well. It said nothing about how I was, other than I was hiding, trying desperately to be anything but myself. (Reynolds 2005:336).

However this raises the problem with trying to achieve status as an 'authentic' musician: identities are constructs influenced by social and cultural factors. Thus we are never communicating a 'real' version of ourselves, only a construction of what we would like to be. Authenticity for musicians such as David Sylvian therefore can be seen to be unattainable, either by the way we construct our own identities or how mediated forms and audiences construct identities for musicians. This is reinforced by Hugh Barker and Yuval Taylor's theory of authenticity:

> Every performance is to some degree 'faked' – nobody goes out on stage and sings about exactly what they did and felt that day. Authenticity is an absolute, a goal that can never be fully attained, a quest. (2007:x).

Conclusion

In conclusion, this studyhas sought to support my original hypostudy: That the utilisation of personae and genre by Sylvian represents his desire to author himself as an 'authentic' performer, although the use of persona and the way it was interpreted by audiences and the media problematises the notion of Sylvian as 'authentic'. The application of theories of authenticity, persona and authorship to Sylvian's musical works and constructed image have proved interesting, challenging and thought provoking, allowing this study to take a more objective viewpoint on a specific moment in Sylvian's musical career.

However the discussions within the two sections have raised a number of critical issues regarding Sylvian's authorial status and use of persona. In considering that Sylvian's ideological position to be perceived as 'authentic' was contradicted by the notion that his persona was actually a character, and that its meaning was authored by the power of audience and media institutions, it can be asked is authenticity a truly unattainable absolute for popular music artists? Lee Marshall suggests that in relation to authenticity and subcultures, using folk as an example:

> A crucial element of authenticity is that performers are understood to be part of a group they represent. (Inglis 2006:23)

However as discussed in the second section, the association of Sylvian with the New Romantic sub-culture contradicted his own ideological values of creating uncommercial music, which he saw as being the way to perceive himself as an 'authentic' musician. Thus it can be argued that like the use of persona and theories of authenticity as binary opposites, popular music is full of contradictions. The authored meaning interpreted by an audience and by the media may not necessarily be the meaning intended by the author – a statement that seems to fit with Sylvian's problematised 'authentic' and authorial status. Thus it can be concluded that although Sylvian may have tried to attain the image of an 'authentic' musician, social and cultural values and institutions will always be there to oppose such an authorial position. This is supported by Keith Negus' statement that:

> Culture, from this perspective, should be understood more broadly as the constitutive context within and out of which the sounds, words and images of popular music are made and given meaning. (1996:62).

Bibliography

Atton, C. (2012) 'Listening to difficult albums'. *Popular Music 31/3*.

Ava-Leach, E. (2009) *Introduction to Music Studies*. Cambridge: Cambridge University Press.

Barker, H. & Taylor, Y. (2007) *Faking it: The Quest for authenticity in Popular Music*. Faber & Faber

Barry, P. (2009) *Beginning Theory: An Introduction to Literary and Cultural Theory: Third Edition*. Manchester University Press.

Barthes, R. (1968) 'The Death of the Author'. In *Auteurs and Authorship: A Film Reader*, edited by Barry Keith Grant, 97-100. Blackwell Publishing.

Bennett, A, Shank, B. & Toynbee, J. ed. (2006) *The Popular Music Studies Reader*. Routledge.

Brackett, D. (1995) *Interpreting Popular Music*. Cambridge University Press.

Branch, A. (2012) 'All the young dudes: Educational Capital, masculinity and the uses of popular music'. *Popular Music 31/1*.

Burke, S. (1995) *Authorship: From Plato to the Postmodern*. Edinburgh University Press.

Caughie, J. ed. (1981) *Theories of Authorship*. Routledge.

Drury, N. (1989) *The elements of Shamanism*. Element Books Ltd.

Frith, M. ed. (2006) *The Best of Smash Hits: The 80's*. Sphere/Emap Consumer Limited.

Frith, S. (1996) *Performing rites: Evaluating popular music*. Oxford University Press.

Gorman, P. (2001) *In their own write: Adventures in the Music Press*. Sanctuary Publishing Ltd.

Kirby, V. (2006) *Judith Butler: Live theory*. Continuum International Publishing Group.

Landy, R.J. (1993) *Persona and Performance: The meaning of role in Drama, Therapy and Everyday Life*. Jessica Kingsley Publishers

Lathrop, T. (2003) *This business of Music Marketing and Promotion*. Billboard Books.

Marshall, L. (2006) 'Bob Dylan: Newport Folk Festival, July 25, 1965'. In *Performance and Popular Music: History, Place and Time*. Edited by Ian Inglis, 16-27. Ashgate.

Middleton, R. (1990) *Studying Popular Music*. Open University Press.

Napier-Bell, S. (2001) *Black Vinyl, White Powder*. Ebury Press.

Negus, K. (1996) *Popular Music in Theory: An Introduction*. Polity Press.

Negus, K. (1999) *Music genres and corporate cultures*. Routledge.

Power, M. (2004) *David Sylvian: The Last Romantic*. Omnibus Press.

Reynolds, A. (2013) 'Classic album: Gentlemen take Polaroids'. In *Classic Pop, March/April 2013: Issue 3*. Anthem Publishing.

Reynolds, S. (2005) *Rip it up and start again: Post-Punk 1978-1984*. Faber & Faber.

Shepherd, J. & Wicke, P. (1997) *Music and Cultural Theory*. Polity Press.

Shuker, R. (2012) *Popular Music: The Key Concepts*. Routledge

Whiteley, S. ed. (2006) *Queering the Popular Pitch*. Routledge.

Audio-Visual

BBC (2004) *Top of the Pops: 40th Anniversary*. BBC Worldwide. DVD.

Discography

Japan (1980) *Gentlemen take Polaroids*. Virgin Records Ltd.

CHAPTER 2

The History & Impact of the Synthesizer: The Real Symbol of the Western Popular Music Revolution?

Tony Turrell

Fifty years ago, October 1964: at the convention of the Audio Engineering Society in New York, a slightly perplexed man by the name of Robert Moog sets up on the exhibition stall that he has been offered due to a late cancellation with four boxes, boxes that he has designed to create sound electronically. Within minutes, a professional choreographer and score writer, an influential academic, and the most successful composer of 'jingles' in America have placed orders – the very first orders taken for what was to be the very first commercially available synthesizer (Pinch & Trocco 2004:29-31).

The advent of the synthesizer could be argued to be one of the defining characteristics in the development of Western popular music. Despite electronic musical instruments being in development and use since the late 18th century, it was the explosion of their usage coupled with their on-going development in the latter part of the twentieth century that popularised the concept of musical sounds made from electronic rather than acoustic sources (Jenkins 2006:313). From the late 1960s onwards, the sounds of the future, as they were perceived, disseminated into and reflected cultural changes through the mediums of film and television, and arguably most powerfully through popular music. The electric guitar had already affected a transformation within the same area of popular music only twenty years previously; making the transition from acoustic to electric and from sound holes to solid bodies, it proved to be the perfect instrument to accompany the new styles being explored and exploited (Trynka 1993:32-37). Capturing the post-war zeitgeist of a teenage culture that had never previously existed, it revolutionized the sound of popular music and became associated with being a symbol of the rebellion against the establishment, and the young against the old (Burrows 2011:9). Still holding a cultural significance within society to this day, the guitar's influence, accessibility and dissemination is not questioned, held up in many ways as a phallic symbol of defiance (Waksman 1999:178), and portrayed as an emblemic image within Western popular music.

However, the synthesizer (or, as it will be referred to a lot, 'synth'), despite not appearing to have the same connotations of rebellion or influence, has conversely seemed to spread much further around the world, and could be argued to have penetrated into more people's lives than the guitar (Du Noyer 2003:74). Its effect on Western popular music and culture, whilst being much less immediately iconic, has also arguably been much more significant, with many of the most popular current genres dominated by synth sounds and sonic textures. This report will attempt to determine if this has indeed been the case, using the impact and developments of the electric guitar as a comparison point. The development of the synthesizer will be charted, and it will be attempted to highlight and document the key technological advances, in relation not only to the progression of Western popular music but also to its history and the culture of the dominant American and British societies of that time.

Research Methodology

The research methodology for this assignment was a combination of secondary desk-based research and sources, supported by primary ethnographical research in the form of interviews with people who have lived through, witnessed and experienced these developments from a professional perspective within the music industry. McNeill & Chapman (2005:14-15) outline the differences between studies carried out under a scientific model of observation and correlation and a sociological one where other factors have to be considered in the study of humans and development. The assumptions for the study subject were made on the basis of much of the research being around historical events and developments that were already well documented in many texts. It was found there were many areas of human and cultural development which also had to be considered, albeit from a retrospective capacity, and whilst the premise of detached study and objective correlation may hold true for many aspects of secondary research, it is not the case for any primary research, where factors of bias and prejudice can influence the outcome (Thomas & Brubaker 2007:92-97). As noted in Pickering (2008:5), primary research (ie. in this case, interviewees experience) and how it relates to the 'social relations in which it occurs and the cultural forms through which [it] is understood, is of major importance to what is investigated within the field'. That importance is relative to the theory the researcher is either attempting to prove or disprove; the findings will be used in conjunction with research theory to provide the bases for the arguments posited (Bryman 2012:20-22). However, those bases are open to criticism due to the understanding being from a subjective rather than objective viewpoint. The research for this particular study being qualitative (word based) rather than quantitative (numbers based: Berry 2005), the possibility of bias in that research is also easier to disguise; it was hoped a better balance could be achieved through combining findings from both primary and secondary areas and triangulating the sources.

As data was gathered, library sources and journals were augmented by media sources such as documentaries and screened interviews; some of the relevant material broadcast in the past was found on YouTube whilst others were available via purchase or from libraries. In an attempt to gain a fresh insight into the topic area, some traditional ethnographic techniques such as semi-structured interviews and unstructured interviews were used. As ethnographic research 'enables us to learn about the social, cultural and artistic life of communities of people…..and the meanings given to the performing arts as they develop over longer periods of time' (Krüger 2008:123), this area was felt by the author to be an important one to help balance the data being accumulated. The primary research here consisted of telephone and face to face interviews with four different subjects: a musical instrument service engineer and three professional musicians, all having a minimum of 35 years of experience. The aim of the interviews was to determine what changes, if any, in their individual work practices were seen due to the advent and development of the synstudyer, whether those changes (or lack of) had positive or negative implications on their chosen career path, and what effects they had noticed on Western popular music and the music buying populace as a whole in the last thirty years. In addition, the author was able to draw upon some of his own experience as a professional musician of some twenty years to help chart development, and this experience was used to help synthesize initial conclusions drawn from the research. However, the result of this is that this study has two potential flaws or shortcomings:

the choice of included material from these interviews is inevitably selective, shaped by the author's own opinions; and as the author's ethnographic undertaking has to be 'recognised as [being] an active participant in the research process whose presence affects situations 'in the field" (Cohen 1993:124), it must be noted the direction of questioning in the interviews may well have been biased or influenced by those opinions.

This study has provided the author with an opportunity to explore a topic of interest much further than had been previously managed. In addition, it has increased awareness of the cultural history of the period, an area that will be seen to be crucial to the development of the synthesizer.

Literature Review

The main focus for the research covers a number of areas; the key ones have been well documented and informed the author's understanding of the overall topic area. The three main groups for study can be identified as: the history of the synstudyer; the history of Western popular music; and the socio-political and cultural history with reference to the music of the same period. As a subsidiary field, the history of the electric guitar must also be considered. Whilst there are many more influencing factors (and therefore texts) to take into account, the main texts described below cover these key domains.

The primary area being the history of the synstudyer, the texts of Pinch and Trocco (*Analog Days: The Invention and Impact of the Moog Synthesizer*, 2004), Jenkins (*Analog Synthesizers: Understanding, Performing, Buying*, 2007) and Vail (*Vintage Synthesizers*, 2000) were identified as core texts within this field, each covering slightly different areas of the development and impact of the synthesizer within popular music from the late 1940s through to the early 1990s. Pinch and Trocco's text covers not only the creations of Dr.Robert Moog, but also that of Don Buchla, the other name synonymous with the synthesizer (Pinch & Trocco 2004:32) and the English company EMS, both contributing to not only the development but also acceptance from audiences and the resulting dissemination. The authors also cover cultural factors that were critical in this history, emphasizing how external social factors provided the backdrop necessary for innovation to not only take place but be encouraged and accepted.

Jenkins' text, whilst outlining the history charted in Pinch and Trocco, expands on this by providing an extension of the history to the present day, encompassing the 'analogue revival' (Jenkins 2007:194) and the software synthesizer available to almost anyone with access to a computer today. The principles invoked by the analogue pioneers of the 1960s now simulated on these instruments, Jenkins demonstrates their enduring popularity and correlates their technological development to the development of Western popular music. Conversely, although providing some background, Vail's text has no reference to modern day practice; it proves important in highlighting the initial impact on society and the amount of market penetration and dissemination within the first ten years' of the synthesizer becoming commercially available.

Spanning both this area and the history of Western popular music and its associated culture are the texts of Taylor (*Strange Sounds: Music, Technology and Culture*, 2001), Theberge (*Any Sound You Can Imagine: Making Music/Consuming Technology (Music Culture)*, 1997), Holmes (*Electronic and Experimental Music*, 2002), Sicko (*Techno Rebels*, 2010) and Braun (*Music and Technology in the Twentieth Century*, 2002), which chart the development of the synthesizer within the framework of the impact of technology on popular music as a whole, each focusing on slightly different areas of music and technological development. An understanding of the approaches taken by avant-garde and experimental electrical composers prior to the 1960s is essential to an understanding of why there was any synthesizer development; Taylor's, Holmes' and Braun's texts outline aspects of the cultural and musical historical background that led to this, detailing the emergence of the *Musique Concrete* and *Elektronische Musik* movements within France and Germany respectively and their approach to sound creation. Theberge and Braun also extrapolate from that background to question the effect on relatively recent music production, cultural attitudes and technological development. Theberge in particular examines the changes in musical practice that have led to an emphasis on the reproduction of sounds rather than their production; this shift has resulted in ambiguity over understanding of the traditional meaning of musical skill and the more modern forms that have emerged since the mid-1990s. Braun's text conversely attempts to draw together its contributor's content to remove some of the departmentalisation that occurs between the fields of musicology and technology. Particularly informing this report were the contributions of Pinch & Trocco (*The Social Construction of the Early Electronic Music Synthesizer*) and Rebecca McSwain (*The Social Reconstruction of a Reverse Salient in Electrical Guitar Technology: Noise, The Solid Body & Jimi Hendrix*), which contributed to the synthesizer/guitar comparison viewpoint the author required for this study. Sicko's insight into this area centres on the inception and global spread of the Techno style of music from Detroit, a genre inspired by synthesizer technology and a crucible for the development and proliferation of the electronic dance music styles we are familiar with today; technological and cultural sidelights on the development of Western popular music are also provided through this framework. These texts have also been augmented by the general history of Western popular music text of Paraire (*Fifty Years of Rock Music*, 1992) which contains a chronological examination of events and developments of popular music in the US and UK since 1942.

Further sociological and historical developmental aspects have been drawn from Shuker (*Understanding Popular Music Culture*, 2008), Longhurst (*Popular Music and Society*, 2008) and Reynolds (*Energy Flash* (Revised edition), 2013 and *Rip It Up & Start Again*, 2005), which tie popular music developments into society and culture and served as a starting point for this strand of the research. Shuker's text provides an introduction to not only the production and consumption of popular music but also the meaning behind it and some of the difficulties that lie behind the analysis of popular music and culture; the author used Longhurst's text to expand on this as he examines these areas informed by wider debates in sociological and cultural studies. Finally, Reynolds provides a historical background in popular musical developments in specific musical areas. His 2013 text deals with the expansion of dance music and its associated culture, from rave's origins in Chicago House and Detroit Techno, through Ibiza, Madchester and the anarchic free-party scene, to the 2000s-shaping genres such as Grime and Electro; the 2005 text deals with the development of popular music in the post-punk era of 1978-84, when Reynolds felt that 'the music seemed inextricably connected to the political and social turbulence of its era' (2005:xi), and encompasses the development of synth-pop and the general widening acceptance of synthesizers within society at this time.

Additional texts by authors such as Du Noyer (*Music; From Rock, Pop, Jazz, Blues and Hip Hop to Classical, Folk and World*, 2003) and Egan (*Defining Moments In Music*, 2007) have been used to augment the historical development of Western popular music, but one key extra text that provided corroborating information for material was that edited by Albiez and Pattie (*Kraftwerk: Music Non-Stop*, 2011). The impact of Kraftwerk and their subsequent influence on the development of popular music has been a factor in the popularisation of synthesizers and technology in music as a whole; much of their work reflects the juxtaposition between humans and machines (*Kraftwerk & The Electronic Revolution*, 2008). As their influence is so important within this field, this text, which pulls together academic analyses of various technological and cultural aspects surrounding them from different authors, was felt to be a valuable addition to the texts outlined above.

The subsidiary field of the history and development of the electric guitar was informed by Trynka (*The Electric Guitar*, 1993) and Waksman (*Instruments Of Desire: The Electric Guitar & The Shaping Of Musical Experience*, 1999). Trynka's primary focus is on the evolution of the guitar, demonstrated through the framework of several iconic, collectible or innovative electric guitars. The historical narrative provides more of a technical perspective in this text, emphasising the technologies and methods used in guitar construction, along with vignettes of their most well-known exponents and their respective influence on development and popularity. Waksman takes a broader sociological approach, centring his argument around the guitar as a bearer of cultural meaning and ideological debate. Constructing a guitar-centred history of (chiefly American) popular music, Waksman explores not only the new sonic possibilities the instrument opened up, but also how those possibilities related to the political and cultural structure of the times, contrasting performers who he believed chose to try and tame the sonics and technology (e.g. Les Paul, Chet Atkins) with those who he felt were attempting to harness the anarchic potential of new timbres and louder volumes (such as Jimi Hendrix and the MC5). In trying to meld together the main political and sonic themes that run throughout the book, Waksman demonstrates how the electric guitar has not only shaped popular understanding of noise and music, but also how for many the instrument has become a pivot or emblem around which larger political and social issues are argued. Both of these texts inform the comparison that needs to be drawn between the history and development of the electric guitar and that of the synthesizer.

All the findings from these sources have informed and expanded the author's prior knowledge of the relevant areas, particularly the backgrounds to both the guitar's and the synthesizer's development and the cultural backdrop that enabled the development to happen; this cultural background that provided the fertile soil for the instrument's germination is the first area outlined below.

Sowing the Cultural Seeds for the Synthesizer

Whilst the historical timeline steps that led to the invention of the modern day synthesizer are summarised in Appendix I, this study is more concerned with its development after its first appearance, and its impact; as a result the musical and cultural background that immediately preceded its development must be considered.

With the early twentieth century came the spread of modernism, a 'cultural movement characterised by certain kinds of cultural product' (Barnard & Spencer 2002:571). New technologies and modern approaches were being incorporated into many areas of daily life; whilst on a domestic level this was evidenced by the increasing use of devices such as vacuum cleaners and electric washing machines, the success of musical instruments such as the Hammond Electric Organ, launched in 1935, also demonstrated a voracity amongst consumers for modernist approaches, new sounds, and a desire for status symbols of modernity (Vail 1997:54-55). Meanwhile, with the ending of the Second World War, many technological developments achieved during its course were being made available to the public for the first time; amongst these items was an invention appropriated from Nazi Germany, magnetic tape. Replacing wire recorders, these were not only used for recording in a traditional sense, but were also employed by the likes of modernist composers Pierre Schaeffer (see fig. 1) and Pierre Henry to approach composition in an entirely new way (Holmes 2002:77). Using tape machines and recorded sounds to compose rather than conventional instruments, tapes would be painstakingly cut and spliced to form organised experimental soundscapes, reflecting a popular techno-scientific cultural outlook of the time; as Taylor

(2001:41) states, 'while it may seem that technology has only recently become a central factor in social and cultural life, the current hype isn't new'. Whilst confounding and alienating many audiences in a similar way to Italian composer Luigi Russolo's found sound experimental concerts of 1914 (*ibid*:45), the manipulation of sound into unfamiliar and new patterns attracted many avant-garde composers; using tape splicing, looping and speed modulation to alter sounds, 'a new sound was born' (Plaide 2010), becoming known as *Musique Concrete*. Meanwhile in Germany, these principles of composing with found and recorded acoustic sounds would be reapplied to recording music entirely from electronically produced signals.

Figure 2.1: Pierre Schaeffer in the studio (1954). Available at http://www.personal.psu.edu/meb26/INART55/concrete.html, accessed 29 April 2014. Reproduced for non-commercial research and educational purpose only (see http://www.ipo.gov.uk/types/copy/c-other/c-exception/c-exception-research.htm).

WDR Koln's Studio for Electronic Music was officially opened in 1953, the creation of physicist Werner Meyer-Eppler and composers Herbert Eimert and Robert Beyer (Jenkins 2007:19). Joined by Gottfried Michael Koenig and Karlheinz Stockhausen, the latter after a stint working for Pierre Schaeffer in 1952, the *Elektronische Musik* movement was born; the key differentiation between that and *Musique Concrete* being the former only utilised sounds recorded from electronic devices, whereas the latter was from recorded acoustical sources (Braun 2002:12). Stockhausen would become famous for his experimental compositions in the electronics field and would eventually meld the two different approaches together in his work, but the key cultural factor was how the acceptance of new electronic sounds was starting to spread (*ibid*:13). As engagement with technology and its usage started to become more commonplace in Western society, a cultural obsession with the future and technology that could possibly be associated with it (Taylor 2001:25-38) began to be reflected in areas such as film soundtracks (e.g. Forbidden Planet, 1956), and the concurrent explosion in popularity of the science fiction genre. The desire for the 'new' in popular Western society, combined with 'Musique Concrete and the spread of its attitudes, created the atmosphere for the development of the synthesizer' (Plaide 2010). This could be evidenced in the UK in the early 1960s by popular science fiction serial Doctor Who; composer Ron Grainer's tune was realised by the BBC Radiophonic Workshop's Delia Derbyshire, and her use of musique concrete tape splicing techniques and electronic oscillators created a sound both memorable and vaguely frightening for the time – it was one of the first TV shows to utilise electronic music for its theme tune. The legacy of this strange sound was that being heard weekly by millions of viewers, it wouldn't seem so strange when it was finally heard by audiences within other contexts (Pinch & Trocco 2004:277-280), and would help society to accept and embrace a different sonic palette. Western audiences were being exposed to the sounds of the future on a gradual basis, preparing the ground for an apparent explosion of new sound later in the decade.

However, the first 'new' to impact upon the Western music buyer in this period was rock and roll, based around the fresh and exciting possibilities of the sound of the amplified electric guitar. This impact was so significant that it 'forever changed the face of popular music' (Harvard University Press 2013), creating a sound that younger people in society particularly related to, and made many crave ownership of one. So far-reaching was this *zeitgeist* that ownership of a guitar 'conferred an aura of coolness upon anyone lucky enough to own one, let alone be able to play it' (Waksman 1999:245-246). With its design origins in the Hawaiian steel guitar, the electric guitar had two names that were chiefly associated with pioneering its design and eventual cultural influence, Les Paul and Leo Fender. By the mid-1950s, they both had iconic designs on the market – the Gibson Les Paul and the Fender Stratocaster – which would prove to be the successful blueprints for all electric guitar design thereafter, and in the case of the Stratocaster would become the most desired, famous and copied electric guitar of all time (Jenkins 2007:324). Popularised by its exposure on national television networks through best-selling artists such as Buddy Holly, it would inspire the youth market that gave rise to the counter-culture of the 1960s. It is against this backdrop of the guitar and its influence that the next stages in synthesizer development and impact must be measured.

The 'New' Sound of Analogue Synstudy

Whilst the use of the electric guitar was exposing audiences to new sounds in the popular music scene, the avant-garde and classical composers were not only becoming more creative but also frustrated with the difficulties and laboriousness inherent in the *Musique Concrete* compositional process. An easier interface was required for electronic music, and with the arrival of the 1960s, this interface would see fruition in two divergent ways. In an odd parallel with the development of the electric guitar, it would mainly be through the efforts of two men: Don Buchla and Robert Moog.

With the end of World War Two, the ready availability of electronic surplus war stock and industrial stock such as vacuum tubes, capacitors and scrap metals were enabling an electronic hobbyist craze, especially in America. Both Moog and Buchla had similarities in their backgrounds (a familiarity with and interest in music, physics degrees, shy and gawky as teenagers (Pinch & Trocco 2006:43)) that they claimed led them into this electronic hobbyist domain, learning their craft by 'tinkering with electronic circuits' (*ibid*:23). Both were keen experimenters within that field and came to the simultaneous realisation of how voltage control [for an explanation of voltage control and how an analogue synth can be made to work using it, see Appendix III] would allow them to create and control pitch and various other elements of timbre. Both men were also working at the same time, albeit on opposite coasts of the USA; and both men were influenced to a greater or lesser degree by the growth of the 1960s counter-culture, which provided the backdrop for synthesizer development and acceptance to take hold and eventually flourish (Taylor 2001:87). It was their degree of immersion into the avant-garde musical culture that would ultimately shape their instrument designs in very different ways. Buchla's greater immersion with the exponents of *Musique Concrete* would lead him to find easier ways to compose than splicing tape, resulting in the analogue sequencer, whereas Moog's lesser immersion but greater involvement with popular and traditional musicians would inform his designs to lead to what the world conventionally accepts as a synthesizer today.

Buchla always saw himself as more avant-garde, and has stated that he 'always enjoyed being on the edge, working on new things.....I always figured that if I made something that was too popular that I was doing something wrong and that I had better move on' (Pinch & Trocco 2006:33). Spending much of his time at the experimental San Francisco Tape Music Centre, Buchla came into contact with *Musique Concrete* and *Elektronische Musik* inspired composers such as Morton Subotnick, Steve Reich and Terry Riley. Attempting to eliminate the need for tape splicing that went with these genres, Buchla produced what is widely regarded as the first playable sequencer in the Buchla Music Box Series 100. However, he was reluctant to call his instrument a synthesizer as for him the name had connotations of imitation; 'He did not regard his new instrument as a vehicle to imitate or emulate the sounds of other instruments' (*ibid*:41). Whilst feeling that something had been created that could cause a genuine revolution in musical sound, Buchla was a true counter-culturist; suspicious of commercial and industrial practice, he refused to engage with bigger corporations to further his work. Although he had achieved a breakthrough, the impact at the time was therefore restricted to academic and avant-garde circles; it was the man working on the East Coast, Robert Moog, who would help popularise the new synthesizer and gain the credit for its subsequent influence.

Moog had realised his first design a year earlier than Buchla; where the Series 100 was built in 1965, Moog had already produced his first Moog Modular prototype in 1964. Connected, like Buchla's modular design, by patch leads between the desired components (see fig. 2), the biggest difference in the design was with a standard keyboard; Moog's design used one whereas Buchla saw no need for one to control what he regarded as a completely new instrument (Holmes 2002:184). Moog also differed in his approach to development of the instrument; 'rather than telling them 'this is the way things are going to be', he listened to what his customers wanted and responded to their needs' (Pinch & Trocco 2006:54). By making his machine 'available to as many musicians as possible and working closely with them to constantly modify his design' (Shuker 2008:35), Moog was trying to ensure his success as a manufacturer. One of these early customers/musicians was a veteran of the Colombia-Princeton Electronic Music Centre, Wendy Carlos.

Figure 2.2: Large Format Modular Synthesizer (2013). Available at http://www.uniquesquared.com/blog/21779/news-2012/modular-synthesizers-at-the-2013-namm-show/, accessed 29 April 2014. Reproduced for non-commercial research and educational purpose only (see http://www.ipo.gov.uk/types/copy/c-other/c-exception/c-exception-research.htm).

Unlike other members of the Princeton music faculty, Carlos had no interest in the experimental sounds that were the majority of the studio's output. She recalled 'I thought….the new technology (should be) used for appealing music you could really listen to. Why wasn't it being used for anything but the academy approved 'ugly' music?' (Holmes 2002:166). Her input and feedback was critical to the development of the Moog synthesizer. Moog remembers that 'every time we visited her there was not one but a whole handful of ideas' (*ibid*:167). Carlos opted to utilise the technology to re-interpret some classical pieces by Bach; knowing the expressive limitations of the instrument she deliberately chose these organ and harpsichord works as they could be transcribed much more easily to the synthesizer (Pinch & Trocco 2006:139). The resultant album, *Switched On Bach* (1968), sold over half a million copies in the first year of its release, went on to top one million and heralded the arrival of the synthesizer into the mainstream pop culture; the release 'singlehandedly inspired such interest in music synthesizers that a new industry was launched overnight' (Holmes 2002:168). Moog modular synthesizers were now selling to pop and rock artists with large record company advances in search of new sounds, and held a particular appeal for the psychedelic and underground progressive musicians of the day. Due to the popularity of the album, "synthesizer' became a household word' (*ibid*:178), and the psychedelic culture of the time encouraged acceptance of the new sounds as the perfect accompaniment to acid trips (Pinch & Trocco 2006:105). However, the synthesizer user was still relatively niche market; it was expensive beyond the means of any but the most well-off musicians, and its general fragility and sensitivity to temperature and humidity changes could cause wild tuning drifts, leading to it being viewed as a studio instrument. There was also a sound revolution occurring at this time in the world of the (much more affordable) electric guitar, and in the hands of Jimi Hendrix, this was in the process of spearheading a much more noticeable sonic agenda to audiences.

Where Carlos's release popularised the synthesizer, musicians such as Chuck Berry and Buddy Holly had already effected a transformation with the electric guitar, and with the adoption of its use by the notable blues players of the day such as Muddy Waters and Buddy Guy, 'interest in the electric guitar helped to define him [ie. a user] as a rebel......[and] stood as the symbol of [his/her] aspirations' (Waksman 1999:285). When musicians such as Hendrix married these influences to new, powerful amplification and effects such as the fuzz-box (distortion) or wah-wah pedal, 'sounds formerly considered to be undesirable – tremendously sustained and distorted notes – came to be aesthetically acceptable, even important, in musical performance'

(McSwain 2002:187). Although some decried these sounds as merely 'noise', the guitar in the hands of Hendrix pointed to a new popular music aesthetic for many, and this unleashing of sonic power was inextricable from the direction that modern life and society were taking, both as a reflection and as an expression. It was indicative of one of the main strengths of the guitar for McSwain, as 'part of the power of the guitar....lies in its flexibility as a metaphor, a sign [ranging from the need] to vent frustration.......to expressing the necessity of reconciling modern life – its speed, urbanisation and noise – with traditional values' (2002:196). Fitting the 'rock' bias and aesthetic of the time, the guitar became 'a focus of energy and attention, leading the audience to concentrate upon the musician rather than the music' (Waksman 1999:281-82). With the synth at this time almost the polar opposite of this – study and fascination rather than energy and attention, music over musician – it would require a change of public perception to engage the audience on the raw, emotional level the guitar had proved capable of and prove as significant a sonic force. Two factors would galvanise this and further the penetration of the synthesizer into popular culture; the first was progressive rock keyboardist Keith Emerson, the second was the development and production of a portable and more reliable version of the bigger modular systems.

Emerson had become aware of the possibilities of the Moog synthesizer whilst still working with his '60s rock/prog/jazz outfit The Nice. Mike Vickers of Manfred Mann had acquired one in 1968 and Emerson was so excited by the instrument's potential that he persuaded Vickers to let him use it at a Nice concert, with Vickers in attendance to perform any patch alterations or onstage maintenance necessary (Emerson 2002:175). Once Emerson moved on to form the progressive rock supergroup Emerson, Lake & Palmer in 1970, he made the decision to invest in his own Moog modular (see fig. 3).

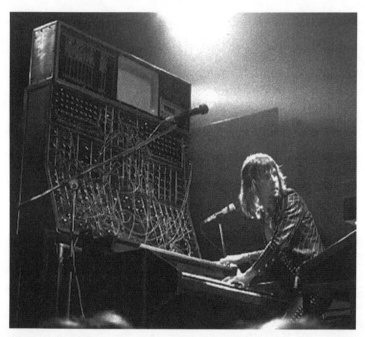

Figure 2.3: Keith Emerson with his Moog Modular and Hammond C3 (1973). Available at http://www.musicmusic.nl/wordpress/?p=483, accessed 29 April 2014. Reproduced for non-commercial research and educational purpose only (see http://www.ipo.gov.uk/types/copy/c-other/c-exception/c-exception-research.htm).

Taking delivery of it just in time for it to be set up for the recording of their debut album, Emerson was fooling around with the first sound he'd patched in, jamming over the end of one of the pieces just recorded. To his surprise (and lasting embarrassment as he did not like what he had just done), the rest of the band, crew and engineer told him he'd just done a definitive take and the solo would stay on the end of the piece (Moog 2005). The track in question was 'Lucky Man'; Emerson's solo section caused 'an audible shock [in audiences]…with the never heard before portamento lead sound' (Jenkins 2007:131), and became used for everything from hi-fi store demonstrations to being played repeatedly on American FM radio. Making more people conscious of the synthesizer at a time when progressive rock was the vanguard musical movement, Emerson had inadvertently opened the ears of young white Western audiences to a fresh sound, making the synth sound almost as 'cool' as the guitar (Pinch & Trocco 2006:212), almost treating it as though it was a lead guitar but with infinitely more power. He also became as crucial as Wendy Carlos to assisting the ongoing development. The challenge for Moog now was to make the monster modular more portable and reliable for gigging musicians to take out on tour; although Emerson did take his huge modular system out with him, Moog realised certain components needed improved stability to be able to withstand constant movement and fluctuating temperatures, and that there was still a limited market for such an expensive instrument. That problem would be solved by the Moog Inc. team that built the Minimoog.

If Emerson's impact with 'Lucky Man' can be likened to Jimi Hendrix's impact with distorted and effected guitar a few years earlier, then the Minimoog could be viewed as the synth's counterpart to the Fender Stratocaster and its initial impact. Developed whilst the stability issues of the big modular were being rectified by making some of the components smaller, the team realised there was more of a focus for most on a few usable sounds and that the massive sonic capabilities of the modular would never be tapped into by many users (Jenkins 2006:313). Taking the most essential parts of the synthesizer signal path they eliminated the need for patch cords by housing everything necessary into one unit, with all the relevant dials and switches still easy to access on the front panel (Pinch & Trocco 2006:214). This machine more than any other synthesizer contributed to the spread of influence and impact as more musicians started to buy and use it; as the first synthesizer to be sold in retail music stores, it went on to sell over 12,000 units and be regarded as a 'classic' (*ibid*:215). Synthesizers started to become commonplace in other types of music, being used by the likes of Bob Margouleff and Malcolm Cecil with Stevie Wonder, explored by Jean-Michel Jarre in material that foreshadowed both New Age and Electronica, and adopted by producers such as Giorgio Moroder who instigated their use in pop with Chicory Tip (*Son Of My Father*, 1972) and disco with Donna Summer (*I Feel Love*, 1977) (Egan 2007:459). Other synthesizer companies started to set up in competition with Moog, such as ARP, Oberheim, Yamaha and EMS. Meanwhile, in Germany some *Elektronische Musik* students were forming an outfit that had arguably the greatest influence on possibly all electronic music that came afterwards, as a result of their focus on the synthesizer. That outfit was Kraftwerk.

Originally formed in Dusseldorf, Germany in 1970, Kraftwerk first came to international prominence in 1974 with the single edit version of their 22 minute track 'Autobahn'. Originally attempting 'a symbiosis of humanity and technology' (Albiez & Pattie 2011:68), Kraftwerk's aim by this time was to be entirely electronically based, focusing on the 'still relatively new and surprising sound of the synthesizer' (Rimmer 2003:88). Using custom built electronic percussion instruments and working with modernist imperatives, a succession of successful albums had an 'enormous influence….that led to the rise of Synthpop in 1980' (Albiez & Pattie 2011:153). Parodying rock music's big posturing (*Kraftwerk & The Electronic Revolution*, 2008) and the 'use of the electric guitar as a technophallus' (Waksman 1999:244), many younger musicians in late 70s Britain would seize upon this and attempt to meld the approach with a punk aesthetic of music being available to anyone to make and play. Many in the industry such as Dennis Brown, instrument and repair technician, noted a shift in prevailing attitudes at this time:

> After working on only two synthesizers in five years compared to the hundreds of guitars and related equipment in the same time, the start of the 80s saw a dramatic increase in the amount of synthesizer based work I started to receive; nowhere near the volume of guitar based work yet but you could already see where things were headed (Brown 2013).

Kraftwerk's influence would spread across the Atlantic later in the decade as the forefathers of House and Techno would be inspired by their approach to attempt to bring synthesizer and electronic based music to the dance floor, and their legacy spans across many of the musical genres now familiar today (*Kraftwerk & The Electronic Revolution*, 2008); in making more of 'the machine' than the performer, Kraftwerk subverted Emerson's approach of 'pseudo-lead guitarist' to the instrument, and succeeded in making more of a 'star' of the synthesizer and widening cultural acceptance of it. It was into this era that Yamaha introduced their new approach to sound synstudy: the digital approach of the DX7, and with it, the seeds of the democratisation of synstudy, sound, and music-making itself.

The Advent of Digital & Electronica

In an era where the guitar and its analogous musical form, rock, seemed only able to reinvent itself by pastiche or repetition, the synth and its associated musical forms of pop and dance appeared to have no such difficulties. Where previously, analogue architecture had inherent issues with stability (including difficulties with keeping the oscillators in tune), the introduction of digital elements into the synthesizer architecture helped stabilise this, enabled by the use of the newly invented microprocessor. Along with the advent of the Musical Instrument Digital Interface (MIDI), a standardised means of communication between units containing a MIDI port, a completely new age of synstudy was born. This began a greater democratization of the music making process as synths became less expensive:

> At one point the synth was a very elitist instrument because of its prohibitive cost, but at the same time had so many possibilities that people wanted to get their hands on….as much as I hated it, digital, with the advent of the Yamaha DX7, helped to start bringing these costs down. (Daniel Miller, *The Shape of Things That Hum* ep.1 & 3, 2001).

The DX7 was very different from its predecessors; notoriously difficult to program, many established synth users refused to engage with its now all too familiar menu based system:

> Although the DX7 was the advent of digital it turned many people off because of the complexity of its programming; suddenly people were merely pressing the preset buttons to see what sounds had already been stored and created, and a sound manufacturing industry for the instrument was born overnight. (Matt Black, *The Shape Of Things That Hum*, ep.3, 2001)

The much cheaper cost and ready availability of these sound libraries obviously compensated for the other perceived deficiencies as sales figures had reached 160,000 units by the end of its production, making it the second-best selling synth ever (only topped by Korg's 1988 release of the M1, with 250,000 units (Vail 2000:181)). Although sound purists bemoaned the stultification of experimentation, many more people were now using synths as the technology became more available and affordable. The obsession with 'the new' led to older synthesizers and technology being used and valued less, second hand values plummeting on them. Professional session musician Foss Paterson found this frustrating:

> There was still so much focus from producers and artists on 'new sounds' but I felt the focus shifted from coaxing new sounds out of equipment that was already there to waiting for or buying the new piece of shiny gear to get new sounds from that. I would be turning up for sessions and be expected to have the newest kit, whether that was a Roland D50 or Korg M1 or whatever. The only way to finance a lot of that in the early days was to sell the kit you already had to buy the new 'best thing'......and whilst I bought into that mind-set with everyone else at the time, I can't help looking back and thinking that was where rock music lost its spirit of innovation. Synth technology started to make some things too easy. (2013)

This reduction in the value of synthesizer technology would have a pivotal effect on fledgling musicians and DJs who would start to blend it with an attitude that was very much dance-floor focused (Sicko 2010:6). Building on foundations laid by Kraftwerk and the British Synthpop scene, the synth in the hands of these artists was arguably set to become the main instrument of the next twenty years, displacing the guitar as the main popular music instrument.

When the Roland synthesizer company brought out its TB303 Bassline Generator, it was intended to be an auto-accompaniment instrument for solo singer-songwriters and organists (*The Shape Of Things That Hum*, ep.6, 2001). Failing in its intended purpose and difficult to program, the unit sold poorly and was quickly discontinued. However, its cheap second hand value led to its adoption in a number of electronic music genres – especially House music - that were now embracing synthesizers and technology as their creative force. Inspired by the likes of Kraftwerk, Gary Numan and Japan's Yellow Magic Orchestra, House pioneers in Chicago such as Jesse Saunders and Vince Lawrence, and Techno artists in Detroit such as Juan Atkins and Derrick May, were employing cheap 'toy' versions of the aforementioned DX7 (the DX100) in their compositions and using the drum box equivalents of the TB303 (the TR707, TR808 and TR909) to provide the dance rhythms (Sicko 2010:72). This blending of synthesizers with a groove and dance driven mentality was not new (cf. Giorgio Moroder and Donna Summer in the mid-1970s), but the access to technology capable of providing this was; as the music gained in popularity (much more so in Europe at the time than America), these sounds became sought after by more people. With the explosion of rave culture in Britain in the late 1980s and early 1990s, the sound of synthesizer based music entered into the cultural fabric of popular music (Reynolds 1998:157), and musical instrument firms started manufacturing more synthesizers with an ever wider range of capabilities and more 'realistic' sound sets. Whilst much emphasis would be placed on sampling within these more modern musical fields (Theberge 1997:187), the synthesizer was still a crucial part of the creative arsenal, and with clubbers and DJs clamouring for the older analogue sounds that came out of boxes such as the TB303, instrument manufacturers started to build modern digital versions of many of these older 'classics' (Jenkins 2006:315). The shift in popular music preferences due to this synthesizer based music was noticed by session guitarist Frank Usher:

> It was in the mid 1990s; we'd had the Brit-pop guitar revival with the likes of Oasis and Blur but my work was starting to tail off. This was down to a combination of decreasing budgets and sampling technology lessening the need for a 'player on the spot', so to speak. But the overriding factor seemed to be that there was simply not as much of a market for guitar based material at that point, and although my work picked up again after 2002, I found it significant that I ended up working mainly with folk or country based artists, playing much more acoustic than electric guitar. Whilst I wouldn't know for sure if there's a direct correlation between my experience and the impact of the synth in popular music terms, I'd dare to stick my neck out and say it's indicative. (2013)

Figure 2.4: Software synthesizer (2009). Available at http://www.synthtopia.com/content/2009/03/28/nekrobat-laborosc-a-free-software-synth-for-windows/, accessed 29 April 2014. Reproduced for non-commercial research and educational purpose only (see http://www.ipo.gov.uk/types/copy/c-other/c-exception/c-exception-research.htm).

Throughout this entire period, guitar development had stymied; most new guitars built were based on copying the design of the 'classics' such as the Stratocaster. Rock music itself, the form most closely associated with the guitar, whilst still prevalent in society seemed to have lost much of the cultural force that made it the dominant white Western medium twenty years previously (Sicko 2010:5). Conversely, electronic dance music was still developing and synth manufacturing was still progressing, searching for new sounds and instrument interfaces; with an 'analogue revival' in full flow, and synthesizer prices decreasing all the time (Jenkins 2007:194), the end of the 1990s saw the development of the first software synthesizer (see fig. 4).

Whether these trends between the instruments development could be read as metaphorical for the musical styles they were popularly associated with or not, with personal computers becoming commonplace in the Western world, it can be argued that the synthesizer was finally poised to take its place in more people's lives than the guitar had ever managed.

The Battle of Significance: Where the Synthesizer is Today

In its latest software incarnations, the synthesizer has become available to anyone who owns a computer; often offered as freely downloadable, there is a bewildering array of synthesizer products available, whether as hardware or software. 80s synthpop musician and producer Thomas Dolby recalls:

> When I started out, synthesizers were a comparative rarity. In those days, the biggest problem was actually affording one; now the hardest thing is choosing one from the scores of different ones on offer that suits your needs. I still find it incredible how freely available they are now – how cheap! – compared with what I had to fork out for my first second hand synthesizer in 1973. (2013)

The digital transition has 'transformed the field of popular music. Technologies that were once considered radical and experimental are now a part of the common sound kit of the digital composer' (Holmes 2002:273). Although there have been many fresh programming architecture ideas introduced since the first digital synths of the early 1980s – Sample and Synstudy, Wave Modulation synstudy, Granular synstudy and others – it could be argued that even the computer systems running the software synths we have today are essentially extensions and progressions of the original digital hardware basis. As hardware synths come under greater threat from software technology equivalents 'which are more reliable, flexible, convenient and cheaper' (Matt Black, *The Shape of Things That Hum*, ep.8, 2001), it could also be argued that this digital development has ultimately ensured many more people have access to a synthesizer than a guitar, as computers and software are now indigenous to most of Western culture. The decreasing cost of synthesizer technology to the average consumer 'has resulted in entirely new kinds of musics that rely on...synths...and other electronic gear' (Taylor 2001:139), and the face of Western popular music has changed radically from where it was at the point of the synthesizer's introduction to it in the late 1960s.

The fact is, the development of Western music, technology, and culture are inextricably intertwined, and the emergence of new instruments and sounds generating fresh musics is one of the constants of that inter-development (Braun 2002:9); the piano effected as much of a transformation in these areas in the eighteenth century as both the guitar and synth did in the twentieth. The main difference in the modern era is that the production of ever-more sophisticated devices 'is eagerly supported by the large rock music industry, which ultimately owes its existence & especially its growth in the last 30 years to.....the parallel increase in the spending power of children's pocket money' (Davies 2002:43). In the initial stages of each instrument's impact, this support was visibly behind the guitar, as music retailers were snapped up into a large distribution network by firms such as CBS, aiming to achieve as wide a market share as possible by mass marketing techniques. For the synth, this sort of market availability was only reached with the advent of digital in the early 80s, twenty years after Moog's first synth was built and marketed; yet the electric guitar's transition from the same beginnings to mass market was a little less than five years, due to a company and design infrastructure already being in place. Cost also played a significant part in this; with a completely new technology, everything has to be designed and built from the ground up, whereas building upon or improving a previous established design, as in the electric guitar's case, is considerably cheaper. However, as the cost of technology has decreased in tandem with its portability and ubiquity in Western society, this position has been reversed; the advent of synthesizers as software instead of hardware 'means they are the instruments par excellence of the digital age. Behind every mp3 file downloaded from the internet lies some form of synthesizer' (Pinch & Trocco 2004:7).

With synth based music more commonplace than guitar driven music in Western society at this time and more musicians working from a computer or laptop basis than working in a traditional pop/rock band set up, it could be argued synths have 'taken over, pushing the guitar into the back seat' (Crombie 1985:5). However, the legacy and original impact of the electric guitar still affords the instrument a more visible presence in popular culture than the synthesizer. Even authors Pinch and Trocco give deference to that presence:

> The synthesizer is the only innovation that can stand alongside the electric guitar as a great new instrument of the age of electricity....the synthesizer may....be the more radical innovation, because, rather than applying electricity to a pre-existing instrument, it uses a genuinely new source of sound—electronics. (2006:7)

Others have lauded the synth as the more radical innovation; Davies (2002, p.43) believes that 'the electronic oscillator.......is the only new principle of sound production that has been discovered since prehistoric times'. Its background as a 'boffin' (and possibly utilitarian) instrument and lack of a romance such as the electric guitar has, disguises the fact that its advent is 'one of those rarest moments in our musical culture, when something genuinely new comes into being' (Pinch & Trocco 2004:6-7). In terms of the battle with the guitar for cultural significance, this has led Brend (2012:x) to state that 'the war is over. Yet it was not won in a single battle, but rather through many skirmishes, land grabs and creeping advances; there was no revolution, but rather a gradual colonisation'. With greater market penetration and wider usage, the synth has continued to evolve, unlike the electric guitar which is still based around the classic 1950s designs. Whether this is because the guitar has been exhausted as an expressive medium as some have claimed (Waksman 1999; Reynolds 2013) is debatable, but its significance now appears to be more nostalgic, with its current perception seeming 'to gain meaning from its association with certain predefined historical moments that ultimately have less to do with history as such than with some version of cultural fantasy about what the past represents' (Waksman 1999:284).

As technology continues to develop, so synths will also have to develop to keep pace because of their position as an integral part of most computer systems. This continuing evolvement can only increase the availability and therefore influence of the synth, and would seem indicative of the fact that although the impact of the synth compared to the guitar is still not as visible, it has had and will continue for some time to have the greater impact and influence on the continuing development of Western popular music. However, that impact and influence is only equal to the ability of the people who choose to engage with it; as Brend (2012:x) states, 'technological advance can suggest possibilities to musicians who are open to suggestion, but it is the musicians who do the creating'. Perhaps, then, the true test of the synthesizer's significance lies not in its cultural penetration to date or the immediate effect of its innovative technology, but whether it is still able to offer users new potential for development, sound creation and inspiration in another fifty years.

Bibliography

Albiez, S, & Pattie, D (Eds). (2011) *Kraftwerk: Music Non-Stop*. London: Continuum.

Anon. (2000) *Timeline: History Of The Synthesizer (before 1900.)* [online] Available at: www.synthmueum.com/magazine/time0010.html. [Accessed 25 October 2013].

Apple Inc. (2009) *A Brief History Of The Synthesizer.* [online] Available at: http://documentation.apple.com/en/logicexpress/instruments/index. html#chapter=A%26section=5%26hash=apple_ref:doc:uid:TempBoo kID-ReplacedWhenAssociatingWithMessierRevision-43982SYN_SC_0908-1006566. [Accessed 19 October 2013].

Bach, J.S. (1968) *Switched On Bach* performed by Wendy Carlos [Vinyl 33rpm]. New York: Columbia Masterworks.

Bailey, S. (2003) *Academic Writing: A Practical Guide For Students*. Oxford: Routledge.

Barfe, L. (2005) *Where Have All The Good Times Gone?* London: Atlantic Books.

Barnard, C & Spencer, J. (2002) *Encyclopedia Of Social & Cultural Anthropology* (2nd Ed). London: Routledge.

Braun, H-J. (Ed). (2002) *Music And Technology in the Twentieth Century*. Baltimore: Johns Hopkins University Press.

Brend, M. (2012) *The Sound Of Tomorrow: How Electronic Music was Smuggled Into the Mainstream*. London: Bloomsbury.

Brown, C; Bischoff, J & Perkis, T. (1996) Bringing Digital Music To Life. *Computer Music Journal*. 20 (2), 28.

Bryman, A. (2012) *Social Research Methods* (4th Ed). Oxford: Oxford University Press.

Burrows, T. (2011) *Guitar Family Trees: The History of the World's Most Iconic Guitars*. London: Apple Press.

Chowning, J & Bristow, D. (1986) *FM Theory And Applications*. Milwaukee: Yamaha Foundation & Hal Leonard.

Cohen, S. (1993) Ethnography & Popular Music Studies. *Popular Music*. Vol. 12, No. 2. (May, 1993), pp.123-138.

Cossar, N. (2005) *This Day In Music: An Everyday Record*. London: Chrysalis Books.

Crombie, D. (1985) *The Synthesizer & Electronic Keyboard Handbook*. London: Pan Books.

Davies, H. (2002) Electronic Instruments: Classifications & Mechanisms. In: : Braun, H-J. (Ed) *Music And Technology in the Twentieth Century*. Baltimore: Johns Hopkins University Press, pp.43-58.

Du Noyer, P; Heatley, M; Lester, P & Roberts, C. (1998) *Encyclopedia Of Albums*. Bristol: Dempsey Parr.

Du Noyer, P. (2003) *Music; From Rock, Pop, Jazz, Blues and Hip Hop to Classical, Folk and World*. Fulham: Flame Tree Publishing.

Egan, S. (2007) *Defining Moments In Music.* London: Octopus Publishing Group.

Encyclopædia Britannica Online. (2012) *Electronic Music.* [online] Available at: http://www.britannica.com/EBchecked/topic/183823/electronic-music. [Last Accessed 2nd November, 2013].

Emerson, K. (2002) *Pictures Of An Exhibitionist.* London: John Blake Publishing.

Forbidden Planet 1956 [film] Directed by Fred M. Wilcox. USA : MGM (98 mins).

Ford, B. (1992) *The Cambridge Cultural History Of Britain Vol.9: Modern Britain.* Cambridge: Press Syndicate of the University of Cambridge.

Friedman, F. (2008) *Moog Polymoog.* [online] Available at: http://www.vintagesynth.com/moog/polymoog.php?comments_page =1#comments_anchor. [Last accessed 1st March 2013].

Frith, S. (1983) *Sound Effects: Youth, Leisure & The Politics of Rock & Roll.* London: Constable.

Giddens, A. (1997) *Sociology* (3rd Ed). Cambridge: Polity Press.

Harvard University Press. (2013) *Instruments Of Desire: About This Book.* [online] Available at: http://www.hup.harvard.edu/catalog.php?isbn=9780674005471. [Last Accessed 20th March 2014].

Holmes, T. (2002) *Electronic & Experimental Music* (2nd Ed). London: Routledge.

Jarre, J.M. (1997) *Oxygene* [CD]. New York: Sony Music.

Jenkins, L (Ed). (2006) *The Illustrated Musical Instruments Handbook.* Fulham: Flame Tree Publishing.

Jenkins, M. (2007) *Analog Synthesizers: Understanding, Performing, Buying.* Oxford: Focal Press.

Kraftwerk & The Electronic Revolution: A Documentary Film. (2008) [DVD] London: Chrome Dreams Ltd.

Krüger, S. (2008) *Ethnography In the Performing Arts.* Lancaster: Palatine.

Lake, G. (1970) *Lucky Man* performed by Emerson, Lake & Palmer [Vinyl 45rpm]. Hamburg: Island Records.

Longhurst, B. (2008) *Popular Music & Society* (2nd Ed). Cambridge: Polity Press.

McSwain, R. (2002) The Social Construction Of A Reverse Salient In Electric Guitar Technology: Noise, The Solid Body & Jimi Hendrix. In: Braun, H-J. (Ed) *Music And Technology in the Twentieth Century*. Baltimore: Johns Hopkins University Press, pp.186-198.

Manning, P. (2013) *Electronic & Computer Music* (4th Ed). Oxford: Oxford University Press.

Moog: A Documentary Film. (2005) [DVD] Hans Fjellestad. Los Angeles: ZU33.

Moroder, G & Bellotte, P. (1972) *Son Of My Father*, performed by Chicory Tip. [Vinyl 45rpm]. New York: CBS.

Moroder, G., Bellotte, P & Summer, D. (1977) *I Feel Love*, performed by Donna Summer [Vinyl 45rpm]. London: GTO Records.

Paraire, P. (1992) *Fifty Years Of Rock Music*. Edinburgh: Chambers.

Pickering, M (Ed). (2008) *Research Methods For Cultural Studies*. Edinburgh: Edinburgh University Press.

Pinch, T, & Trocco, F. (2004) *Analog Days: The Invention and Impact of the Moog Synthesizer*. Cambridge: Harvard University Press.

Plaide, J. (2010) *The New Sound Of Music 1979*. [video online] Available at: http://www.youtube.com/watch?v=6MsyOe7xCqg&list=PLE41F23D 582CF32A4. [Last Accessed 24 March 2014].

Pressing, J. (1992) *Synstudyer Performance And Real Time Techniques*. Oxford: Oxford Press.

Prior, N. (2008) *OK Computer: Mobility, Software & The Laptop Musician*. London: Routledge.

Reynolds, S. (2005) *Rip It Up And Start Again: Post-Punk 1978-84*. London: Faber and Faber.

_____ (2013) *Energy Flash: A Journey Through Rave Music & Dance Culture* (Revised Edition). London: Faber & Faber.

Rimmer, D. (2003) *New Romantics: The Look*. London: Omnibus.

Russ, M. (2004) *Sound Synstudy And Sampling* (2nd Ed.). Burlington: Focal Press.

Russolo, L. (2004) *The Art Of Noise (Futurist Manifesto 1913)*.Burlington: Focal Press.

Sadie, S & Tyrrell, J (Ed & Ed). (2001) *The New Grove Dictionary Of Music And Musicians*. Oxford: Oxford University Press.

Schneider, F & Hutter, R. (1974) *Autobahn* performed by Kraftwerk [Vinyl 45rpm]. London: Vertigo.

Sicko, D. (2010) *Techno Rebels: The Renegades Of Electronic Funk* (2nd Ed). Detroit: Wayne State University Press.

Shuker, R. (2008) *Understanding Popular Music Culture* (3rd Ed). Oxford: Routledge.

Taylor, T.D. (2001) *Strange Sounds: Music, Technology & Culture*. London: Routledge.

The Shape Of Things That Hum ep.1-8. (2001) [TV Programme] Allied Forces/Watchmaker Productions, Channel 4, 30 January 2001 20:00.

Theberge, P. (1997) *Any Sound You Can Imagine: Making Music/Consuming Technology (Music Culture)*. Middletown: Wesleyan University Press.

Thomas, R.M & Brubaker, D.L. (2007) *Theses & Studys: A Guide to Planning, Research & Writing*. Thousand Oaks: Corwin Press.

Tobler, J & Frame, P. (1980) *25 Years Of Rock*. London: WHSmith.

Trynka,P (Ed). (1993) *The Electric Guitar*. London: Virgin Books.

Vail, M. (1997) *The Hammond Organ: Beauty in the B*. San Francisco: Miller Freeman

_____ (2000) *Vintage Synthesizers*. Milwaukee: Miller Freeman.

Waksman, S. (1999) *Instruments Of Desire: The Electric Guitar & The Shaping Of Musical Experience*. London: Harvard University Press.

Warner, T. (2003) *Pop Music – Technology & Creativity: Trevor Horn & the Digital Revolution*. Farnham: Ashgate Publishing.

Wikstrom, P. (2009) *The Music Industry: Music In The Cloud.* Cambridge: Polity Press.

Wonder, S. (1972) *Talking Book* [Vinyl 33rpm]. Los Angeles: Motown.

Appendix I: The Earliest Origins of Synstudyers

The earliest origins of the synthesizer can be traced back to the late eighteenth century. The Clavecine Electrique or Electric Harpsichord was the invention of Jean-Baptiste Delaborde, and used a harpsichord-like keyboard to activate clappers that were charged with static electricity to ring bells (Anon 2000). Despite this surprisingly early beginning, it was a century later before another electrical instrument was created. Inspired by German scientist Hermann von Helmholtz's experiments with sound wave motion, American inventor Thaddeus Cahill (1867-1934) designed and built an instrument he called the *Telharmonium*, a 'formidable assembly of rotary generators and telephone receivers (designed) to convert electrical signals into sound' (Encyclopaedia Britannica Online). At 200 tons, it predated public address systems and had to be played into the public telephone network to be heard. Despite the previous existence of the Clavecine, his instrument is now widely regarded as the first true electronic instrument, and the next stepping stone towards the modern synthesizer; ahead of its time, the design principles would eventually find their scaled down home within the design of the Hammond Organ.

Where Cahill's instrument was the result of planning and considered construction, the Russian inventor Leon Theremin (1896-1993) invented the instrument that bears his name accidentally, after fitting a tone generator to the radio 'motion sensor' he had already developed. Discovering the tone altered in pitch in relation to where his hand moved around the antenna, he started giving concert performances using his new monophonic sound source as early as 1920 (M.Jenkins 2007:17). Although a synthesized sound, it had no controller keyboard, everything being reliant on the proximity and movement of the hand to the antennae; this made it difficult to control accurately. However, the legacy of the Theremin can be seen in the later work of Moog and

Buchla; Moog commenced building his own theremins at age 19 and would return to building them again in later life.

Whilst instruments such as the Ondes Martenot (1928, see (a) below) and the Trautonium (1930, see (b) below) proved interesting developments in their own right, the next step towards the modern synthesizer can be recognised in Edouard Coupleux and Joseph Givelet's 1929 device, the Automatically Operating Musical Instrument of the Electric Oscillation Type. This instrument married electronic sound generation to automated control via mechanically punched tape, making it the link between the Player Piano and the RCA synthesizer (Apple 2009). Due to its lengthy name, its builders shortened it and as a result it was the first instrument to be named a 'synthesizer'. However, the first recognisable synthesizers from the modern perspective of the word were the Electronic Sackbut, designed and built in 1948 by the Canadian Hugh Le Caine, and the RCA Electronic Music Synthesizer, designed in 1956 by Americans Herbert Belar and Harry Olson (L.Jenkins 2006:312).

The Sackbut was designed for the musician to play the keyboard with their right hand and to control the sound with their left, using 'expression buttons' and a device extremely akin to the modulation pads we see on some more recent modern day synthesizers. Although never developed into a commercial prospect, its design is significant for the use of two innovative techniques; the use of adjustable wave forms as timbres and the development of voltage control, both of which would be implemented in the synthesizers of the 1960s and '70s. Conversely, the RCA Electronic Music Synthesizer, whilst innovatively allowing continuous automated control of pitch, timbre, envelopes and volume by information punched onto a roll of paper tape, was complex, unwieldy and volatile due to its tube circuitry. With the advent of the transistor in 1948, a more stable, rugged and portable replacement became available for vacuum tubes, enabling the next stage in the synthesizer's development, and the breakthroughs of Buchla and Moog.

(a) The Ondes Martenot was sonically similar to the Theremin; on the Martenot the sound was generated by pulling a wire back and forth. The instrument has been revived in popular music quite recently by bands such as Radiohead.

(b) Freidrich Trautwein and Oskar Sala worked in 1930s Berlin on the instrument they called the Trautonium. Operated by pressing a steel wire against a bar, it could either play variable pitches like a fretless string instrument or incremental pitches as per a piano. Sala, who moved into industrial film scoring, continued to develop the instrument throughout his life and most famously used it for the 1952 Alfred Hitchcock movie 'The Birds'.

Appendix II: Modular Design

A modular synth consists of separate modules, each performing a separate specialised function (Voltage Controlled Oscillator, Low Frequency Oscillator, Voltage Controlled Amplifier *et al*), which would be connected to each other by patch cords to create a patch. Each module output would create a signal, generated by voltage; combining these module outputs together into a single audio source could provide a potentially infinite variation of sound. Theoretically it was possible to have as many modules as you physically had space – and means – for. However, this resultant instrument would still only be able to play one note at a time.

Appendix III: Voltage Control Synthesizer Components

In simple form, the basis of a synthesizer is an oscillator (an electric signal which oscillates), often made of two transistors (electrical control switches) and a couple of resistors (which resist the passage of electrical current to a greater or lesser degree). A steady power supply (a few volts from a battery is enough) is fed into one end of this circuit, and the other end produces a rapidly varying voltage. Potentiometer resistors (or 'pots') control variations in frequency, amplitude, wave shape and the like, and the resultant signal is then sent to speaker outputs. This gives a rough, simple (and possibly not very tuneful) analogue synth (M.Jenkins 2007:.9).

Appendix IV: Interviewees

Dennis Brown is an instrument repair technician based in South East England. He has been involved with everything from servicing and working on Cream bassist Jack Bruce's musical equipment through to repairing school musical equipment, guitars, amps and home organs and keyboards. Starting this career in 1972, he has over 40 years' experience in the industry.

Thomas Dolby is a musician and producer best known in the UK for his 80s solo hits 'She Blinded Me With Science' and 'Hyperactive'. His session work has encompassed artists such as Foreigner, Def Leppard, George Clinton and David Bowie, and his production credits include Joni Mitchell and Prefab Sprout. Film score work includes George Lucas' 1986 film 'Howard The Duck',and videogame credits include 'The Gate To The Mind's Eye' Continually involved with new technological developments, he has designed software synthesizers for mobile phones and created hundreds of digital polyphonic ringtones (including the famous Nokia ringtone). He is often a speaker at technology conferences.

Foster ('Foss') Paterson is a keyboard player and composer who has worked with artists as diverse as progressive rockers Camel, Bee Gee Barry Gibb and Christian singer Julia Fordham, and was singer-songwriter John Martyn's keyboard player of choice between 1978 and 1990. Foss has also recorded much of the incidental and title music found on the Discovery and History satellite channels.

Frank Usher is a Scottish guitarist who began his career doing 'dep' work with The Incredible String Band at the end of the 1960s. Since then, along with continuing projects with Incredible String man Mike Heron, his work has 'taken in countless small-time sessions in all genres' and seen him play and compose with artists such as ex-Marillion singer Fish, folk legends Aly Bain and Phil Cunningham and work regularly with top session musicians such as bassist John Giblin and drummer Mark Brziezcki. Outside of playing Frank has spent his spare time working as a guitar luthier, building and repairing.

CHAPTER 3

Issues with Culture: Rihanna as the Tourism Ambassador for Barbados

Rebecca Sanders

In 2011 Rihanna was elected the 'Barbados Tourism Ambassador', in which she signed a 3 year contract with the Barbados Tourism Authority (Barbados Free Press 2011). Wirth-Nesher (1996) states:

> The duty of the ambassador is to bring the symbols of his own country into the very centre of another. (1996:115)

By examining Rihanna's music, lyrics and the image which she chooses to portray, and taking into account Wirth-Nesher's definition of the duties bestowed upon a tourism ambassador, I hope to determine whether or not Rihanna is a suitable candidate for the role. Perhaps more importantly, this will involve exploring to what extent Rihanna is reflective of the Barbados tourism brand identity, as well as looking at whether or not she displays an authentic depiction of the traditional music and entertainment sector of her West Indian homeland Barbados.

In the first section, I will be observing present trends in the Barbados tourism sector and, more specifically, the current tourism statistics of the nation. This information is important to my research as it shows the present state of the island's tourism sector. I will then explore how the Barbados Tourism Authority promotes the cultural industry of the island by analysing the tourism marketing concept of 'place branding'. *The White Paper on the Development of Tourism in Barbados* (2013) and official tourism websites for the nation will be utilised to establish and examine the brand identity of the island.

In the second section, I will analyse how Rihanna's media presentation fits into the desired Barbados brand. From a musicological stance, I will analyse the foundations of her music by exploring its lyrical content and instrumentation, while also implementing semiotic analysis of her music videos. It is my intention to compare and contrast the characteristics of the traditional music of Barbados with the musical features of Rihanna's compositions. This exploration will inform whether or not Rihanna represents and displays an authentic depiction of the traditional music of her West Indian homeland.

In the final section, I will contemplate other reasons for Rihanna having been appointed as the tourism ambassador of Barbados. This will encompass applying notions of 'stardom', 'the demonstration effect' and 'commoditisation' to her role, all factors which contribute to her validity as an ambassador. In this section, I broaden the scope of this research by analysing past marketing strategies that have seen 'stars' or 'celebrities' used as commodities to promote towns, cities, nations and regions. This analysis may perhaps give valuable insight into Rihanna's appointment as ambassador by identifying how other tourism authorities have used 'celebrities' as part of their marketing strategies to promote cultures.

Methodology

Having already established the basic theoretical outlook of this study, it would be pertinent to note that this is an original study and thus there is no existing discourse considering Rihanna and her role as the Barbados Tourism Ambassador, and perhaps more importantly whether she displays an authentic depiction of her native homeland. This study uses a qualitative research approach and is reliant upon both primary and secondary sources. Literature is a particularly important source within this study as it is abundant in history and traditional aspects of the Barbadian music culture. Gathering background information on the culture will be imperative to this study to establish whether Rihanna negotiates characteristics of the music of the island. Furthermore, I also anticipate that detailed analyses of Rihanna's music videos and discography will play a central role as part of this research. Findings will be presented in the form of a case study, and will implement musicological analysis to determine whether or not she brings the symbols of her native homeland to the centre of other countries.

Wirth-Nesher's (1996) writing is a comparative analysis of diverse cityscapes. It is her third chapter 'Translated Cities: Domesticating the Foreign' which is vital to my research, as she explores how places are experienced differently by the ambassador and tourists. In her work she defines the duties of the ambassador, which is a critical foundation for the outlook of this study, since I shall be taking into account her definition of the duties bestowed upon the ambassador in correlation with Rihanna's presentation. Wirth-Nesher's (1996) discussions of the ambassador shall inform my understanding of the duties Rihanna should be conforming to, and in this study I will continually revert back to this definition.

The desired brand image of the island is outlined in the Barbados governments policy paper *The White Paper on the Development of Tourism in Barbados* (2013). It lays down the foundations and develops the framework of how the nation's tourism industry shall sustain growth by addressing improvements of the existing product. The current situation of the island's tourism sector is discoursed, whilst also identifying the aspects of the culture that will be promoted in campaigns. This is a key source for this study as it proposes the brand elements of Barbados' culture, which are vital in regards to understanding the extent to which Rihanna is reflective of the tourism's brand identity.

Curwen Best (2004) has musicological and cultural tendencies in his analysis of the popular music of the Caribbean. It is his comprehensive discourse in regards to the Caribbean music genres of Calypso, Soca, Spouge and Dancehall that are most relevant to this study. In his analysis he explores the composition of the musical forms through exploration and identification of the traditional instrumentation, time signatures and lyrical themes of the aforementioned music genres. Gathering information from a musicological perspective in regards to the music genres that are intrinsically linked to Barbados is central to this study to establish whether Rihanna negotiates musical characteristics of Barbadian music. Michael Veal (2007) and Carolyn Cooper (2004) have musicological tendencies, but delve further in depth than Best (2004). Their writings take on a social and cultural perspective of Caribbean music styles wherein they explore the use of creole language in lyrics and dance movements originating from the island. These are key sources for this study for establishing signs and symbols of the Barbadian culture in the semiotic analysis of Rihanna's music videos.

Rihanna's discography is critical for this study as her recordings allow for the textual analysis of her body of works from a musicological approach. This is imperative to this research as it informs the styles of music which she chooses to incorporate in her songs and more importantly to the extent she depicts Caribbean musical characteristics in her music. YouTube will allow me to gain in-depth analysis of the image she chooses to portray in her music videos through exploring signs and symbols associated with Caribbean culture. Rihanna's music and music videos will be a key element in this study to inform an understanding whether or not she brings the symbols of her native homeland to the centre of other countries.

Tourism, Statistics and the Branding of Barbados

In this section, I will be exploring present trends in the Barbados tourism sector and more specifically the current tourism statistics of the nation. This information will be important to my research as it will clarify the dependence of the nation upon tourism while identifying the present state of the island's tourism industry. I aim to establish how the Barbados Tourism Authority promotes the cultural industry of the island as this shall inform why Rihanna's attributes are beneficial to the brand identity of the nation.

Smith (2005) defines tourism as 'activity whereby the host country or region provides services to visitors who, in turn, bring in foreign exchange and essentially hold a vital role in the social, cultural and economic development of most nations' (2005:1). Visitor expenditure on commodities such as accommodation, food and drink, local transport, entertainment and shopping contribute greatly to the economy of many countries. The United Nations World Tourism Organisation's (UNWTO) 2013 report states that 'for some 90 countries, receipts from international tourism were over US $1 billion in 2012' (UNWTO 2013:5). The UNWTO (2013) report illustrates the importance of tourism; many nations are dependent solely upon the money generated by visitors.

Barbados has endured decreasing visiting figures since 2012. The nation's tourism figures of 2013 indicated that in comparison to 2012, Barbados' visiting figures were down month on month, fluctuating from -12% at the lowest visiting and decreasing to -0.1% at its highest (CTO 2013:2). Figures released by the Caribbean Tourism Organisation show that from January through to September 2013, Barbados' overall stopover tourist arrivals were down -6.2% from the previous year to only 379,865 tourist arrivals (CTO 2013:2). *The White Paper on the Development of Tourism in Barbados* (2013) policy outlines that tourism is 'a major catalyst for wealth creation and poverty reduction' and that 'the industry can provide the fastest way to create jobs, grow the economy and generate revenue for social services, which benefits all Barbadians' (Hall 2013:30). This epitomises that decreasing tourist arrival figures are an extremely problematic situation for the Barbados government who stress the importance of tourism arrivals for the 'economic survival of the nation' (Hall 2013:29).

The White Paper on the Development of Tourism (2013) identifies that Barbados has become a 'mature and tired product that is in urgent need of rejuvenation' in order for it to 'compete effectively within the current highly competitive global marketplace' (Hall 2013:x). The policy identifies tourists as being 'different from any other time in the history of tourism', who have aspirations for 'authentic experiences' and who is longing to immerse themselves into the local culture to 'learn and experience' the way of life of Barbadians (ibid). This type of tourist demands 'more unique experiences' and is 'less satisfied with sun, sea and sand alone'; they have desire to get to know the local culture, the people and to eat local food (ibid). To satisfy the tourist's yearnings, the tourism sector intends to promote the traditional aspects of the culture. Given that the origins of 'what is referred to as the 'old' phenomenon of culture in terms of tourism travel can be traced back to the cultural practises of the education-motivated travel of the European Grand Tour during the 17th and 18th centuries' (Ivanovic 2008:30), this marketing strategy is not an original approach for destinations that anticipate an influx of tourists.

Littrell (1997, cited in Richards 2001:8) suggests that 'culture can be viewed as comprising what people think (attitudes, beliefs, ideas and values), what people do (normative behaviour patterns, or way of life) and what people make (artworks, artefacts, cultural products)'. Given this definition of culture, it is presumed that cultural tourism is concerned with the lifestyle, the history, art and cultural products of the host country's culture and various other elements that facilitate its way of life. It would be pertinent to note that, since Rihanna is the tourism ambassador, her music and imagery in music videos should to some degree convey aspects embedded in the Barbados culture to adhere to the tourism authorities' intentions of promoting the traditional elements of the nation.

In *Cultural Heritage and Tourism: An Introduction*, author Dallen J. Timothy (2011) writes, 'One prevailing marketing concept of the modern era is place branding, place promotion or destination branding' (2011:276). This method of sustained marketing and promotion sees towns, cities, regions and countries publicised as 'holistic destinations that can be promoted to tourists, investors or potential new residents' (ibid.). The Barbados brand offers much more than the island's promotional tourist slogan 'Long Live Life' and is rather a product blend of the nation's cultural characteristics (VisitBarbados 2014). This product mix is what makes the Barbados brand unique and different from other destinations, thus creating a desirable brand identity.

The images mediated of Barbados generally display the cultural and natural attractions of the nation, including the sun, sea, beaches, rum and traditional food and music unique to the island. These primary cultural attractions of Barbados are reinforced on official tourism websites and discussed within *The White Paper on the Development of Tourism* (2013) policy. Milena Ivanovic, author of *Cultural Tourism* (2008), summarises the roles of primary cultural attractions in a destination as follows: 'they are the main reason for a trip: they define a destination's authenticity and uniqueness, and they form the basis for developing a destination's image' (2008:132). Obviously, Rihanna alone does not possess adequate pulling power to attract a momentous amount of tourists; however her celebrity status ensures that her promotional videos are seen around the world and that the context of these campaigns includes the primary attractions of the island. Furthermore, as Ivanovic (2008) states these 'primary attractions' are the 'main reason for a trip' and define a destination's 'authenticity and uniqueness', so it is crucial that an authentic representation of the Barbadian culture is endorsed by Rihanna as not to misinform prospective tourists to the island (ibid).

Ivanovic (2008) further states, 'Unlike primary attractions, the roles of which involve enticing tourists to a destination', the secondary attractions alternatively 'provide a cultural menu for a destination' (2008:132). The secondary attractions of the island, also known as supporting attractions, include the entertainment sector and can be a 'huge factor' for tourists when booking a holiday. Although they are said to 'not possess any pulling power of their own' they enhance and diversify the tourist's experiences thus providing more attractions for the tourist (ibid). It will be crucial to my research to analyse as to whether Rihanna gives an accurate appropriation of the music of the island, which, as part of her role as tourism ambassador, is to 'bring the symbols' of her 'own country into the very centre of another' (Wirth-Nesher 1996:115).

The Barbados Tourism Authority's website Visit Barbados identifies the music of the nation as a combination of 'diverse genres and influences, most notably of British and African origins, that include Barbadian folk melodies, Western Classical, religious, Caribbean Jazz and Opera to the undulating rhythms of Calypso, Spouge and Soca' (Visit Barbados 2014). It is calypso which appears to be the most prominent music style of the island as it is the most frequently promoted genre on dedicated tourism websites (Best 2014:14). Henry Pariser, author of *Explore Barbados* (2000), discusses the reputation of Calypso, stating that 'next to Reggae, it is the best known music to come out of the English-speaking Caribbean' and is one of the main features of the Crop Over festival (2000:55).

Each tourism website, including Visit Barbados (2014), Barbados (2014) and Totally Barbados (2014), amongst many others, promotes different festivals around the nation, but all endorse visiting the Barbados Crop Over festival. Its origins can be traced back to the 1780's, a time when Barbados was the world's largest producer of sugar (Barbados 2014). It is said that at the end of the sugar-cane harvest, 'there was always a huge celebration to mark the culmination of another successful sugar cane harvest - the Crop Over celebration' (ibid). In the 1940's, the festival was terminated and only revived in 1974 when 'other elements of Barbadian culture were infused to create the extravaganza that exists today – an event that attracts thousands of people from across the globe' (ibid). The history of the Crop Over festival exemplifies the importance of the Calypso music genre and how deeply embedded the music style is within the culture of Barbados.

Additionally, the Visit Barbados website (2014) showcases a video on Bajan music, featuring a performance by The Mighty Gabby, a Bajan

Calypsian artist, as he sings his song 'Emmerton' (The Mighty Gabby 2014). Again, the promotion of Barbadian music appears to be heavily centred on the Calypso music genre. The video displays the musician playing his acoustic guitar in hills that look over the beautiful scenery of the sun, sea and sand. This is clearly iconic and in direct correlation to the Barbados brand. The Mighty Gabby says that 'Emmerton' is a folk song which 'speaks a concept of who we are and where we have come from' (ibid). It is a political song in which the artist bellows, 'yuh tell me tuh fuhget yuh bring bull dozers an push-down de houses' in his homeland (ibid). It will be interesting to find out whether Rihanna addresses any social or political matters within her current music, or more specifically whether she negotiates the musical characteristics of Calypso in her own music. Thus it will be fundamental to assess whether Rihanna negotiates characteristics of the Calypso genre.

To conclude, this first section has clarified the vital role of tourism in Barbados for the social, cultural and economic development of the nation. I explored the current situation of the Barbados tourism sector in which statistics show that the nation is recently suffering from consistent decreases in tourist arrivals. It would be pertinent to note that this decrease in tourism figures has become an issue after Rihanna's appointment as ambassador, which influences my curiosity further to understand and explore to what extent Rihanna is supportive of the Barbados culture and brand identity.

Additionally, *The White Paper on the Development of Tourism* (2013) policy outlines that the brand image of Barbados has become a 'mature tired product that is in urgent need of rejuvenation and image overhaul' (Hall 2013:x). This would explain the appointment of Rihanna as a promoter for the Barbados brand as she portrays a fresh, invigorated and youthful image for the brand identity. Furthermore, since the Tourism Authority declares promoting the traditional aspects of Barbadian culture, it is understood that Rihanna must display an authentic depiction of the island through her status as tourism ambassador. However, taking into account Wirth-Nesher's definition of the duties bestowed upon a tourism ambassador, I wish to explore and challenge this notion in the following discussions.

Rihanna, Caribbean 'Riddums' and the Representation of Culture

So far I was able to show that Barbados is intent on promoting its culture for tourism, and this section aims to explore and analyse Rihanna's media representations. This will involve examining some of her music's lyrical content and instrumentation, as well as carrying out semiotic analysis of her music videos. Through comparing and contrasting her music's characteristics with those of the traditional music of the island, this analysis will illustrate whether Rihanna depicts an authentic representation of the music of her West Indian homeland, Barbados.

Rihanna's 2005 debut album *Music of the Sun* (Rihanna 2005) combines various musical characteristics associated with Caribbean music. For instance, Barry Walters defines her debut single 'Pon De Replay' as 'a poppy piece of dancehall reggae with slapping, syncopated beats recalling big-band jazz' (Rolling Stone 2005). The track is driven by syncopated dancehall reggae rhythms and even includes Bajan creole with the title 'Pon De Replay', meaning to repeat a song again (Artists Direct 2006). Rihanna explains, 'It's broken English. Pon is on, De means the, so it's just basically telling the DJ to put my song on the replay' (Kidzworld 2014). Here, Rihanna's use of language draws directly from her native culture, which, combined with Caribbean musical influences, suggests to me that in 2005 she was in fact somewhat representative of Barbados.

Furthermore, Rihanna also employs creole language in her track 'That, La, La, La', in which she sings, 'You tell Mr. D.J. wanna rub a dub' (Rihanna 2005). 'Rub a dub' could signify one of two things: First, Michael Veal (2007), author of *Dub: Soundscapes and Shattered Songs in Jamaican Reggae*, writes that 'Dub was a style of erotically charged dancing which involved holding the women close to you and rub on her, you would call it a rub a dub' (Veal 2007:61). Second, another understanding of the term is expressed by Carolyn Cooper (2004), author of *Sound Clash*, who defines 'rub a dub' as a style of 'Jamaican popular music, alternatively labelled Dancehall, Ragga and Dub' (Cooper 2004:16). Either way, the term derives from the Caribbean islands, and through her use of the creole language she is promoting her culture, as well as sustaining a relationship with the region of Barbados.

The second track on her debut album titled 'Here I Go Again' (Rihanna 2005) is driven by a relaxed reggae drum rhythm and off beat staccato electric guitar. The instrumentation comprises of syncopation, which is a characteristic of the Calypso music genre (BBC 2014). Additionally, the song includes steel pans, which are intrinsically associated with the Caribbean, since the origins of the instrument lie in that region, as well as being the 'foremost musical instrument in…Trinidad and Tobago' (Horner, Fletcher and Rossing 2010:667). Rihanna's style of musical composition that is associated with the characteristics of the Calypso genre thus demonstrates how she has brought the symbols of her culture into her music and disseminates this on a global level.

Additionally, lyrics by J-Status featured in the song make reference to the Caribbean when he raps 'Cause you really miss 'dem days when we used to chill up on the hill watch the sunset in West Nigril' (Rihanna 2005). Here, the lyrics symbolise Rihanna's attachment to the island as West Nigril is a beach area situated in the Caribbean (Expedia 2014). In this track, J-Status also highlights Rihanna's ethnicity as he raps to her 'Girl yuh Bajan beauty it a gimme di chill' (Rihanna 2005), reinforcing her birthplace and native land of Barbados to listeners.

In the album's title song 'Music of the sun' (Rihanna 2005), a dancehall drum rhythm drives the track, however it is the acoustic guitar which is distinctive and most prevalent. The melody and rhythm of the guitar resembles the style of the music performed by the aforementioned Calypso artist The Mighty Gabby in his track 'Emmerton', which is promoted on Visit Barbados as Bajan Music. Given the similarities between 'Music Of The Sun' and 'Emmerton' and the aforementioned use of steel pans in 'Here I Go Again' (Rihanna 2005), it could be suggested perhaps that Rihanna's 2005 debut album was heavily influenced by Calypso musical characteristics. So at this stage in her career, Rihanna's music was indeed representative of the traditional music of the island of Barbados.

In other words, my analysis of the tracks on Rihanna's *Music of the Sun* (2005) album reveals a strong association and sense of belonging to her West Indian homeland, and this is established through her appropriation of music qualities related to the Caribbean region. Additionally, when Rihanna was asked in an interview with Kidzworld, the leading safe social network for kids and teens launched in February 2001, 'What could fans expect to hear when they purchase the album?', she answered, 'The word sun represents my culture where I'm from, the Caribbean. It represents me. So the album consists of music of the sun' (Kidzworld 2014). Thus Rihanna deliberately represents her nation by embracing both Bajan dialect and Creole language, and by embedding musical characteristics of the Caribbean culture throughout her *Music of the Sun* (2005) album. Rihanna succeeds in reminding her fans of her ethnicity and conveys an authentic depiction of her homeland.

Her subsequent album *A Girl like Me* (Rihanna 2006) is also embedded within Caribbean musical influences, borrowing elements from the Dancehall and Reggae genres in tracks, such as 'Kisses Don't Lie', 'Break it off' and 'Crazy little thing called Love', as well as incorporating some RnB tracks, such as chart toppers 'We Ride' and 'Unfaithful'. However, her third album release *Good Girl Gone Bad* (2007) represents a departure from the Caribbean sound of her previous albums, *Music of the Sun* (2005) and *A Girl Like Me* (2006). *Good Girl Gone Bad* (Rihanna 2007) instead absorbs elements and characteristics synonymous with RnB, 'the genre which emerged from American Blues and Soul music in the United States' (Gazzah 2008:98). The Dancehall and Reggae-syncopated drum rhythms that are present in Rihanna's earlier albums are replaced here with four-on-the-floor drum patterns with a steady accented beat in 4/4 time. Additionally, new instruments replace guitars, steel pans and violins used in her debut album *Music of the Sun* (2005). The evolution of Rihanna's music could be understood as paralleling her migration to America. From her third album onwards, her musical output is for the most part profoundly dependent upon R&B and Hip-Hop genre characteristics.

More recently, however, Rihanna's albums *Rated R* (Rihanna 2009), *Loud* (Rihanna 2010), *Talk That Talk* (Rihanna 2011) and *Unapologetic* (Rihanna 2012) return to her roots once again and feature a couple of tracks that employ characteristics of Caribbean music. For example, in the track 'No Love Allowed' from her *Unapologetic* album (Rihanna 2012) album, the rhythm guitar is strummed on the offbeat and the 'tonal qualities are set to emphasise the high end frequencies' of the instrument in 'order to contrast the low end frequencies' of the walking bass line (Miller and Shahriari 2012:386). This style of guitar playing and the tonal qualities that are given to the instrument are associated with Reggae music, and through the implementation of these characteristics she is connecting herself once again with the music of the Caribbean (ibid.). Additionally, 'Rude Boy' from her *Rated R* album (2009) is given a touch of Rihanna's Caribbean roots. Not only does the track include steel pans, the instruments which originate in the Caribbean, but the drums also follow the 'offbeat' characteristics of Reggae, whereby the emphasis of the beat is placed on beats 2 and 4, instead of 1 and 3 (Miller and Shahriari 2012:386). This Reggae rhythm is also present on the singles 'Whats My Name?' and 'Man Down' from her *Loud* album (Rihanna 2010), utilising syncopated instrumentation as well as reliance upon Caribbean rhythms. West Indian and Caribbean tones also radiate through her single 'You Da One' (Rihanna 2011). It could be suggested that this song is built around characteristics of the Barbadian musical genre Spouge, as the song incorporates a typical 'prominent strumming of the rhythm guitar' and once again a strong reliance on beats 2 and 4, an aforementioned characteristic associated with Reggae music (Best 2004:14). By embracing the region's musical rhythms on some tracks on her later albums, Rihanna clearly displays an authentic representation of the traditional music of Barbados.

However, the majority of Rihanna's later musical output makes less and less musical references to the island of Barbados, whilst focusing on R&B characteristics rather than Caribbean music styles. Here Rihanna tends to pay homage to America through the imagery depicted in her music videos. In her 'Pour It Up' (Rihanna 2013) music video she appears brandishing American US dollars, which does not represent or put the Barbadian culture in the spotlight as the nation uses the Barbadian dollar as its currency. Additionally, in her music video for the single 'We Found Love' ft. Calvin Harris (Rihanna 2011) 'filmed in Belfast Ireland', Rihanna is displayed dancing in a traditional English 'fish and chip' shop, with her jacket and bikini embroidered with an American flag pattern (Vena 2011). There is also an American flag hanging on the wall and an English person narrating at the start of the video. As tourism ambassador, her duty involves projecting the cultural symbols of Barbados, and yet her music videos show her promoting the United States of America as opposed to her native homeland, Barbados.

Having said this, Rihanna does continue to makes subtle references to the Caribbean, which is evident in her popular single titled 'Rude Boy' (Rihanna 2009). The rude boy subculture arose from the poorer sections of Kingston, Jamaica and was associated with violent discontented youth described as the 'dangerous roodie', the 'stepping razor' and the 'youthful hooligan who resisted police enforcement' (King 2002:37). However, in regards to the context of this song, her appropriation of the 'rude boy' could simply be referring to the sexual nature of the man and the acts she is asking him to perform: 'Can you get it up, Come here Rude boy, boy Is you big enough' (Rihanna 2009). It would be important to note the success of this track: it reached the top ten in 28 countries and number one in Australia, and featured on the UK R&B Chart and the US Billboard Hot 100 chart (Pietroluongo 2010). Thus if this song is to be associated with Kingston, Rihanna is not only portraying the Caribbean in a negative light, but also contradicting her role as an ambassador due to the negative connotations related with the 'rude boy' culture.

Throughout Rihanna's career, she can be seen performing a kind of 'Wukking up' dance movement in her music videos, such as 'You da one' (2011), 'What's My Name' (2010) and 'Pon De Replay' (2005). 'Wukking Up' is a traditional Bajan style of dance that involves waistline and hip gyration and movement of the pelvis (Besigiroha 2010:237). She performs this dance move in her music video for 'Pour It Up' (2013) where the camera slows up as her bottom gyrates. This is a display of highly sexualised imagery and in complete contrast to the 'Wukking Up', which can be seen in videos of the Crop Over festival. Linda Besigiroha (2010) writes that there is a certain shame attached to the Caribbean dance move and 'this shame is still perpetuated today, evidenced in the carnival season when dichotomies exist between ordinary carnival bands and more respectable bands where the style of dance is not tolerated' (2010:237). Rihanna thus chooses to perform her womanhood in a highly sexualised manner, although, aside from the stigma attached to the body movement, she is still performing a dance that originates in the Caribbean and is therefore performing an authentic aspect of her native culture.

One might question her role as an ambassador of a country in terns of her highly explicit lyrical content within her music, asking how this would benefit Barbados' tourism industry. For instance, the lyrics in her single 'S&M' (Rihanna 2010) include 'sex in the air I don't care I love the smell of it sticks and stones may break my bones but chains and whips excite me'. Additionally in 'Birthday Cake' (2011), Rihanna sings 'I want to fuck you right now, just get up on my body', while in 'Cockiness' (2011) she raps 'I want you to be my sex slave, anything that I desire'. Her use of sexual preferences and desires within her lyrical content could be reflective of the Caribbean's Dancehall genre. Moskowitz (2013) writes that 'lyrics of Dancehall songs run the gamut from conspicuous uplifting of the oppressed Jamaican underclass to discussions of sexual encounters, drug use or criminal activity' (2013:330). Although these lyrics would not be suited to everyone's taste, they could be understood as a characteristic of the Dancehall genre, and then it could perhaps be suggested that she displays an authentic representation of the traditional music of that region.

To conclude, in this section I have explored how Rihanna represents and displays an authentic depiction of the island. Through musicological and semiotic analysis, I have illustrated her use of the creole language, instrumentation and musical characteristics, which are bounded to the traditional music of the Caribbean region. Additionally, through semiotic analysis of her music videos it is apparent that she utilises the 'Wukking Up' dance movement that derives from the Caribbean (Besigiroha 2010:237). Having said this, I have reservations to the extent to which she displays an authentic representation of the music of the island since the vast majority of her work is influenced by the R&B genre, and so in the following section, I will discuss the notion of authenticity from a sociocultural perspective.

The Demonstration Effect, Authenticity and Rihanna as a Commodity

In section two, I established that Rihanna displays an authentic depiction of the island through parts of her musical works. However, it could be suggested that these representations of the island are surpassed by the R&B characteristics that are intrinsically linked to the vast majority of her back catalogue. Therefore, in this section I will explore other reasons for her appointment as ambassador for the tourism sector of Barbados. This will encompass notions of 'the demonstration effect', 'stardom' and 'commoditisation', as well as looking at past marketing strategies.

It is an inevitable fact that culture changes occur as a result of tourism. Macleod (2004) writes that 'tourism is part of the globalisation process', implying here that as tourists travel through different cultures, there is an 'exchange and flow of economic and intellectual items in terms of goods, knowledge, values and images, as well as people on a global scale' (Macleod 2004:4). The homogenisation of culture is sometimes intensified by tourists whose behavioural patterns are often copied by locals of a host country, which Smith (2009:53) refers to as the 'demonstration effect'. Smith (2009) explains this notion as being 'the desire for locals to learn and indulge in the same forms of entertainment, non-local food and drink and non-traditional fashions which the tourists consume' (ibid). It could perhaps be suggested then that as tourists pass through the island, the locals of Barbados acknowledge what appeals to the incoming travellers, and the Barbados Tourism Authority then appropriates the tourist's favourite entertainment into its brand identity.

Given that *The White Paper on the Development of Tourism* (2013) discloses 'three of Barbados' traditional source markets, namely the USA, the UK and Europe, the brand could perhaps be targeting these regions due to Rihanna's influence throughout these regions (Hall 2013:30). Thus Rihanna's promotion as tourism ambassador was perhaps not to portray an authentic depiction of the traditional music of her West Indian homeland. Graburn (1989) furthers this idea by suggesting that the package holiday tourist who is most commonly attributed to Barbados would prefer a non-authentic holiday. The author refers to this type of tourist as carrying a 'home-grown bubble' of their lifestyle around with them, in which 'they can live whilst on vacation' and thus have 'a tendency to expect western amenities' (Graburn 1989, cited in Macleod 2004:13). Applying this critique to Rihanna's ambassador role would suggest that perhaps her duty does not include instilling the traditional cultural values of Barbados into the typical package holiday tourist's mind, and rather she is used to exemplify the diverse cultural attractions a prospective tourist can expect.

To assess other motives and reasons regarding Rihanna's role as tourism ambassador, my research could revealed valuable insights by analysing past marketing strategies that have seen 'stars' or 'celebrities' used as a means to promote towns, cities, nations and regions. The Balearic Ministry of Tourism has previously contracted Claudia Schiffer as tourism ambassador, and prior to her appointment actor Michael Douglas, who both signed multi-million euro deals. The reason for their nomination as ambassadors was that they were both 'high profile celebrities and owned properties on the island' (Telegraph 2010). In this instance, the strategy employed by the Balearic Ministry of Tourism defies the definition of the duties bestowed upon a tourism ambassador (see Wirth-Nesher 1996), as both Claudia Schiffer and Michael Douglas were given the duty to promote the region based upon their celebrity status, as opposed to bringing the symbols of the Balearic state into other countries.

Given Rihanna's high profile celebrity status, it could be suggested that the Barbadian Tourism Authority are using her public image as a recognisable trademark and powerful source to promote and sell the Barbados brand. Laura Ahonen (2008) furthers this idea by arguing that an artist's celebrity value and image aid in the marketing of products (2008:41). This is indeed applicable to Rihanna whose aura of image has remained a potent strength in the last couple of years to sell diverse products. Her endorsement deals have included Nivea's '100 Years of Skincare' campaign, collaborations with MAC Cosmetics in 2011, in which she released her own line of makeup called RiRi hearts MAC, and promotions for lager production company Budweiser in July 2013, in which she would become part of their 'Made for Music' campaign to be promoted in an 85 country campaign. Additionally, Rihanna was announced as the face for French fashion range Balmain in December 2013 as well being elected the CFDA Fashion Icon award 2014 (Grow 2012, MAC Cosmetics 2014, Hampp 2013, Alexander 2013, Holmes 2014). Rihanna's persona as a commodity adheres to Shuker's (2008) evaluation of 'stardom' in which he notes, 'stars are individuals who, as a consequence of their public performances or appearances in the mass media, become widely recognized and acquire symbolic status' (2008:70). Applying this critique to Rihanna's role as tourism ambassador, it could perhaps be suggested that the Barbados

Tourism Authority is using her symbolic status and recognisable image as a platform to upsell the island.

This shows that Barbados could simply be utilising Rihanna's fame and superstardom to endorse the island, rather than using her fame to bring the symbols of Barbados into the forefront of potential tourist's minds. This is clearly shown as part of a recent 'multi-million marketing arrangement' with Rihanna, whereby a campaign video was produced and aired (Loveridge 11.10.2013). This 2013 promotional video, which was uploaded via Rihanna's official YouTube account, is the second component of an advertising campaign launched by the Barbados Tourism Authority (Barbados Tourism Authority 2013). The visuals exhibit Rihanna exploring and immersing herself into the cultural heritage of the island. Rihanna is displayed conversing with the locals during a game of beach dominoes, wheeling a bicycle on a country lane and walking along a desolate hillside with the ocean visible behind. She can also be seen playing in the sea and frolicking on the sand at Six Men's Bay, 'a secluded cove towards the north-west corner of the island, near Colleton' (DailyMail 2013). Additional scenes reveal her gazing out to the sea from a cabana and show her floating in the water at Animal Flower Cave, 'an attraction in the remote far north of the island which rarely features on the traditional tourism radar' (ibid). Rihanna is portrayed in the film as if the video recorder is capturing a real moment in the everyday life of a Barbadian. Evidently the campaign is actually staged and packaged as a commodity. Within this package, Rihanna is shown to present an innocent and childlike idyllic life in stark contrast to the image of her that is usually depicted; often clad in little clothing and carrying out explicit behaviours. Rihanna and the Barbadian heritage have been emphasised and exoticised for the pleasure of potential visits to the island, as the video makes visible the incredibly beautiful local Barbadian culture as opposed to the West Coast commercial beach resorts usually associated with the island.

This appears to be an attempt to showcase a different side of a country that is largely known for its West Coast beach resorts, which is all part of the plan to offer its travellers more than the standard package holiday. Her track 'Diamonds' (Rihanna 2012) is the soundtrack to the commercial and is played throughout. The song itself is a mid-tempo electronic and pop ballad performed with heavy synthesizers, orchestral sounds and electronic rhythms with a four on the floor drum rhythm driving the track. The music used in this campaign differs from the aforementioned traditional music of the island, which usually incorporates 4/4 time with syncopation, guitar, trumpets, saxophones and percussive cowbells. It could be suggested that in this promotional video, Barbadian culture is made a commodity and thus packaged and sold for consumption to present the tourist with ever more diverse cultural attractions.

Closely linked to the notion of commoditisation is the concept of authenticity. MacCannell (1973) argues that commoditisation may sabotage the authenticity of local cultural products, and in fear of this, a surrogate 'staged authenticity' emerges in host cultures (1973:591). Implicit in his critique is the notion that tourists are misled 'to accept contrived attractions as authentic', whilst the host culture's social reality is sustained through 'the conscious product of an individual effort to manipulate a social appearance', which MacCannell (1973) refers to as 'mystification' (ibid). In *Staged Authenticity: Arrangements of Social Space in Touristic Settings* (1973), he explores notions of 'front' and 'back' regions in touristic settings, suggesting that in tourists' desire for authentic experiences they are often led into what is taken to be a 'back' region, but is in fact a 'front' region that has been totally set up in advance for touristic visitation (MacCannell 1973:597). Given that the Barbados Tourism Authority's website identifies the music of the nation as 'a combination of Caribbean Jazz and Opera to the undulating rhythms of Calypso, Spouge and Soca', it is evident that the song 'Diamonds' (Rihanna 2013) does not negotiate the musical characteristics of these genres. Thus applying MacCannell's (1973) theory would render the promotional video campaign as merely a product of 'staged authenticity'. Implied here is that the tourist is presented with 'Diamonds' (Rihanna 2012) what is presumed to be representative of the traditional music culture of Barbados, while the authentic music experience they desire lies in the 'back' region that is closed to tourists.

However, to critique the use of Rihanna's 'Diamonds' (Rihanna 2012) into the promotional campaign as a form of 'staged authenticity' would be to suggest that Barbadian music and culture has not developed or changed. As Naremore and Brantlinger (1991) argue, 'culture, like language, is forever in a condition that Raymond Williams describes as emergent and its various forms are constantly subject to transformation, combination, and dissolution' (1991:15). And so to apply MacCannell's (1973) theory of 'staged authenticity' would imply that 'the posited authenticity' of the traditional Barbados music culture 'serves to denounce an inauthentic present', in this case Rihanna's music (Fabian 1983:11).

There is a preconception around the notion of authenticity, wherein traditionally it has been applied to music that 'purports to be historically informed or historically aware' or more simply 'faithful to sounds of past performances' (Ahonen 2008:101). This objective understanding of authenticity renders artists who do not conform to original traditions and values of a culture as non-authentic, since they do not continue those established ideals. However, situating authenticity as a sociocultural construct carries the corollary that the notion is 'constantly being reshaped within different cultural practises' and more importantly 'all music can conceivably be found authentic' (Ahonen 2008:101; Moore 2002:210). Therefore, applying this theory to the 'Diamonds' (Rihanna 2012) track used in the promotional campaign and, more importantly, the body of Rihanna's work, which is predominantly made up of R&B musical characteristics, would classify her discography as an authentic representation of the music of Barbados as it could be deemed to represent a modern day Barbados.

To continue, the *White Paper on the Development of Tourism in Barbados* (2013) outlines that the nation would be employing the best attributes of the island to add 'diversification of the product offering' (Hall 2013:103). Though the vast majority of Rihanna's musical characteristics may not be representative of the island's traditional music, it could be argued that her artistic image is more than likely to represent a modern day Barbados. This in turn would not only rejuvenate and diversify the Barbados brand but allow it to move away from what the *White Paper on the Development of Tourism* identifies as a 'mature tired product' (Hall 2013:x). Connell and Gibson (2003) suggest that 'music is a cultural resource bound up in how places are perceived and how they are promoted' (2003:221). Thus employing Rihanna as tourism ambassador 'expresses and embodies the new social identities', which have emerged as products of 'urbanisation and modernisation' throughout Barbados through her modern musical attributes (Manuel 1988:17). Therefore, the promotion of her music and association with Barbados tourism celebrates the evolution of the island's music culture and must be seen as 'paralleling the evolution of new societies', whilst diversifying the tourist product and influencing the images that attract tourists (ibid).

To conclude, in this section I have explored other reasons for her appointment as ambassador for the tourism sector of Barbados. These notions have encompassed 'the demonstration effect', 'stardom' and 'commoditisation', as well as looking at past marketing strategies, and I have argued that these notions do not necessarily depict Rihanna as an authentic purveyor of the Barbadian culture. As discussed in this section, situating authenticity as a social and cultural construct carries the corollary that authenticity is 'constantly being reshaped within different cultural practises', and more importantly 'all music can conceivably be found authentic' (Ahonen 2008:101; Moore 2002:210). Therefore, applying authenticity from this perspective would incur that Rihanna's discography is an authentic depiction of the island and her appointment as ambassador serves to represent a modern day Barbados that 'expresses and embodies the new social identities', which have emerged as products of 'urbanisation and modernisation' throughout Barbados (Manuel 1988:17).

Conclusion

The intention of this study was to determine whether or not Rihanna was a suitable candidate for her role as tourism ambassador of Barbados. Taking into account Wirth Nesher's (1996) definition of the duties bestowed upon a tourism ambassador, I aimed to determine whether or not Rihanna displays an authentic depiction of the traditional music of her West Indian homeland. This research also established reasons that I perceive to have justified Rihanna as a suitable candidate for her employment as tourism ambassador. This is despite the fact that these justifications do not necessarily depict Rihanna as an authentic purveyor of Barbadian culture. To further this theory, I explored how it could be suggested that the Barbados Tourism Authority have sought an opportunity to benefit from Rihanna's 'stardom'; perhaps exploiting her recognisable image and symbolic status as a marketing strategy and more specifically a platform to upsell the island.

Additionally, I also highlighted Smith's (2009) theory of the 'demonstration effect' and how this could have impacted on her employment as ambassador. Implicit in Smith's (2009) proffered notion is the idea that as tourists pass through the host country, the locals are inclined to copy behavioural patterns of the tourists. In applying this theory to Rihanna's role as ambassador, it could be understood that the Barbados Tourism Authority is appropriating the tourist's favourite popular music into the nation's brand identity, irrespective of whether she purveys an authentic depiction of the island, although, as Graburn (1989) suggests, the package holiday tourist has a tendency to expect Western amenities while on holiday. If Rihanna's appointment was to be the result of her 'stardom' or 'the demonstration effect', it would contradict her duties as ambassador 'to bring the symbols' of her 'country into the very centre of another' (Wirth-Nesher 1996:115).

In the case study approach used in section two, I analysed a large body of Rihanna's music. Through musicological and semiotic analysis, I identified that a number of her songs incorporate lyrical themes that could be influenced by the Dancehall genre, traditional instrumentation and syncopation intrinsically linked to Caribbean music alongside her use of Creole language and Bajan dialect. This illustrates that she conveys the symbols of her own country and its surrounding region to other countries worldwide due to the popularity of her songs. Her negotiation of these characteristics would concur that Rihanna represents and displays an authentic depiction of the island, however by taking into account her entire music works that for the most part are influenced by the R&B genre, I harboured reservations in declaring her representation as an authentic depiction of the traditional music of Barbados.

In section three, I challenged the use of her song 'Diamonds' (Rihanna 2012) in the promotional video campaign by the Barbados Tourism Authority, as its characteristics were not representative of the traditional music of the island. Additionally, since *The White Paper on the Development of Tourism in Barbados* (2013) policy paper identified the promotion of the island's traditional culture, MacCannell's (1973) theory would render the use of 'Diamonds' as a product of 'staged authenticity'. However, his critique would have implied that the culture of Barbados has not developed or changed.

As previously mentioned, authenticity has traditionally been applied to music that 'purports to be historically informed or historically aware' or more simply 'faithful to sounds of past performances' (Ahonen 2008:101). However, by situating authenticity as a sociocultural construct it carries the corollary that authenticity is 'constantly being reshaped within different cultural practises', and more importantly 'all music can conceivably be found authentic' (Ahonen 2008:101; Moore 2002:210). Therefore, applying authenticity from this perspective would incur that Rihanna's discography is an authentic depiction of the island, and her appointment as tourism ambassador helps to represent a modern day Barbados that 'expresses and embodies the new social identities', which have emerged as products of 'urbanisation and modernisation' throughout Barbados (Manuel 1988:17). Taking into account Wirth-Nesher's definition of the duties bestowed upon a tourism ambassador, I wish to conclude that Rihanna does in fact purvey the symbols of her native homeland in her music, albeit from a modern day perspective, and thus I concur from a social and cultural understanding of authenticity that she depicts an authentic depiction of the Barbados music culture.

Bibliography

Besigiroha, Linda (2010) 'Independant women? Feminist Discourse in Music Videos'. In Gymnich, Marion & Ruhl, Kathrin & Scheunemann Klaus (eds) *Gendered (Re)Visions: Constructions of Gender in Audiovisual Media*, 227-240. Germany: Bonn Univeristy Press.

Best, Curwin. 2004. *Culture @ the Cutting Edge: Tracking Caribbean Popular Music*. Jamaica: University of the West Indies Press.

Connell, John and Gibson Chris. 2003. *Sound Tracks: Popular Music, Identity, and Place*. London: Routledge.

Cooper, Carolyn. 2004. *Sound Clash: Jamaican Dancehall Culture at Large*. New York: Palgrave Macmillan.

Fabian, Johannes.1983. *Time and the Other: How Anthropology Makes Its Object*. New York: Columbia University Press.

Gazzah, Mirian. 2008. *Rhythms and Rhymes of Life: Music and Identification Processes of Dutch – Moroccan Youth*. Amsterdam: Amsterdam University Press.

Horner Fletcher & Neville and Rossing, Thomas D. 2010. *The Physics of Musical Instruments*. New York: Springer.

Ivanovic, Milena. 2008. *Cultural Tourism*. Cape Town, South Africa: Juta & Company Ltd.

King, Stephen A. 2002. *Reggae, Rastafari, and the Rhetoric of Social Control*. US: University Press of Mississipi.

Kuss, Malena. 2007. *Music in Latin America and the Caribbean: An Encyclopaedic History*. USA: The Universe of Music, Inc.

Macleod, Donald V. L. 2004. *Tourism, Globalisation and Cultural Change*. New York: Channel View Publications.

Manuel, Peter. 1988. *Popular Musics of the Non-Western World: An Introductory Survey*. Oxford: Oxford University Press.

Miller, Terry E & Shahriari, Andrew. 2012. *World Music: A Global Journey*. Oxon: Routledge.

Moore, Allan. 2002. *Authenticity as Authentication*. Popular Music. Volume 21: 209–223.

Moskowitz, David. 2013. 'Reggae'. In: Torres, George (eds) *Encyclopedia of Latin American Popular Music*, 330-32. Greenwood: California.

Pariser, Harry S. 2000. *Explore Barbados*. San Francisco, CA: Manatee Press.

Richards, Greg. 2001. *Cultural Attractions and European Tourism*. Oxon: CABI Publishing.

Smith, Melanie. 2009. *Issues in Cultural Tourism Studies*. Oxford: Routledge.

Smith, Stephen L J. 1995. *Tourism Analysis*. Second Edition. Essex: Long Man Group Limited.

Timothy, Dallen J. 2011. *Cultural Heritage and Tourism: An Introduction*. Bristol: Charlesworth Group.

Trevor G. Marshall and Elizabeth F. Watson. 2007. 'Barbados'. In Malena Kuss (eds). *Music in Latin America and the Caribbean: An Encyclopedic History*, 345-358. USA: Universe of Music.

Veal, Micheal. 2007. *Dub: Soundscapes and Shattered Songs in Jamaican Reggae*. Middletown: Wesleyan University Press.

Wirth-Nesher, Hana. 1996. *City Codes: Reading the Modern Urban Novel.* Cambridge: Cambridge University Press.

Online Sources

Alexander, Elle. 17.12.2013. 'Rihanna For Balmain'. Available at > http://www.vogue.co.uk/news/2013/12/17/rihanna-for-balmain---campaign-star. Accessed on 03 April 2014.

Artists Direct. 12.05.2006. 'Rihanna Answers Her Fans' Questions!'. Available   at http://www.artistdirect.com/nad/news/article/0,,3655358,00.html. Accessed on 07 March 2014.

BBC. 2014. 'Music of the Caribbean'. Available at > http://www.bbc.co.uk/schools/gcsebitesize/music/world_music/mus ic_carribean4.shtml. Accessed on 18 February 2014.

Barbados. 2014. 'Barbados Crop Over Festival'. Available at > http://www.barbados.org/cropover.htm.

Barbados Free Press. 18.06.2011. 'Rihanna as Tourism Ambassador: Smart move, Good deal, or drowning man grasping at a life preserver?' Available   at> http://barbadosfreepress.wordpress.com/2011/06/18/rihanna-as-tourism-ambassador-smart-move-good-deal-or-drowning-man-grasping-at-a-life-preserver/. Accessed on 09 April 2014.

Billboard. Caulfield, Keith. 30/05/2013. 'Rihanna Earns Sixth Million-Selling Album'. Available at > http://www.billboard.com/articles/news/1565445/rihanna-earns-sixth-million-selling-album. Accessed on 06 March 2014.

CTO. 12/12/2013. 'Caribbean Tourism Organization –Latest statistics 2013'. Available at > http://www.onecaribbean.org/wp-content/uploads/DEC12Lattab13.pdf. Accessed on 23 January 2014.

Daily Mail (10.08.2012) 'What, no bikini? Caribbean cutie Rihanna bathes in a sundress as she becomes the official face of Barbados'. Available at> http://www.dailymail.co.uk/tvshowbiz/article-2186387/Rihanna-smoulders-beach-official-face-Barbados.html. Accessed on 06 April 2014.

Expedia. 21.03.2014. 'Beach Hotels in West End, Negril. Available at> http://www.expedia.co.uk/West-End-Negril-Hotels-Beach-Hotel.0-n6160037-0-tBeachHotel.Travel-Guide-Filter-Hotels. Accessed on 21 March 2014.

Grow, Kerry. 2012. 'Rihanna Loses Nivea Deal After Year-Long Sexiness Campaign'. Available at> http://www.spin.com/#articles/rihanna-loses-nivea-deal-after-year-long-sexiness-campaign/. Accessed on 01 April 2014.

Hall, Kerry. 2013. 'White Paper on the Development of Tourism in Barbados'. [Government Document] Obtained from > http://barbadosunderground.files.wordpress.com/2012/12/draft-white-paper-revised-13-feb-2012-final-version.pdf. Accessed on 08 October 2013.

Hampp, Andrew. 17.09.2013. 'Exclusive Premiere: Watch Budweiser-Sponsored Rihanna Documentary 'Half Of Me''. Available at>http://www.billboard.com/articles/news/5695561/exclusive-premiere-watch-budweiser-sponsored-rihanna-documentary-half-of-me. Accessed on 07 April 2014.

Holmes, Sally. 24.03.2014. 'Rihanna to Receive CFDA Fashion Icon Award'. Available at> http://www.elle.com/news/fashion-style/rihanna-to-receive-cfda-fashion-icon-award. Accessed on 04 April 2014.

Kidzworld, 2014. 'Rihanna Interview'. Available at >http://www.kidzworld.com/article/5853-rihanna-interview. Accessed on 07 March 2014.

Leadbeater, Chris. 2013. 'Rihanna shows her playful side in new video shoot for her home island Barbados'. Available at > http://www.dailymail.co.uk/travel/article-2256039/Rihanna-stars-new-advertising-campaign-Barbados.html?ITO=1490&ns_mchannel=rss&ns_campaign=1490. Accessed on 18 February 2014.

Loveridge, Adrian. 11.10. 2013. 'Barbados tourism performance worst of 25 Caribbean Tourism Organisation members'. Available> https://barbadosfreepress.wordpress.com/tag/rihanna/ Accessed on 20 March 2014.

MAC Cosmetics. 2014. 'RiRi MAC Fall'. Available at > http://www.maccosmetics.com/whats_new/11626/New-Collections/RiRi-Hearts-MAC-Fall/index.tmpl. Accessed on 08 April 2014.

Nicholas, Anne. 2010. 'Game over for Rafa Nadal and Majorca tourism'. Available at > http://my.telegraph.co.uk/expat/annanicholas/10140603/game-over-for-rafa-nadal-and-majorca-tourism/. Accessed on 18 February 2014.

NME. 12.06.2011. 'Rihanna made Barbados ambassador by tourist board'. Available at > http://www.nme.com/news/rihanna/57376. Accessed on 18 March 2014.

Pietroluongo, Silvio (March 17, 2010) 'Rihanna Rules Hot 100 with 'Rude Boy' Track'. Billboard. Available at> http://www.billboard.com/articles/news/958936/rihanna-rules-hot-100-with-rude-boy-track Accessed on 20 March 2014.

Totallybarbados. 2014. 'Barbados Festivals' [Online] Available at > http://www.totallybarbados.com/barbados/Entertainment/Festivals/. Accessed on 07 March 2014.

Vena, Jocelyn. 2011. 'Rihanna's 'We Found Love' Video Tells 'Everybody's' Story'. Available at > http://www.mtv.com/news/articles/1672957/rihanna-we-found-love-melina-matsoukas.jhtml. Accessed on 18 February 2014.

Visit Barbados. 2014. 'The music of Barbados'. Available at > http://www.visitbarbados.org/bajan-music.aspx. Accessed on 24 February 2014.

Walters, Barry. 08.09.2005. 'Rihanna'. Available at > http://www.rollingstone.com/music/albumreviews/music-of-the-sun-20050908. Accessed on 07 March 2014.

World Tourism Organization. 2013. 'UNWTO Tourism Highlights'. Available at> http://dtxtq4w60xqpw.cloudfront.net/sites/all/files/pdf/unwto_highlights13_en_hr.pdf. Accessed on 22 January 2014.

Videos

Barbados Tourism Authority (2013) *Rihanna Barbados 2013 Campaign Video* [Online video]. Available at> https://www.youtube.com/watch?v=V5kbjC96oss. Accessed on 20 December 2013.

Rihanna (2005) *Pon de Replay (Internet Version)* [Online video]. Available at> https://www.youtube.com/watch?v=oEauWw9ZGrA. Accessed on 03 January 2014.

Rihanna (2010) *Rihanna - What's My Name? ft. Drake* [Online video]. Available at> https://www.youtube.com/watch?v=U0CGsw6h60k. Accessed on 04 January 2014.

Rihanna (2011) *Rihanna - We Found Love ft. Calvin Harris* [Online video]. Available at > https://www.youtube.com/watch?v=tg00YEETFzg. Accessed on 03 January 2014.

Rihanna (2011) *Rihanna - Man Down* [Online video]. Available at> https://www.youtube.com/watch?v=sEhy-RXkNo0. Accessed on 05 January 2014.

Rihanna (2011) *You Da One* [Online video]. Available at> https://www.youtube.com/watch?v=b3HeLs8Yosw. Accessed on 02 January 2014.

Rihanna (2013) *Rihanna - Pour It Up (Explicit)* [online video]. Available at > https://www.youtube.com/watch?v=ehcVomMexkY. Accessed on 01 January 2014.

The Mighty Gabby (2014) *Emmerton.* Available at > http://www.visitbarbados.org/bajan-music.aspx. Accessed on 03 January 2014.

Discography

Rihanna. 2005. *Music Of The Sun.* London: Def Jam Recordings 9885146. Compact Disc.

Rihanna. 2006. *A Girl Like Me.* London: Def Jam Recordings 9878575. Compact Disc.

Rihanna. 2007. *Good Girl Gone Bad.* London: Def Jam Recordings 1736599. Compact Disc.

Rihanna. 2009. *Rated R.* London: Def Jam Recordings 602527259901 Compact Disc.

Rihanna. 2010. *Loud.* London: Def Jam Recordings 0602527523651. Compact Disc.

Rihanna. 2011. *Talk That Talk.*London: Def Jam UK 602527904542. Compact Disc.

Rihanna. 2012. *Unapologetic.* London: Def Jam Recordings 3722236. Compact Disc.

CHAPTER 4

Music, Memes and Metaphors: An Analysis of the Construction of Meanings in Popular Music

Chris Cawthorne

> In and of itself, music is not so full of meaning for our inner life, so profoundly moving, that it can claim to be a *direct* language of the emotion . . . The intellect itself has *projected* this meaning into the sound, as it has also read into the relationship of lines and masses in architecture a meaning that is, however, actually quite foreign to mechanical laws. (Nietzsche 2004:128)

The pages that follow deal with but one question: how does music *mean?*[1] As such, what is 'good' or 'bad', 'authentic' or 'fake', 'exciting' or 'insipid', is neither here nor there. It is not *what* music means that is of interest here. Instead, our task is to consider the manner in which *meanings are represented in music,* and set out a system through which such meanings can be discerned and explicated.

Considerations into the putative links between music and language are by no means unprecedented in academic discourse (see 'Source Review'). Between the various strands of cultural studies, linguistics, literary theory and philosophy, the ground work has been well covered. But what these studies dispense in observation, they take back in their self-containment and dissension towards other disciplines. For what remains the greatest threat to the study of meaning is the unyielding bent of scholars to follow the well-trodden paths that preceded them and to stay within the confines of their own discursive parameters. It is, in other words, only upon traversing the conceptual fissures between these disciplines that the full understanding of musical meaning can be realised. Interdisciplinarity is thus essential.

---

[1] I wish to make it clear from the outset that, in the present context, 'music' will be understood as referring to its structural features alone. That is to say, the analysis of secondary elements—such as lyrics—will not be undertaken herein. In broad terms, the object of inquiry here is anything that can be represented on a 'stave'.

In appearing at the outset, Nietzsche's remark is as about as productive as it is damaging, as aside from framing that which is to follow here, he also expresses in a single phrase what I have required an entire essay to demonstrate—although it is hoped that this account will be significantly more substantial. Paradoxically, the theory of meaning that follows here is something quite abstract from music itself, whilst, at the same time, inextricably bound to it. This is the principle focus of section one, 'Language and Functionality', in which the abstract rules and systems that govern the representation of meaning in language is dealt with at some length.

Section two, 'Music, 'Man' and Metaphor', building on the theories set out in the previous section, attempts to outline the fundamental differences that separate music from other forms of language. Beginning with an analysis of the inherent difficulties in rendering music distinct, the concluding pages aim to illustrate a cohesive theory for distinguishing between music and 'verbal language' without, in so doing, undermining the structural foundations on which they are each upheld.

In the final section, 'Cultural Evolution', we consider how meanings enter into language. For if language, as we shall see, is merely a conduit for the representation of meaning, there must necessarily be a contrast between that which enters at one end and that which is received at the other. Moreover, upon concluding, we look at the prognostic value of the theories set out in the section, contrasting their application now (2014) with the context of their origin.

In the bringing together of hitherto disparate theories, I aim to demonstrate a theory of musical meaning that is both encompassing and satisfactory. For it is only in the full understanding of musical meaning that we can grant ourselves a full understanding of music in *toto*.

Source Review

The antecedents to the critical consideration of the relationship between music and language can be said to stretch right across the history of 'Western philosophy', with some vestigial strands reaching as far back as Greek antiquity (Bowie 2007; Thomas 1995). However, properly speaking, it was not until the turn of the twentieth century that the study of language began to take the form in which we know today, with theorists such as Ferdinand de Saussure (1916a; 1916b) emphasising language as both a veritable object of scientific inquiry and a means for the construction of meaning in society (ibid.).

Shortly after Saussure, philosophy split into 'two camps', which can be followed right into the latter half of the twentieth century—and indeed thereafter—along two longitudinal traditions: 'Analytical' and 'Continental' (Edgar and Sedgwick 2010). The former, initiated by the likes of Bertram Russell and Ludwig Wittgenstein, regarded language as a set of tools for accurately and *logically* describing the world; a tradition that subsequently gave rise to theorists such as Noam Chomsky and Donald Davidson (Davidson 1978, 1986; Edgar and Sedgwick 2010). The latter, whose exact origin is perhaps less determinate, has its roots in hermeneutics and phenomenology and has come to be more closely associated with disciplines in sociology and cultural studies (Burke et al. 2000; Edgar and Sedgwick 2010; Storey 2012).

Of course, it is not entirely necessary that this division should be so easily deduced, as each tradition follows a not-dissimilar trajectory into the mid-twentieth century, both holding language as fundamental to the way in which we interpret and ascribe meaning to the world. However, its evocation here serves only to guide us in the right direction, as it will be the Continental tradition that our analysis will be principally, though not invariably, concerned with.

One of the prevailing themes in Continental philosophy, then, is the idea that all meaningful communication, and therefore meanings overall, can be mapped onto a complex 'system of representation', which is based on the work of Ferdinand de Saussure (Edgar and Sedgwick 2010; Hall 1997; Saussure 1916a, 1916b). As such, *semiology* is now synonymous with the Continental traditional; and in particular, with the French 'structuralist' thinkers of the early 1960s, such as Barthes (2013), Derrida (2001) and Foucault (2002).[2] Of these theorists, it was Roland Barthes in particular who used the linguistic structures—of the 'signifier', 'signified' and 'sign'—set out by Saussure

---

[2] The term structuralism is used here in the inclusive sense - encompassing structuralism, post-structuralism, deconstructionism, etc.

(1916a) to model his *system of signification* that will be so heavily relied upon over the following pages—foremost, sections one and two.

Saussure's work (ibid, 1916b) is also elicited in section three, apropos of the ways in which meanings can be traced across the development of language. Setting up a two-dimensional axis—*the axis of successions* and *the axis of simultaneities*— Saussure suggest that the construction of meaning can be shown to evolve both horizontally—through time— and vertically—across a cultural space (1916b). This, again, provides a solid foundation for the theories discussed throughout the section—in particular, those regarding memetics—and a cohesive way of binding together the accepted themes in philosophy and cultural studies (Burke et al. 2000; Derrida 2001; Tagg 2012), with the more unorthodox themes derived from psychology and evolutionary biology (Blackmore 1999; Dawkins 2006). Saussure, then, and the Continental tradition, has thus been essential to the following study, as both an inaugural framework and a subsequent means of theoretical cohesion

Language and Functionality

If music is a language, then our first question is simple: what is language? Stuart Hall describes it thus: 'in language, we use signs and symbols—whether they are sounds, written words, electronically produced images, musical notes, even objects—to stand for or represent to other people our concepts, ideas and feelings' (Hall 1997:1). In other words, the function of language lies in the *externalisation* of concepts. If we accept this, then our second question should be thus: *how* do signs and symbols come to stand for our concepts and feelings? If we are to understand how music has come to have meanings, then we must first consider language as a whole.

Signs and Systems of Representation

Nothing in the inscription of 'left' is inherently leftward; this is also true of its utterance, 'l-ɛ-f-t'.[3] Nevertheless, on seeing or hearing the term, the average Anglophone will have no trouble comprehending its meaning: *that which is westward when facing north*. In this way, we seem to

---

[3] This is, perhaps, poor example if we include the discernible semblance of an 'L' suggested in the extension the left hand thumb and forefinger. However, an oversight of this anomaly is surely justified as coincidental.

receive meanings intuitively; and as long as your 'left' is the same as mine—when, say, driving a car—we need not ever think about it. But how can we explain this phenomenon?

In semiology, it is said that meanings are communicated via a 'shared system of representation' (Hall 1997); a process based on the relationship between what Ferdinand de Saussure termed the *signifier*, the *signified*, and the *sign* (Saussure, 1916a). At each end of the division between the *word*, 'left', and the *concept* of 'leftness', is where Saussure places the signifier and the signified: the signifier represents or *refers to* the signified. Moreover, when we hear/see the word 'left', the association of the signifier and signified is seamless and presupposed: we apprehend the two as essentially combined. Saussure called this the *sign* (ibid.).

That written language is itself a signifier makes this a particularly difficult concept to explain; even a fairly prosaic example, such as that offered above, only frames what Roland Barthes terms the 'primary' or '*denotative*' aspect of signification (Barthes 2013).

The expression of denotative meanings—e.g. directions, descriptions, etc.—adheres to the same structure set out in the example above: (signifier → signified) = sign. However, language also expresses what semioticians call the connotative signification. In order to express this second meaning, Barthes argues that the *sign* of the primary signification must become the *signifier* of the secondary signification. For both clarity and economy, I have reproduced the example from Barthes' celebrated essay, 'Myth Today' (2013), below: [4]

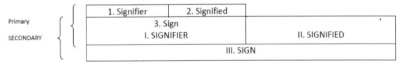

Figure 1.1 (ibid: p.224) [4]

---

[4] (*Figure 1.1*). In Barthes' original table, he enumerates the two semiological systems as 'Language' and 'MYTH' (2013). Replicating this here would cause unnecessary confusion; I have therefore substituted his designation with the terms 'Primary' and 'SECONDARY'—terms amiable with both Barthes' and my own intentions.

The *denotative* meaning of 'left' –that which is westward when facing north—can be mapped on to the 'Primary' stage of Barthes' table (*Figure 1.1*). However, in its 'SECONDARY' signification, 'left' can also *connote* a particular political persuasion. Although nothing in the phenomenology of Socialism is *literally* leftward, any more than the phonology of the letters L-E-F-T, we see that meanings are built up in holistic structures, constituted by monadic and interdependent units. Thus the phrase, 'on the left', carries two meanings.

Having established the role of semiotics in the functionality of language, we can now begin to conceptualise an acceptable model for the discernment of *musical* meaning. For if music is, indeed, a form of language, then it must necessarily adhere to this same system of signification. The following example may provide a suitable explanation of how this is so.

To the ear of those whose tastes are derived from a Western Christian tradition, a 'sad' chord is constituted by the notes that make up a 'minor chord'. On the primary plain of analysis, these denote the formal features that make up the sign, 'minor chord'. In its secondary signification, the 'minor chord' also connotes the emotion, 'sadness'. Thus, as with verbal language, musical meanings are holistic and comprised of minimal units of signification that are layered on top of one another. However, while the current model seems to satisfy the examples delineated above, a singular minor chord does little by way of reflecting a full musical experience. If we are to accept this model, and the notion of meanings as built up from holistic units, then we must first consider what constitutes a musical 'unit'.

Charles Seeger coined the term 'museme' to describe a unit of music comparable to that of the morpheme in language (Tagg 2012).[5] According to Tagg, the museme can designate anything in a song, from a particular chord in a Beatles track, to a mistake left in the final mix of a Sex Pistols track, to a discernible use of 'close-miking' in a Tori Amos recording –i.e. anything present in the aural musical experience (ibid.). However, as we have seen, it is not always these *minimal* musical units that constitute our experience of music. Take, for example, The Rolling

---

[5] Morpheme: 'A meaningful morphological unit of a language that cannot be further divided (e.g. in-come-ing, forming incoming)'. (Oxford Dictionaries [ONLINE]).

Stones' 'Midnight Rambler' (1969): over the course almost seven minutes, the song's tempo steadily—but noticeably—increases, before another transition into almost total inertia. This particular meaning— i.e. speeding-up and slowing-down—can only be communicated in the context of the whole performance. But whence has the museme emerged?

Tagg suggests that musemes are interdependent and, though significant in their singularity, best understood in terms of 'museme stacks' (ibid.). We also see this in verbal languages; for example, there are very few instances in which a word can have meaning when considered in total abstraction. Even the word, 'no', has little significance if it is not situated in the context of other words: "do you like Bob Dylan?' . . . 'No!".[6] In this manner, if Barthes' system can be used to explain the process by which the museme represents meanings, then Tagg's notion of 'stacked signification' provides a way of viewing how meanings can be understood as holistic structures.

So far, then, we have established the semiological process through which language represents meaning. However, the problem with Barthes earlier model (*Figure 1.1*) is its narrow admission of interpretive meanings, regarding the process of stacked signification as though it existed independently of any context. That is to say, if the 'speeding-up/slowing-down' in 'Midnight Rambler' (1969) can be said to constitute *one* museme stack, then how can we account for everything else that is happening in the text? Where, for example, does the interplay between the harmonica and the lead guitar fit into this stack? Of course, the obvious answer is that songs are built up of many different stacks, merging and intertwining throughout the song's duration. But this is far from unproblematic; such a system would result in a very complex, almost completely incomprehensible enterprise.

In the late 1960s, the structuralists began to consider the limitations of the *sign*, with theorists such as Jacques Derrida, Michel Foucault and Barthes himself moving into the realms of what we might now refer to

---

[6] In fact, Donald Davidson claims that words can be understood perfectly well in abstraction as they are almost always supplemented by other forms of language, such as gesture: "[points to a Bob Dylan CD]' . . . 'No!" (Donaldson 1986). See section two.

as post-structuralism (Storey, 2012). They claimed that the 'science of the signifier . . . has taken its place in the work of the period and its purpose is less the analysis of the sign than its dislocation' (Barthes 1971:166). It is to this school that we shall now turn.

After the Sign: Différance *and the Third Meaning*

When we listen to music, we are not simply listening to a succession of chords, but a succession of *differences*. A song is not merely its score; it is the differences between the notes of a melody, between the melody and its harmonies, the pitch and its rhythm, etc: music only exists in the spaces between the notes. Even a singular, long, monotonous note, when presented as music, exists only in its relation to the notes and rhythms that have been excluded from that piece. In this way, music is temporal, in that it exists and is experienced in real-time. As such, musemes—and therefore meanings—are racing past our ears each second. We cannot stop the music to contemplate them, as they would then disappear. Music is thereby constantly shifting in meaning. Moreover, because musical meaning is built up from *differing* signifying units that are constantly shifting between one another, meaning is therefore always being *deferred*. This is why, to resort to predicates, music 'ebbs and flows', has 'depth' and 'nuances', it 'takes us on a journey': in a word, music is *expressive*.

This flux, in which meanings are both *different* and *deferring*, is what Jacques Derrida called '*différance*'—simply an amalgamation of the two terms (Storey 2012). Derrida described this as 'the indefinite referral of signifier to signifier . . . which gives the signified meaning no respite . . . so that it always signifies again and differs' (Derrida 2001:29). Furthermore, 'it is only when located in a discourse and read in a context that there is a temporary halt to the endless play of signifier to signifier' (Storey 2012:129).

There are two contexts in which musical *différance* can be located. The first we have discussed above in the form of the museme stack, whereby each musical unit is bound up in both its difference to the proceeding unit and its anticipated deference to the following unit. Hence the motional predicates that are so often ascribed to music. The second context deals with musical meaning on a much more *individualised* level: a signification that is only perceptible and discernible to the listening subject alone. Barthes (1970), in an essay of the same name, called this 'the third meaning'.

Proposed during his analysis of the photographic image, Barthes' third meaning, under a little revision, offers further possibilities for the case at hand. Using as a basis the primary and secondary modes of signification set out above (*Figure 1.1*), Barthes suggests that this system should be extended by a further signification: the *sign* of the secondary signification becoming the *signifier* of the third (ibid.). Viewed in this way, an object now signifies three meanings: a primary meaning—denotation; a secondary meaning—connotation; and a third meaning—connotation/*différance*).

The secondary signification, or the 'obvious meaning', serves the same purpose as it did prior to this annexation (ibid.): minor chord = sadness. The third signification, or the 'obtuse meaning', however, takes on a different role, signifying something far more subtle and far more subjective. It is a hidden meaning that is at once *different* to, and *deferred* from, the former:

> The obtuse meaning, then, has something to do with disguise . . . it declares its artifice without in so doing abandoning the 'good faith' of its referent . . . without one disguise destroying the other; a multi-layering of meanings which always lets the previous meaning continue, as in a geological formation, saying the opposite without giving up the contrary.(ibid:58)

In other words, *the third meaning* is a kind of paradox. Emerging from the secondary signification, it is at the same time entirely independent of it. Furthermore, it is not simply a fixed or latent quality of the obvious meaning that is amenable to scrutiny and objectively discerned. It is, in part, carried over from the secondary signification and constituted by the contingency of the reader's subjectivity.

Take, for example, R.E.M.'s 'Shiny Happy People' (1991). To 'western ears', we might reasonably describe it as a 'happy' song. On a denotative scale, the music exemplifies its formal features: the 'major key'; the '90s Alt./Trad. Folk' instrumentation and genre conventions; the rising canon melody in the call-and-response section, etc: all of which are, *prima facie*, 'happy' elements. Moreover, on a connotative level, the 'jingling' guitars, the hand-claps that punctuate the mandolin refrain, Kate Pierson's 'bright' and 'chirpy' vocals, the 'upbeat' rhythm and overall *'feel'* of the track, all signify a certain 'cheerfulness', 'happiness' and 'positivity'.

In its third signification, however, it is possible to say that 'Shiny Happy People' (1991) is a 'creepy' song. The very insistence of its 'happiness', the 'disingenuousness' of the vocal timbre, the 'ghostly' resonance of the mandolin: something in all of these elements imbue the song with a surreal and perturbing quality. In the verses the key changes to minor, on one level, emphasising the exuberance of the chorus, providing a 'release' for the tension built up throughout. However, I would argue that this only adds to the torment of the track, unearthing an even 'darker' underpinning. Similar can be said for the 'waltz' style middle-8, evoking the image of bourgeois complacency, depressing by way of its very indifference. But still, amidst this general 'creepiness', the song remains contagiously 'upbeat', and almost infallibly 'happy': the 'good faith' of the referent remains intact.[7]

We began the present section with a question: if music is a language, then how does language come to have meaning? Language can be viewed as a *system of representation* through which meanings are represented and understood. Drawing from themes in Continental philosophy and semiology, we have seen that musical meanings are constructed from minimal units of signification - or musemes - that can be mapped onto a *three-tiered* system (*Figure 1.1*). Each layer of signification has a different function: denotation, connotation and *différance*. Furthermore, units can be 'stacked' up and intertwined, creating a complex nexus of signification that is always shifting. In light of this, the following section will begin to consider the ways in which music is unique as a language, how musical significations differ to those of speech, or video, etc.

Music, 'Man' and Metaphor

Music is a language, but it also different to language. One reason for this may be that we receive music through different mediums, such as instruments or CD players, etc; but this is highly unsatisfying for two reasons. First of all, languages share mediums: we sing through the

---

[7] Of course, as Barthes suggests, meaning—especially the third meaning—is a highly subjective phenomenon. As follows, the foregoing example is purely heuristic and based entirely upon my own interpretation.

same medium with which we speak; we use CD players for our 'Learn French' audio-books, etc. Secondly, as we saw in section one, different languages are represented, and therefore apprehended, via the same *system of representation*. Accepting this, it follows that languages cannot be differentiated by way of their structural features but by the meanings they represent, rendering the 'different mediums' argument redundant.[8] I shall therefore begin with this section, as I did the first, with a simple question: how is musical meaning *unique*?

A Brief Archaeology of Language

'Man' [sic] features in the present section heading for two reasons: [i] alliteration; and [ii] the notion of anthropocentricism—and indeed, patriarchy—can be traced across the entire historical development of language and meaning (Tagg 2012). Robert Oliphant, to give just one example, said that 'music and language are both uniquely human activities, they set us apart from the other creatures of this planet' (Oliphant 1972:60). Borderline dogmatism aside, there is certainly some truth to this claim. However, is it not true that animals 'sing'?

Phillip Tagg, in his self-inferred *magnum opus, Music's Meaning* (2012), dedicates a surprising amount of wordage to this issue. Take, for example, his treatment of the whale song:

> As [humpback whales] migrate or swim around their breeding grounds, they piece together repeated phrases, singing song after song for up to twenty-four hours . . . Humpback whale song also contains rhythms and phrases which, strung together, build forms of a length comparable to ballads or symphonic movements. It also seems that their songs contain recurrent formulae which end off different phrases in much the same way as we use rhyme in poetry. (Tagg 2012:55)

Despite this appearance, Tagg suggests that the whale song cannot be conflated with the structural and aesthetic conventions of 'human music'. Their use of sound in this way bears a closer resemblance to our use of verbal language; and even then, it is a far less sophisticated

---

[8] The term 'structural features' is used here in a strictly semiological context, as it is the tradition on which we have based our analysis. For another perspective see Feld and Fox (1994), who argue that the relationship between music and verbal language can be viewed as essentially linguistic and explained in terms of grammatical structures such as syntax, semantics and pragmatics.

system (ibid.). Though animals use language, in that they apprehend shared sign systems, it serves only as a kind of *proto-language*. The difficulty with this view, at least for Tagg, is that it is essentially *anthropomorphic* in that it 'interpret[s] *non-human* behaviour on the basis of *human* experience, perception and behaviour' (ibid: p.55). In other words, the very fact that we perceive, and thereby label, the utterances of animals as essentially musical, supports the view that music is a distinctly human conception: put tersely, birds do not *hear themselves* as 'singing'.

The implications of this kind of assertion are far too numerous to exhaust here. However, if we are to distinguish music from language proper, then the foregoing considerations must not be overlooked. Indeed, if we have learnt anything from modern science and evolutionary biology, it is that human language itself must have evolved from an antecedent proto-language (Darwin 2011). Further, if we are to accept this theory, then the very possibility of abstracting music from language is thrown into question.

Downing A. Thomas, in his consideration music's role in the French Enlightenment, offers one way of thinking about this:

> Conceived of as a natural sign of the passions, music predates all language. As such, it constitutes a natural model for all representation . . . and thus paves the way for the subsequent elaboration of conventional sign systems and signifying practices . . . As a signifying practice which is nonetheless still part of the natural world, a primordial system of musical tones sets the stage for conventional language and the culture that exists within language. (Thomas 1995:9-10)

One interpretation of this is that music represents an ideal form of semiotic signification, a *pièce de résistance* of Barthes' system of representation covered in section one. Even if this is not Thomas's precise intention, we can at least conclude that both music and language have emerged from the same nebulous origin. But we have yet to properly answer the question set out above.

There is also another, perhaps more fruitful implication to Thomas's claim however; one we see again and again in related literature (Schopenhauer 1970; Bowie 2007). It is that we conceive of music as *a natural sign of the passions*. In other words, as Schopenhauer once put it, it would seem that 'music speaks not of things but of weal and woe . . . that is why it speaks so much to the heart [the emotions], while it has nothing to say directly to the head [reason]' (Schopenhauer 1970:162). Thus we have two propositions: [i] at the very moment that we began to use language reflexively, and as a means of conceptual externalisation, language also began its diversification; and [ii] upon this diversification, each different aspect of language aligned itself with a particular aspect of signification - music became the language of *the heart* thereof.

In other words, despite sharing the same system of representation for the dissemination of meaning, the differing forms of meaning generated by, say, music and verbal language remain ultimately incommensurable as they are apprehended by different modes of our cognition—i.e. reason and emotion.[9] This is why simply explaining to someone, in words, the way you feel when listening to a particularly 'affective' or 'moving' piece of music does very little in turn to 'affect' or 'move' your listener. That they may recognise, conceptually, the feelings you aim to express, your verbal expression does nothing by way of evoking those same feelings in that individual.

How, then, can we begin to identify these modes without reducing them to mere romanticisms? To stay with the foregoing example, it is clear that music and verbal language occupy different roles in our lives. The purpose and functionality of verbal language, for instance, necessarily relies on its ability to articulate concepts in a way that is precise and unambiguous: music, on the other hand, communicates meanings that exist outside the scope of verbal language. Andrew Bowie offers an astute designation, marking a distinction between 'the conceptual, that is communicated by [verbal] language, and the pre- or extra-conceptual, that is communicated by music' (Bowie 2007:221).

Therefore, we now have three suppositions: [i] all language, from a semiological perspective, adheres to a sovereign *system of representation* of the kind we saw in section one; [ii] languages are aspectual in that their

---

[9] Here, 'emotion' can be taken in its broadest sense; this includes what is often referred to as 'feelings'. For as Andrew Bowie suggests, 'the line between feelings, which supposedly has no cognitive content, and emotion, which does . . . [is] less clear-cut than is often thought (Bowie 2007:20).

respective meanings appeal to different modes of apprehension—
emotion/reason, etc; [iii] as such, music communicates *extra-conceptual*
content in that it is apprehended by the emotions—as opposed to
reason, which is the realm of verbal language: those who understand
the term 'left', turn when they hear it said; those who understand
sadness, feel so when they hear it played.

In accepting these claims, we are well on our way towards a satisfying
conception of how musical meanings are represented through language
and apprehended thereof. Yet, our project is still too skeletal; it
requires more substance and cohesion, a way of grounding our analysis
in comprehensible and familiar terms. I therefore dedicate the
following to this task.

Meaning and Metaphor

In section one, we agreed that language has three levels of signification:
denotative, connotative, and *différance* (Barthes 1971, 2013; Derrida
2001). My first aim, here, is to suggest that each of these levels
correspond with the different modes of apprehension discussed above
(Bowie 2007). That is to say, the former—denotative signification—is
apprehended conceptually; the latter, apprehended extra-conceptually.
Secondly, I aim to suggest that it is via the concept of *metaphor* that
these parallels can be upheld.

Jenefer Robinson asserts that a musical work has two expressive
functions: to [i] *literally exemplify* its formal features, and [ii] *metaphorically
exemplify* its expressive features (Robinson 2010). However, while there
should be no problem in accepting this claim, it is of little consequence
here, as Robinson offers nothing in terms of how this exemplification
is achieved. Thus, it is only through the full comprehension of
metaphor that we can begin to understand this phenomenon.

The common conception of *metaphor* has undergone little change since
Aristotle, who described it as simply 'the application of a noun which
properly applies to something else' (Aristotle 1996:34). This, however,
will not be the conception used here, as it is far too broad and
deductive. Instead, we might look to Donald Davidson, who, flying in
the face of the Aristotelian view, suggested that 'metaphors mean what
the [expressions], in their most literal interpretation, mean, and nothing
more' (Donaldson 1978:209). That is to say, figurative language is in

fact literal, in that it is simply another way of expressing a literal meaning. Take, for example, the sports commentator who exclaims, 'she's on fire'. On hearing this, we know that the competitor has not burst into flames but instead demonstrated a vivacious athleticism. Hence, the locution, 'she's on fire', expresses two meanings - one denotative, one connotative - both of which are apprehended literally.[10]

It is this conception of metaphor that is essential to a comprehensive and cohesive understanding of musical meaning. Consider, for example, Roger Scruton's remark concerning expressivity in the music of Bedřich Smetana:

> It does not seem strained to suggest that Smetana's music expresses the shining and silken qualities that we hear in it. Smetana's music is not *literally* shining or silken. But its expressive power is revealed in its ability to compel these *metaphors* from us, and persuade us that they fit exactly. Of course, it is a mystery that they fit. But the mystery is immovable. (Scruton 1999: in Boghossain 2010:122 [my emphasis])

Paradoxically, Scruton's claim is at once agreeable, and yet, woefully amiss. Indeed, it does not seem strained to talk about music in this way; and indeed, the metaphors, 'shining' and 'silken', seem an apt choice for the music in question. However, that the metaphor is simply a *mystery* is a view that I do not share.

Ultimately, Scruton reduces the metaphor to a purely verbal phenomenon: it is only by ascribing to it words such as 'shining' or 'silken' that the music obtains, and thereby expresses its meaning. This, however, is problematic; for if such words did not exist, then, following Scruton's argument, Smetana's music would be devoid of meaning entirely—which is inconceivable. Instead, the metaphor must be viewed as a kind of transaction, a state of reciprocity. For if music and verbal language are simply variations of the same abstract system then their meanings must be expressed equally, and indeed symbiotically, by both. Each expression is different, but only insofar as we apprehend them differently. Taking a metaphysical perspective, the

---

[10] Lest being reductive, I would not hesitate in referring the reader to Davidson's 'What Metaphors Mean' (1978), in which the concept of the literal-metaphor is rendered with far greater clarity.

'quality-of-shining' is not a property of language *per se*, but an abstract concept; language serves only to express this concept. The *word*, 'shining', expresses the 'quality-of-shining' *conceptually*—denotatively; in Smetana's *music*, it is expressed *extra-conceptually*—connotatively; both of these instances constitute a literal expression of this quality.

This is not to suggest, however, that metaphors have no function; on the contrary. Their role is to make us *notice* things, to foreground certain qualities, to illuminate underlying connections (Davidson 1978). When Walter Benjamin described the volumes of Proust's *À La Recherche Du Temps Perdu* as 'the Nile of language, which here overflows and fructifies the region of truth' he was revealing a perhaps hitherto-unrealised quality of the work (Benjamin 1929:197). So too, in Smetana's music, we are made to notice a *particular property* of shininess that cannot be expressed in other forms of language. The *visual* expression of shininess represented by, say, a mirror, therefore supplements the *aural* expression of shininess represented in Smetana's music. It is also in this heuristic function of the metaphor that musical meaning has its seat.

The problem with this, however, is that it is essentially Platonic, in that it posits meaning as something fixed and objective –a view I am not altogether satisfied with. As we saw in section one, meanings are not fixed in this way, but instead, highly subjective and always shifting. As Donaldson suggests, a 'metaphor is the dreamwork of language and, like all dreamwork, its interpretation reflects as much on the interpreter as on the originator' (Donaldson 1978:209). In other words, Scruton's interpretation and identification of meaning in Smetana's music is not sustained by a universal concept of shininess, but by his individual experience of the music apropos of his general experience of 'shininess'. As such, each time Scruton experiences a new or different expression of shininess, in *any* form of language, he is forced to review it. Consequently, in this involuntary re-evaluation, Scruton's interpretation of Smetana's music is, perforce, repositioned in reference to his renewed understanding. Its meaning is in a constant state of *différance*, lingering only momentarily before changing again as the process is repeated. The apprehension of musical meaning is thus *reflexive* and based on an unstable, three-way relationship between the subject, the object, and the subject's prior experience of the quality that the object represents.

Marcel Proust—as interpreted by Deleuze (2008)—saw the heuristic function of metaphor, as a means of revealing hidden truths about the world, to be essential in the role of art. Incidentally, Proust refers to such truths as 'signs', suggesting that their meaning is not concealed within an object of representation, but in the unique perspective of its beholder (ibid.). The artist is therefore a purveyor of 'coiled meanings', whose unique perspective of the world is drawn out and made conspicuous in his/her work. Unfortunately, Deleuze takes no liberty in expatiating on Proust's concept of the 'sign', and it is therefore unclear—and unlikely—that it has its basis in the Saussurean conception. It is useful, however, to consider the obvious parallels between the Proustian 'sign' and Barthesian 'third meaning' (1970) or Benjamin's concept of 'the aura' (1936).[11]

How, then, is musical meaning unique? Music, emerging as it did from an ambiguous 'proto-language', can be differentiated in terms of its apprehension. Represented by a semiotic system of signification, its meaning is an expression of extra-conceptual content (Bowie 2007). In using Donaldson's conception of metaphor (1978), we can devise a cohesive blueprint for mapping these modes of apprehension onto Barthes' system of signification (2013). Moreover, in briefly returning to the notion of *différance* (Derrida 2001), we saw that musical signification is a reflexive process, in which meanings are suspended between listeners and all their experiences with a particular expression of meaning.

Cultural Evolution

Our purpose here is to formulate a full and broad-gauge account of musical meaning. We have seen how meanings are represented in language; we have seen how such meanings, on account of their respective modes of apprehension, have come to occupy different expressive roles. In short, we have seen *how* music means. If, however, we are to grant our study its rightful certitude, then it must also be

---

[11] By necessity of space, I am enjoined from further discussion on Benjamin's concept of 'the aura'. However, in short, it is best understood as a kind of unique perception of the natural world: 'If, while resting on a summer afternoon, you follow with your eyes a mountain range on the horizon or a branch which casts its shadow over you, you experience the aura of those mountains, of that branch' (Benjamin 1936:216).

answerable to the question of *why* music means: or rather, how do these meanings *come into* language in the first place?

Spreading the Word

There is something inherently intuitive about language, a principle that, by way of its striking lucidity, has often lead theorists to the most counterintuitive of conjectures. Noam Chomsky, for instance, argued that the foundations of language are upheld by an innate syntactic capacity that is common to all humans, regardless of their socio-cultural differences (Edgar and Sedgwick 2010). I find this view to be vastly deficient.[12] Instead, I aim to argue that language and meaning can be explained in purely material terms, and that the 'intuitiveness' of language is simply an 'unconscious foundation' of culture (Storey 2012).

In section one, we agreed, provisionally, that the functionality of language relies on a necessarily predetermined vocabulary of 'shared sign systems' (Hall 1997). But this is not *strictly* true because, again, it frames language as something fixed and universal; which is, of course, not the case.[13] In other words, whilst the system by which meanings are represented in language is universal, the representations of these meanings are not *interpreted* in a fixed or universal way. Instead, as we saw in section two, meanings stand in a reflexive relation to the interpreter's subjectivity.

The trouble with this view is that it is essentially idiolectal, in that it places an unwieldy emphasis on the subject. That is, if meanings come into language by way of an interpreter's subjectivity alone, then surely the link between shared or mass languages and the conditions under which they can occur is forestalled and the very possibility of

---

[12] It is astonishing that Chomsky's theory ever gained the critical currency that it did. Using the capacity of children to construct new sentences from a limited exposure to words and phrases (Edgar and Sedgwick 2010), Chomsky seems to entirely negate the fact that [i] children are submerged in sounds and conversation from the moment they enter the world—whether it is directed at them or not; and [ii] world languages have completely different syntactical structures—even, say, French and English, which share a close etymological lineage.

[13] It is now more or less axiomatic that there is no such thing as a 'universal language' (Lévi-Strauss 1958; Tagg 2012).

meaningful communication between two or more people is obviated. Davidson (1986), however, argues the contrary:

> It is an enormous coincidence that many people speak in similar ways, and therefore can be interpreted in more or less the same way. But in principle communication does not demand that any two people speak the same language. What must be shared is the interpreter's and the speaker's *understanding* of the speaker's words. (ibid:256-257 [my emphasis])

In any case, it would seem that *subjectivity* is of central importance here. And indeed, if, as Davidson suggests, it is not so much a *shared system* but a shared *understanding* of that system on which meaningful communication relies, then there must also be a 'shared subjectivity'.

Tagg argues that in order for musical meanings to have a cultural significance there must be a degree of, what he terms, '*intersubjectivity*' (Tagg 2012): '*intersubjectivity* arises when at least two individuals experience the same thing in a similar way. The same (or a similar) experience is in other words shared between (*inter*) two or more human subjects' (ibid:196). For instance, not only can one be sure that there are others who apprehend R.E.M.'s 'Shiny Happy People' (1991) as essentially 'happy', it is also reasonable to assume that others will recognise its 'creepiness'.

'The fact of agreement', as Stanley Fish argues, 'rather than being a proof of the stability of [language], is a testimony to the power of an interpretive community to constitute the objects upon which its members . . . can then agree' (Fish 1981:338). As such, what we have is a conception of language that is suspended somewhere between a reading subject and his/her 'interpretive community', and in which the stability of the representation of meaning is upheld by the intersubjective knowledge and experience of that community (ibid.). Which is to say, if meanings, as we saw in section two, are simply the object of an individual's subjectivity, then the transmission of meaning from 'speaker'[14] to 'interpreter(s)' is not a neutral one, but an act of both refinement and authentication. Thus, language is not simply an *a priori* phenomenon, received by intuition alone, but a reciprocal process

---

[14] I use 'speaker' to refer to any purveyor of language in its broadest sense—i.e. musician, orator, filmmaker, etc.

between 'speakers' and interpreters within their respective communities. As such, the locus of meaning can have but one emplacement: culture itself.

Anthropologist, Claude Lévi-Strauss, argued that the seemingly 'natural' state of meaning within language is simply a product of its intrinsic coordination with the cultural environment from which it emerges:

> Language can be said to be a condition of culture because the material out of which language is built is of the same type as the material out of which the whole culture is built: logical relations, oppositions, correlations, and the like. Language, from this point of view, may appear as layering a kind of foundation for the more complex structures which correspond to the different aspects of culture. (Lévi-Strauss 1958:402)

Moreover, it is not only in verbal language that this process takes hold. In music, for example, the 'sad' signification of a 'minor chord' is a conspicuous facet of the 'Western' musical tradition, traceable across the wide-spread propagation of Roman Catholic ideologies in Central Europe during the Middle Ages (Moy 2000). In this manner, *received* Western tonalities are derived from the same ideological 'materials' as the predominant Christian belief systems in which they were conceived.

Just as the *apprehension* of meaning, discussed in section two, is based on a reflexive relationship between the subject, the object, and the subject's knowledge—whereupon meanings are in a constant state of *différance*—the *construction* of meaning is based on this same complex relationship, only extended across a field of shared and intersubjective ideologies.

In popular music, we can conceptualise this in terms of genre development. A *very* brief overview of rock music's early ancestry, for example, would illustrate a general structural development from austere blues/R 'n' B styles in the early-1960s, to experimental styles of garage/acid rock in the late-1960s, to the ostentatious whims of progressive rock in the early-1970s, and an 'ironic' return to austerity with punk in the late-1970s (Shuker 2012; Frith 2002). Over the course of this development, the accepted paradigms of rock music are constantly mutating, constantly *evolving*, constantly *deferred from*, and *different to*, the paradigms that preceded it: some are gained—e.g.

'virtuosity'—some fall away—e.g. 'virtuosity'—some remain steadfast throughout—e.g. 'auth-enticity' (ibid.). Furthermore, these alterations tend to follow a more or less demonstrable lineage: hence, the term 'sounds like'.

It is perhaps unsurprising, then, that meaning comes into language via its usage and subsequent mutation. But this is not a necessarily one-dimensional process. In fact, Saussure (1916b) suggests that the development of language should be viewed as positioned on the following axes:

> [i] *the axis of simultaneities* . . . which stands for the relation of coexisting things and from which the intervention of time is excluded; and [ii] *the axis of successions*, on which only one thing can be considered at a time but upon which are located all the things on the first axis together with their changes. (ibid:55).

On one hand, it could be argued that the different 'eras' of rock, delineated above, correspond with Saussure's *axis of simultaneities*. From this perspective, the various significations common to, say, progressive rock in the early 1970s—e.g. virtuosity = authenticity—are upheld in the same way that we have already seen: between the object, the subject, and the intersubjective collectivity of the respective interpretive community. On the other hand, the axis of successions allows us to trace the particular paradigms and significations that run through rock music's historical development—e.g. authenticity—independently of the sub-genres as a whole. Moreover, it is only when the two axes are considered in tandem that we can begin to map out the emergence of meanings within music.

It is not necessarily the structural features that matter in genre development, but the meanings assigned to them by particular interpreters at particular times. 'Virtuosity', for example, was valued in the early seventies for connoting 'authentic musicianship' before, paradoxically, being thrown out by the punks who saw it as 'authenticity's' precise antistudy. The signifier, 'virtuosity', is therefore purely contingent to the meaning, 'authenticity' (Shuker 2012).

From the evidence above, then, we are justified in the following deductions. Firstly, because meanings emerge from the same conditions as a culture itself, and are thereby transmitted primarily within that culture, it is possible for communities to interpret meanings in similar ways—intersubjectively. Secondly, while no *individual*, in their singularity, can infuse language with meaning, meanings are *evolved from* the constant adaptations and aberrations that must ultimately occur in a subject's usage of language—as a speaker or interpreter both. Finally, and perhaps most importantly, musical meanings are in no way 'natural' or 'inherent' within their significations, but constructed arbitrarily and *culturally contingent.*

Power and Memetics

Our final consideration is one that, in truth, deserves far more attention than it will consequently receive here. It is that, as many authors have observed, it is almost impossible to talk about the construction of meaning within language without falling upon the notion of *power relations* (Hall 1997). Unfortunately, of the many perspectives associated with this concept, the limitations of space enjoin their proper reproduction here. A *very* basic summery of these arguments, if ever one existed, would plausibly lead us towards a quasi-Marxist conception of language construction, in which meanings could be said to emerge from the hegemonic, discursive practices of top-down institutions, which are manipulated and controlled in the interests of a sovereign minority (Burke et al. 2000; Foucault 2002; Gramsci 1935).[15] An example of these themes can be found in the work of Pierre Bourdieu (2010).

In his analysis of taste construction and cultural evaluation in 1960s France, Bourdieu argued that construction of taste was an essentially stratified process (ibid.). For Bourdieu, his subjects' evaluation of what was 'good' and what was 'bad' revealed a close correspondence with traditional high/low cultural distinctions and could be mapped onto a distinctly Marxist model of society: meanings acquired a kind of 'cultural capital' that was designed and designated by the 1960s French Bourgeoisie (ibid.).

---

[15] In truth, such an outstanding oversimplification is barely justified by the reasons given, for the discourse surrounding culture, language and power relations remains, in my opinion, among the most relevant and critical debates still today. The proper elicitation of these arguments, however, would almost certainly require a project of their own. As such, I would refer the reader to the following discussions: Bourdieu (2010), Burke et al. (2000), Foucault (2002), Gramsci (1935), Hall (1997), Moy (2000).

So far, we have considered a whole range of theories in our analysis of musical meaning. However, we must also accept that it is an analysis deeply rooted in Western traditions of philosophy and cultural theory. However, in my view, we have yet to come up with a truly satisfying account of how musical meanings are generated. The point I make here, is that, though important, power relations do not provide a wholly satisfying answer to the question of why meanings *mean*. For if it is, in fact, the hegemony of institutionalised and/or market forces that ultimately inscribe meaning in language, then what is the impetus for that particular inscription in the first place? That is to say, if it was the Church who decided that the minor chord would be the 'sad' chord, what led them to that decision?

Memetics is, in truth, still a kind of pseudo-discipline, and has yet to gain credence within the respective critical discourses; it seems that many are either unsure of what to make of it or are simply reluctant to 'take it seriously' (Blackmore 1999). However, as I aim to demonstrate, memetics offers an insightful and cohesive way of viewing the modern world and its dealings—with particular regard to construction of meanings and language.

Foremost, and contrary to the common misapprehension, memetics is a *psychological* discourse (ibid.). Any confusion around this subject is generally answerable to the way in which it emerged. In a spirited passage of his seminal book, *The Selfish Gene* (2006), evolutionary zoologist, Richard Dawkins, suggested that 'cultural transmission is analogous to genetic transmission in that, although basically conservative, it can give rise to a form of evolution' (Dawkins 2006:189). Correlating particular cultural units with genes, he coined the term, 'meme' (ibid.). If then, as we have seen, the idea that languages *evolve* has become widely accepted (Saussure 1916b), it should not be a stretch to afford memes their due consideration. As follows, we must first look at the meme's biological counterpart.

The ideas set out in Darwin's *The Origin of Species* (2011) are by now well established and not worth reproducing at length here. The crux of his study, however, is indicated by his coinage of the phrase, 'the survival of the fittest'. This is the idea that species that are most aptly suited to their environment will propagate with the greatest fecundity, 'passing on' their traits to their offspring (Darwin 2011). Following Darwin, schools of evolutionary biology, of which Dawkins was a part, discovered that it was in fact genes that harboured such traits and *replicated* them down the generations. Furthermore, as Dawkins (2006) later suggested, genes were replicating agents in themselves, acting largely in their own interests and doing whatever it would take to be replicated.[16]

In short, it could be argued that the meme corresponds with the signifying cultural units considered in section one—i.e. 'musemes'. Moreover, if we accept memetic theory, then it would follow that these units are in a sense 'replicators', constantly striving towards their own propagation and improvement.

In her consideration of why musical phrases get 'stuck in our heads', Susan Blackmore provides an example of how memes might work in terms of popular music:

> The imitating machinery of the brain is an excellent environment for copying tunes. So if a tune is memorable enough to get lodged in your brain and then passed on again then it will - and if it is really memorable . . . it will get lodged in lots of brains . . . [this] is just an inevitable consequence of having brains that can imitate tunes. (Blackmore 1999:55)

The problem with this idea is the difficulty one faces in accepting the meme as an *analogue*, as something abstract, when it seems to demand personification. It is almost impossible, by way of the predicates that we attach to it, to conceive of the memes as anything other than autonomous agents that act for themselves. This is not the case. Again, the notion of memetics is only *analogous* to biological evolution and cultural transmission and is upheld in purely non-genetic terms (ibid.). In fact, as Blackmore alludes to, it is not the 'will' of the meme to replicate itself, but something in the brain that seems to pick and choose what is most memorable and worthy of replication.

Ultimately, psychology has a long way to go before its theories can be rigorously tried and tested. Although, while we cannot truly predict what memetics might hold for the future analysis of musical meaning,

---

[16] Although this is a highly reductive explanation of contemporary evolutionary theory, we need not go further here. For further discussions, see Darwin (2011) and Dawkins (2006).

it has certainly opened up a number of theoretical doors for further inquiry. However, if memetics—or rather, psychology—cannot yet provide us with a satisfying answer to the problem of meaning, then is there not a regression? Are we not immediately returned to the notion of power relations and the top-down manipulation of meaning? I believe not.

As we have seen, it is only through the collective use of language within a community that change can be brought about in language— and therefore in meaning. Moreover, that which separates us from those who first posed the question of the power relations, in the early-twentieth-century, is the dawning of mass communication. This, I argue, has the most compelling implications for the origin of meaning today. For it is in mass communication that reversal of power relations and top-down hegemonies has its seat proper. In response to Bourdieu, Simon Frith argued that 'a similar use of accumulated knowledge and discriminatory skill [used by 'high culture', hegemonic institutions] is apparent in low cultural forms, and has the same hierarchical effect. Low culture . . . generates its own capital' (Frith 2002:9). That is to say, in the age of the internet and hyper-connectivity, the boundaries that once demarcated cultures and communities are dissolving, opening up the field to the 'universalisation' of language and culture; less and less is the dissemination of cultural capital the domain of institutionalised hegemonies and market forces. Thus, whilst memetic evolution may not provide us with a veritable answer here, we can certainly say that meanings are subject to a kind of 'cultural evolution'. As such, in light of the ever-expanding armature of the web and global connectivity, and the slow but gradual reversal of hegemonic mediation, we stand at threshold of a cultural *revolution* in the universalisation of meaning.

Conclusion

The impetus for this project emerged from that most curious of cocktails: genuine surprise and moderate frustration. Surprised, at the paucity with which theorists of music and language refer to disciplines outside of their own; and frustrated, with the apparent impenitency with which they do so. On one hand, in, for example, sociology or anthropology, we are constantly reminded of the salience of *people* in the theorisation of meaning (Frith 2002; Lévi-Strauss 1958). In literary theory, on the other hand, *people* are often rendered as secondary to the system with which their meanings are expressed (Barthes 2013). And so on. In any case, regardless of the theoretical perspective, it has so often seemed that the various theories of meaning set out across these disciplines—especially theories of musical meaning—have failed to do justice to the object of inquiry.

Thus, in bringing together these disciplines, I have attempted to synstudye a legitimate framework onto which musical meanings can be mapped and rendered explicit. Within this framework, meanings can be traced from their usage, in both individual and societal terms, and related back to their roots in culture. And all the while, in tracing this archaeology, musical meanings are rendered proper in their distinction from the meanings represented in other forms of language.

We might at this point return to Nietzsche (2004)—cited at the outset—whose remark, when reconsidered in light of the foregoing pages, may be understood with greater clarity.[17] As we have seen, the structural features of music—i.e. their musicological constitutions—do not correspond directly with the apprehension of their meaning. Instead, such meanings are *projected* into music by their interpretive communities, and are therefore purely contingent and 'actually quite foreign to [their] mechanical laws' (ibid:128).

The system, however, is, of course, a complex one, and not without its limitations. Because whilst I have placed great emphasis on the differences and similarities between music and *verbal* language, I have not factored in their similarities and differences with the representations of, say, the visual aspects of language—i.e. filmic, photographic, or bodily gesticulation. My project is therefore lacking in this respect. However, while I accept these limitations, I would uphold the possibility that such instances, given the requisite consideration, could themselves be analysed by way of the systems set out in this work. An undertaking best left for a later, more substantial work, perhaps.

---

[17] 'In and of itself, music is not so full of meaning for our inner life, so profoundly moving, that it can claim to be a *direct* language of the emotion . . . The intellect itself has *projected* this meaning into the sound, as it has also read into the relationship of lines and masses in architecture a meaning that is, however, actually quite foreign to mechanical laws' (Nietzsche 2004:128).

Finally, what of the value of memetics in regard to our knowledge of the future? Certainly, it too must be answerable to a number of just criticisms, as it is without a doubt 'not there yet'. However, as alluded to in the section's concluding pages, the possibilities of viewing signifying units as a kind of cultural replicator are many; particularly, it should be added, in the age of mass communications. Of course, where this theory may subsequently lead us is unclear; and, until it is given the theoretical consideration it deserves, it may never lead us anywhere. In spite of this, it remains, in my view, among the few existing theories that provides a satisfying framework for the discernment of precisely *how music means*, neither directly linked to our modes of apprehension, nor bound to the mechanical laws of language.

Bibliography

Aristotle (1996) *Poetics*. London: Penguin Books.

Barthes, R. (1970) 'The Third Meaning': in Barthes, R. (1977) *Image-Music-Text*. London: Fontana Press. 52-68.

Barthes, R. (1971) 'Change the Object itself': in Barthes, R. (1977) *Image-Music-Text*. London: Fontana Press. 165-169.

Barthes, R. (2013) 'Myth Today': in Barthes, R. (2013) *Mythologies*. New York: Hill & Wang. 215-274.

Benjamin, W. (1929) 'The Image of Proust': in Benjamin, W. (1999) *Illuminations*. London: Pimlico. 197-210.

Benjamin, W. (1936) 'The Work of Art in the Age of Mechanical Reproduction': in Benjamin, W. (1999) *Illuminations*. London: Pimlico. 211-235.

Blackmore, S. (1999) *The Meme Machine*. Oxford: Oxford University Press.

Boghossain, P. (2010) 'Explaining Musical Experience': in Stock, K. [ed.] (2010) *Philosophers On Music: Experience, Meaning, and Work*. New York: Oxford University Press. 117-129.

Bowie, A. (2007) *Music, Philosophy, and Modernity*. New York: Cambridge University Press.

Bourdieu, P. (2010) *Distinction*. London: Routledge Classics.

Burke, L. Crowley, T. & Girvin, A. [ed.] (2000) *The Routledge Language and Cultural Theory Reader.* London: Routledge.

Darwin, C. (2011) *The Origin of Species.* London: Collins Classics.

Dawkins, R. (2006) *The Selfish Gene.* 30th Anniversary Edition. Oxford: Oxford University Press.

Davidson, D. (1978) 'What Metaphors Mean': in Lepore, E. & Ludwig, K. [ed.] (2006) *The Essential Davidson.* Oxford: Oxford University Press. 209-224.

Davidson, D. (1986) 'A Nice Derangement of Epitaphs': in Lepore, E. & Ludwig, K. [ed.] (2006) *The Essential Davidson.* Oxford: Oxford University Press. 251-265.

Deleuze, G. (2008) *Proust and Signs.* London: Continuum.

Derrida, J. (2001) *Writing and Difference.* London: Routledge Classics.

Edgar, A. & Sedgwick, P. [ed.] (2010) *Cultural Theory: The Key Concepts.* 2nd Edition. London: Routledge.

Feld, S. & Fox, A. A. (1994) Music and Language. *Annual Review of Anthropology:* Vol. 23. 25-53.

Fish, S. (1981) *Is There a Text in This Class?: The Authority of Interpretive Communities.* Cambridge: Harvard University Press.

Foucault, M. (2002) *The Archaeology of Knowledge.* London: Routledge Classics.

Frith, S (2002) *Performing Rites: Evaluating Popular Music.* 2nd Edition. Oxford: Oxford University Press.

Hall, S. [ed.] (1997) *Representation: Cultural Representations and Signifying Practices.* London: Sage.

Lévi-Strauss, C. (1958) 'Linguistics and Anthropology': in Burke, L. Crowley, T. & Girvin, A. [ed.] (2000) *The Routledge Language and Cultural Theory Reader.* London: Routledge. 401-409.

Moy, R. (2000) *An Analysis of the Position and Status of Sound Ratio In Contemporary Society.* New York: The Edwin Mellen Press.

Nietzsche, F. (2004) *Human, All Too Human.* London: Penguin Books.

Robinson, J. (2010) 'Can Music Function as a Metaphor of Emotional Life?': in Stock, K. [ed.] (2010) *Philosophers On Music: Experience, Meaning, and Work*. New York: Oxford University Press. 149-177.

Saussure, F. de (1916a) 'The Nature of the Linguistic Sign': in Burke, L. Crowley, T. & Girvin, A. [ed.] (2000) *The Routledge Language and Cultural Theory Reader*. London: Routledge. 21-32.

Saussure, F. de (1916b) 'Language and Linguistics': in Burke, L. Crowley, T. & Girvin, A. [ed.] (2000) *The Routledge Language and Cultural Theory Reader*. London: Routledge. 53-63.

Schopenhauer, A. (1970) *Essays and Aphorisms*. London: Penguin Books.

Shuker, R. (2012) *Popular Music Culture: The Key Concepts*. 3rd Edition. London: Routledge.

Storey, J. (2012) *Cultural Theory and Popular Culture: An Introduction*. 6th Edition. Harlow: Pearson.

Tagg, P. (2012) *Music's Meanings: A Modern Musicology for Non-Musos*. Huddersfield: Mass Media Music Scholars' Press.

Thomas, D. A. (1995) *Music and the Origin of Language: Theories from the French Enlightenment*. Cambridge: Cambridge University Press.

Discography

Berry, B., et al. (1991) 'Shiny Happy People': on *Out of Time*, performed by R.E.M. [CD]. California: Warner Brothers Entertainment.

Jagger, M. & Richards, K. (1969) 'Midnight Rambler': on *Let It Bleed*, performed by the Rolling Stones. [CD]. New York: ABKCO Records.

Online Sources

Oxford Dictionaries [ONLINE]: Available at http://www.oxforddictionaries.com/ (accessed on 06/04/2014).

CHAPTER 5

A-Gendered Rap: An Analysis of Gender, Sexuality and Ethnicity in Rap music

Sindy Kavanagh

> By playing close attention to female rappers, we can gain some insight into how young African-American women provide for themselves a relatively safe free-play zone where they creatively address questions of sexual power, the reality of truncated economic opportunity, and the pain of racism and sexism. (Rose 1994:146)

'Is this the thanks I get for puttin' you bitches on?
Is it my fault that all of you bitches gone?
Should've sent a thank you note, you little hoe,
Now I'm a wrap your coffin with a bow.'
Nicki Minaj 'Roman Reloaded' (2010)

Hip-Hop and more specifically Rap music, has long been demonised within the media and academia for apparently being a sexist, racist and homophobic genre. This attention is often placed on the music of male rappers and their discussions of women within their music, but also the 'objectification' of females within their music videos. This study situates female rappers within the 'hyper-masculine' world of rap and discusses the negotiation of their gender, sexuality and ethnicity and the implications this has upon existing stereotypes regarding African-Americans and African-American women.

The study of this study is that female rap artists often reinforce these stereotypes regarding women and black female sexuality. The messages they claim to portray of female empowerment and strength are often contradicted by their own objectification and exploitation of females within their songs and lyrics.

The first section in this study will trace the subculture of Hip-Hop from the inner-city areas of New York through to 'Gangsta Rap' and the globally successful business of rap today. This section discusses 'blackness' and the problematic use of this term. Section one also discusses masculinity and authenticity within the genre and how these terms relate to the idea of an 'authentic black masculinity within rap music. This first section lays the foundation for section two; the analysis of female rap artists. Section two is concerned with the contradictory nature of female rap artists' lyrics. This section discusses pioneering female rappers and how the 'gangsta era' changed the lyrical content and behaviours of female rappers.

Section Three brings this study into a new and, as of yet little researched area discussing rap artist Nicki Minaj. This section analyses Minaj's videos and lyrics in an attempt to understand how female artists in the modern era negotiate their ethnicity, gender and sexuality. Section Three also discusses the broader issues relating to the construction black female sexuality in the United States.

Methodology and Literature Review

The idea for this study came last summer (2013) whilst travelling in America. I spent a period of time in New York City and visited the boroughs of the city including Bronx, Brooklyn, Harlem, Queens and Staten Island. My interest in Hip-Hop culture and in particular rap music led me to various historical sites for any Hip-Hop fan. My interest in the discourses of Gender and Sexuality paired with my undergraduate degree in Popular Music Studies meant that a study on all three of these areas focused within Hip-Hop and Rap music would make for a study that I would find interesting and stimulating whilst simultaneously offering some fresh insight in this area.

Whilst researching hip-hop, rap music and issues such as gender, sexuality and ethnicity, I had plenty of literature to work with and to explore. However, what was lacking in areas of research was any academic writing on modern hip-hop and new female artists such as Nicki Minaj. This is due to how new these artists are, however I thought Nicki Minaj would be an interesting case study that would bring fresh insight to the study of rap music.

Through time consuming exploration of books and journals, questions started to develop around these issues; what is the role of female rappers within rap music? How do they fit into this 'hyper-masculine' world? Is rap hyper-sexual, sexist or misogynistic? What effect has

'Gangsta rap' had on commercial rap? How do modern female rappers such as Nicki Minaj, compare to older female artists? These are some of the questions I attempt to answer through my research and study.

However, a number of the key pieces are no longer current. For example, Tricia Rose's *Black Noise* (1994) is still considered as one of the definitive texts on hip-hop culture and rap music despite being twenty years old. Rose's work explores the social and political conditions that defined Rap in its early years, race and gender is discussed heavily within the text. The chapter 'Bad Sistas: Black Women Rappers and Sexual Politics in Rap Music.' (1994:100-146) discusses the first wave of female rappers such as MC Lyte and Salt 'n' Pepa. The text praises these female artists as 'liberating black women' and for voicing concerns regarding black female sexuality. Although this text was key in my understanding of these first wave artists and the historical roots of Hip-Hop, the text was published just before the 'Gangsta Era' of Rap and therefore misses the second wave of female artists and the controversial themes within the music of males and females during this period.

Michael. P. Jeffries *Thug Life; Race, Gender, and the Meaning of Hip-Hop* (2011) proved to be an invaluable text, which situated Hip-Hop and Rap music in its modern context, discussing issues such as sexism, misogyny and violence within the genre and subculture. Jeffries depiction of female representation within music video provided a framework of analysis that I could use when analysing other videos.

Much of the research was journal based and many of the journals I came across helped to construct my arguments, for example Michael Oware's 'A Man's Women? Contradictory Messages in the Songs of Female Rappers, 1992-2000' (2009).This text employs content analysis of lyrics to explore the messages within female rap artists' music; this text was the basis for my argument in suggesting that contradictory messages nullify any of the positive messages. Various other journals such as Adams and Fuller (2006) and Balaji (2010) also brought more current debates regarding images within rap's music videos. Whilst also exploring the underlying political and social issues and helping to root my arguments in solid theory, this allowed me to explore the broader issues concerning the treatment and representation of Black women within the media in the United States.

Whilst discussing the historical role of female and male rappers I also wanted to analyse Nicki Minaj and her role in modern Rap music. As suggested earlier there was no specific research analysing Nicki Minaj therefore existing literature discussing female artists and black sexuality within rap was used as the framework upon which I built and drew from, my own ideas about these musical texts. Through questioning the aforementioned questions, I hope to give a new slant on what is essentially an insecure area of research.

Historicised Hip-Hop to Racialised Rap

This section will discuss the evolution of Hip-Hop culture and Rap music in an attempt to understand the political, social and cultural landscape and background of the genre. The relationship between gender, authenticity, ethnicity and Rap music will be explored within this section, with particular attention paid to 'blackness', 'masculinity' and sexism within the genre.

Roots and Antecedents

As with any musical genre it is difficult to pin point an exact birth date as both critics and scholars often dispute this matter, however Borthwick and Moy suggest that rap music has a clearer history when compared with other musical genres and that rap music can be traced both historically and geographically; 'Rap's story beings in the early 1970's with street parties in the Bronx and Harlem, inner-city areas of New York City' (2004:156). Rap or 'rapping' became a staple of Hip Hop culture around this time. The other distinct elements of hip-hop culture include turntablism (DJing), breaking (dancing) and graffiti (art). These parties are often referred to as 'block parties' where all of these elements were combined to be performed in front of and consumed by the African American and Hispanic communities of New York City (Longhurst 1995:150-151).

DJs such as DJ Kool Herc and Afrika Bambaataa would perform at these 'block parties' using portable PA systems and would mix together records using two turntables and an audio mixer/controller. As Borthwick and Moy explain; Herc (Clive Campbell) was a Jamaican Immigrant, his Jamaican nationality is of importance as he drew upon the tradition of the Jamaican sound system, reggae deejay and 'selector' (2004:156). Therefore we can suggest that reggae had an important influence on rap music and hip-hop culture. The 'selector' in reggae music, however would be known as the DJ in rap music (the person who chooses and plays records and is responsible for the 'turntabling') whilst the deejay in reggae would be known as the MC (Master of Ceremonies) within rap music. Herc could be suggested as gaining authentic merit due to his nationality.

The use of two turntables and a mixer allowed for the DJ to cut from track to track but also to use the drum breaks from the track, these break beats are then rapped over by an MC or the DJ himself. 'The DJ ruled during hip hop's early day, and it was the DJ who established the foundations for the lyricist (the MC)' (Perkins 1996:6). This relationship is one that has changed during the evolution of hip-hop and rap music with the MC or rapper now being the main focus of attention. The MC (more commonly known now as a 'rapper') would rap over the DJs mix through a microphone. Rapping or MCing is a vocal style in which the artist speaks lyrically, in rhyme and verse usually to an instrumental or synthesized beat.

DJ Kool Herc and Coke La Rock provided an influence on the vocal style of rapping by delivering simple poetry verses over funk music breaks, before this they had attempted to introduce reggae style toasting into their sets; however this was not received as well by American audiences. When discussing rap music it is often implied that we are only referring to the vocal and lyrics that are 'rapped' however, it is important to differentiate between hip-hop music (which does not always contain rapping) and rap music and to understand that rap music applies to the entirety of the music not just the vocal delivery.

During the nineteen eighties many significant technological advances including sampling technology and drum machines impacted hugely on the way that rap music was being produced, recorded and performed live via DJing and DJs. It could be suggested that during this time the role of the DJ within the production of recorded rap music became less important as the technology available could easily replace the techniques mastered over time by these DJs. For example the use of drum machines such as the Oberheim DMX and Roland 808 allowed artists the freedom to create their own drum beats without relying on break beats. Sampling also allowed for looping a break beat without the need for a DJ (Perkins 1996:7).

The advancements in technology were not the only changes to happen to rap music during this period; the focus within lyrical content became much more socially reflective and politically charged. The inner-city areas of New York that hip hop emerged from during the nineteen seventies is suggested by Rose as being the catalyst for such creativity 'Hip Hop culture emerged as a source for youth of alternative identity formation and social status in a community whose older local support institutions had been all but demolished along with large sectors of its built environment.' (1994:34). Rose suggests that many youths felt alienated from American society, this feeling of alienation and abandonment was often the focus of and reflected in lyrical content. Some of hip- hop's first commercial successes contained highly politically charged lyrics; for example Grandmaster Flash and the Furious Five's track 'The Message' became a hit in 1982. Following on from this, artists such as Public Enemy gained success with their often political and aggressive style of music.

The Gangsta Era

Rap music has gone through a number of changes and has been the focus of much attention for academics studying issues such as gender, ethnicity and authenticity within popular music and culture. This focus on gender has often been placed on the lyrical content of rap songs but also on artwork, music video, music press and media, live performance and general persona of artists portrayed across this media. It is within these forms that artists have been accused of promoting or glamorising violence against women (including sexual and domestic violence), misogyny and the subordination of women. The issue of gender is of course deeply rooted in other issues and debates, in particular issues of race and ethnicity.

The sub-genre 'Gangsta Rap' has been given the most attention in this area. Hilson Woldu discusses how Rap music transitioned from the political messages within Grandmaster Flash and Public Enemy's music to a more aggressive and negative form:

> There followed in the late 1980's and early 1990's a particularly notorious period in popular rap, the so-called 'gangsta era' , in which the image of the black male as violent, profane, woman-hating, sex-obsessed criminal was imprinted in popular culture. (2006:90).

Hilson Woldu states that; 'Arguably this genre occasioned more bad press than any other black popular music' (ibid). Artists such as NWA, Dr. Dre, Tupac Shakur and Notorious BIG are a few of the most popular gangsta rappers to be accused of promoting violence against women and misogyny in their music. Jarman-Ivens suggests that: 'Thanks to acts such as NWA, The Geto Boys, Tupac Shakur, D12 and 50 Cent, rap music has come to be perceived as a violent, aggressive, misogynist, and male-dominated genre.' (2006: p199). Consequently and perhaps not surprisingly, this sub-genre of rap or style of rap is the best known to mainstream listeners and as Hilton Would suggests 'is the type most fans or audiences associate as being representative of the whole genre.' (2006:90). This is of course problematic as these artists become the main representation of the genre due to the media attention that the negative aspects of the genre attract, meaning that other forms of rap with perhaps more positive messages are ignored or forgotten, in favour of this controversial form instead.

In more recent times Gangsta rappers such as Eminem, 50 Cent and Lil' Wayne have continued to produce songs and music videos with violent and sexual themes, so much so that many social commentators have argued that these artists are glamorising violence and sexual violence against women. Jeffries suggests that these artists use lyrics and music video to 'rhetorically objectify, degrade and insult women.' (2011:154). Jeffries goes on to suggest that women within these music videos are 'Frequently cast as objects for sexual consumption and the justified objects of male scorn by commercially successful hip-hop artists.' (ibid) The 'casting' Jeffries refers to is that of the 'hip-hop honeys' or 'video vixens' as these women have come to be known as and are referred to as 'bitches' and 'hoes' by many male rappers. Section two will discuss the issue of gender in relation to female participation more thoroughly.

Popular music scholars have suggested that certain forms of Hip Hop are racist and sexist and have stated that the genre projects only one representation of young black males which reinforce stereotypes. However it could be suggested that this stereotypical image has now become the 'authentic' image or adoptable 'persona' that new Hip Hop artists must embody; social commentators would argue that this has an effect on popular culture and this has led to Hip Hop/rap being blamed for promoting violence to impressionable youths. The gangster 'persona' is adopted by most rap artists, in an attempt to situate them as 'hyper-masculine' beings.

Scott (2009:305) uses Frith's earlier analyses of different personae (see Frith, 1996:186-212) to create three individual personae that can 'function simultaneously' (ibid) these are; 'the real person' (the performer as human being), 'the performance persona' (the performer as social being) and 'the character' (the songs personality; the role of lyrics) (Scott 2009:305). He also suggests that there are many different avenues in which an artist is said to perform their persona (e):

> Popular musicians do not perform their persona exclusively in live and recorded performances, they also perform them through the visual images used in the packaging of recordings, publicity materials, interviews and press coverage, toys and collectables and other venues and media including music video. (ibid)

The range of media and products that Scott notes here as being platforms for performing persona suggest that the audio visual element to music is very important, the success of music video in the last thirty years is further evidence of this. Within Hip-Hop, music video has been a vital platform for artists in which to perform their 'persona', a lot of the content that is deemed misogynistic or sexist comes from music video and the representation of females within this media.

Authenticating 'Black' Masculinities

Authenticity within this genre is reliant on what we will call 'the struggle', without reference to a struggle during childhood and adolescence the artist could be suggested as being less 'authentic' or 'real'. The 'struggle' that is referred to here is often financial but could also be a struggle against racism, domestic abuse, violence, drug and alcohol issues and crime. The track 'In Da Club' by rap artists 50 Cent (2003) makes explicit reference to sex, drugs, violence and guns. 50 Cent adopts the gangster persona throughout this song; however, are we to assume that this is the real 50 Cent or that he is adopting a persona? Whilst referencing his own struggle 50 Cent also projects his new found fame and wealth upon the listener, he raps about owning a Mercedes Benz, how he 'made a mill' out the deal' (meaning a million dollars from his recording contract with Interscope Records) and also how he owns jewels, cars, cribs and pools. This new persona that 50 Cent adopts here is of a rich and powerful 'gangster', this persona is just as important as the 'struggle' within gangsta rap, where riches and a luxurious lifestyle are celebrated. This second persona often becomes more important as the artist continues to release more music and as a result earns more money. The 'commerce' versus 'art' debate could be viewed as less important within rap music as money-making is viewed as an 'authentic indicator' for an artist within this genre.

The term 'authenticity', from the Latin 'authenticus' meaning 'coming from the author' (Shepherd 2003:164) is a term that has been used heavily within the field of popular music scholarship and journalism to evaluate and categorise music as 'genuine' or 'real' and is often used to place value judgements on popular music texts or musicians. 'Authenticity' is a problematic term as there are no definitive guidelines as to what can be deemed 'authentic', this is largely due to individual interpretation and meaning making; each person has their own idea of an 'authentic' sound, song, performer or performance. There is also the argument as to whether authenticity actually exists or is merely constructed and reinforced by the 'cultural industries' (e.g. the music industry) to aid the sale of cultural artefacts such as music by injecting it with ideology:

> On the one hand it could be doubted whether there is such a thing as an authentic-autonomous-musical form in the first place; on the other hand it is apparent that authenticity here functions as an ideological construct- a construction of commercial (and academic) discourse.' (Frith 2007:152)

Frith states that any notion of authenticity within popular music as being 'natural' is false and that authenticity is a construct in itself, constructed by musicians, the music industry, audiences and scholars alike. Many other academics have accepted the term as once important but now believe that 'authenticity' is no longer worthy of academic study and that it 'has been con- signed to the intellectual dust-heap' (Born and Hesmondhalgh 2000:30). However, Moore (2002:211) disagrees with any abandonment of the study of authenticity within popular music on the grounds that it still serves as an important ideological function. He also points out that the study of authenticity in relation to music has often been used to make distinctions between so called 'serious music' such as Rock and 'less serious' music such as Pop. Within Hip-Hop and rap music the term 'authentic' is crucial to the success or failure of an artist's career; the artist as an individual must be viewed as being 'authentic' or 'real' in order for audiences or fans to take the artist seriously.

Authenticity is often performed through lyrics, however, lyrical analysis has been subject to much criticism within the field of popular music due to the interpretative nature of analysing the intent of lyrics and the level of autobiography contained within them. Although it does seem that within certain genres such as Hip Hop it would be almost impossible to discuss how the genre relates to concepts such as gender, ethnicity and authenticity without mentioning lyrics. Lyrics within Hip Hop attempt to position the artist as 'authentic'. Within commercialised Hip Hop and more specifically 'gangsta rap', lyrics frequently discuss issues such as crime, sex, guns, violence and drugs. These lyrics are often used to 'authenticate' the performer with the audience, as Price (2006:79) suggests Hip Hop is described as a culture that came from the 'street' therefore it is important that Hip Hop performers reference the 'streets' within their music.

Within popular music and in particular genres such as Hip-Hop, the label 'black' has been subject to much criticism and often regarded as suspicious. Despite these criticisms some writers have continued to argue that the concept of 'black' music has some importance; Hatch and Millward state that 'The music made by 'black' people is related to their oppression in the United States and the importance of 'black' musicians within the development of certain musical forms such as Blues should not be overlooked' (1987:129). However what Hatch and Millward also suggest is that the label 'black' is often used in an overly simplistic manner and can lead to the assumption that certain forms of music are in some way 'authentically black'. It could be suggested that within popular music the label 'black' is used as a symbol of 'authenticity', Ramsey (2003) argues that the association of certain genres of music such as hip- hop with an 'authentic blackness' is a powerful marketing tool and helps to promote and sell records on a global scale. It could be suggested then that the industry responsible for the production, marketing and dissemination of these musical texts are using the label 'black' to 'authenticate' certain artists and that this authentication reinforces dominant hegemonic ideologies and hinders the breaking down of racial barriers and 'otherness'.

Longhurst further problematizes the labelling of certain styles of music as 'black'; questioning the ways in which music can be defined by such a term; 'The concept of 'black music' has sometimes been used in an unreflective way, where it is assumed that it is the music performed by black people.' (1995:128). This assumption that 'black' music is performed by 'black' people would situate the individual performers as the singular auteurs of the piece and would fail to recognise the large amount of people that work on producing popular music texts. Therefore if music is to be categorised as 'black' then we would be expected to assume that every person involved in the music making production process is of the same race/ethnicity. This quest for authenticity could and has resulted in the exclusion or inclusion of musicians or audiences based purely on race and although it is of course important not to overlook the influence of 'black' musicians within genres such as Blues and Soul and here Hip-Hop their race should not be a defining signifier of 'authenticity' or used to make value judgements on popular music texts. However it is apparent that the use of the label 'black' has become a signifier of authenticity within hip-hop culture and rap music. Hip-Hop culture is often described as black with many Hip-Hop artists referencing the term black in album titles such as Jay-Z's 'Black Album' (2003) and Kanye West's track 'Black Skinhead' (2013). Both are contemporary examples of how the term is still used within rap music and how artists themselves refer to themselves as being black.

Frith's analysis of authenticity, as discussed earlier in this essay, is also relevant in discussing race within rap music. If authenticity is to be constructed and reinforced by the cultural industries i.e. the music industries, then we are to question the use of such an outdated term and who stands to benefit from the use of such an essentialist label. If we are to question the use of labels such as 'World Music' and deem this a racist or reductionist label then we should certainly treat the term 'black' to describe certain forms of music or humans with an even higher level of suspicion.

Jeffries states that, 'The relationship at the root of the debate over hip-hop and resistance: white men distribute and consume commercially successful rap music, and black men perform it.' (2011:9). As Queeley asserts, 'Hip-Hop now lives in the ghetto of the white imagination' (2003:2). The ownership of these industries and the consumers of this music are often white, middle class men. Therefore, the stereotyping and single representation of black males within this genre then needs to be treated with caution, suspicion and out right mistrust. We could argue here that this ownership is exploitative and not accurately representative of African American culture; however it promotes these musics as being so. With the sole purpose of generating income from these artists, owners of these industries are perhaps less concerned with the morality of such actions and rather more concerned with the economic power of these artists.

It has been the purpose of this section to explore Hip-Hop and its evolution throughout the last three decades and to discuss the issues of race, gender and authenticity. What is apparent is that for black male artists within hip-hop there is perhaps only one 'authentic' persona that can guarantee success, however this success comes at the risk of stereotyping large communities or cultures. So far gender has been discussed in regards to masculinity, and women's participation has been analysed within male performers' music, lyrics and music video. Section Two attempts to restore the balance, discussing female participation in regards to artists and performers and their role within hip-hop culture and rap music.

Voices from the Margins

This section is focused on the first commercially successful female rap artists and the role of women within hip-hop and rap music. Previous discussions within this paper have centred around females within male artists' music and media such as music videos and lyrics, however this section is focused on women as artists and performers within this genre and how they fit into the, so called, 'hyper-masculine' world of rap.

Exaggeration or 'Marginalisation'?

As suggested earlier, hip-hop and rap music has often been criticised for being 'male-dominated' and sexist. However, other genres such as Rock and its sub-genres have faced similar scrutiny within the media and academia. However, rap music is not, nor has it ever been strictly the domain of men (Emerson 2002; Keyes 2004; Rose 1994). Jarman-Ivens states that 'In accordance with the generalised exscription of women from a great deal of music history, women tend to appear in forms of hip-hop culture as marginal figures.' (2006:199), this marginalisation of females within hip-hop culture and rap music has been discussed heavily by academics such as Tricia Rose (1994, 2004) and Michael P. Jeffries (2011). Rose suggests a different understanding of the issue, 'Sexism in rap has been gravely exaggerated by the mainstream press.' (2004:291) Rose discusses journalism as amplifying and exaggerating the issue of sexism within the genre in order to demonise its performers and audiences. However, it is difficult to dispel these notions of sexism when even the most popular and revered Hip-Hop critics are also failing to recognise the achievements or the presence of women within the genre.

In 1989, George Nelson the pro-Hip Hop music critic published a sentimental rap retrospective to mark the tenth anniversary of rap's musical debut in the recording industry. In this publication Nelson traces all of the major shifts within rap music, naming artists, albums, titles and producers. He names over twenty artists/groups but fails to name any female artists; Rose suggests that this analysis is common; 'Nelson George's analyses is not unusual; his is merely the latest example of media critics' consistent coding of rap music as male in the face of a significant and sustained female presence.' (2004:292). This analysis that Nelson gives at this time negates to acknowledge the success that many female rappers have had, artists such as Salt 'n' Pepa, MC Lyte and Queen Latifah have all had commercial success before 1989, yet Nelson does not feel that any of these successes are worthy of including in his writings on rap.

The failure to make separate mention of these female artists has often been passed off as media critics' view that these female artists are just 'one of the boys'. Perhaps for George and most media critics generally, it is as Rose suggests; 'far easier to re-gender women rappers than to revise their own gender-coded analysis of rap music' (2004:292). As these female artists are tough and arguably as tough as males they can be said to fit into George's one dimensional view of rap artists and leave him able to justify his exclusion of female artists.

Other academics have been much more critical in their writings on the issue of sexism within the genre, 'Rap music written and performed by men has generally either ignored the existence of women or defined them as commodities, objects of male pleasure, or ornaments.'

(Goodall 1994:85). Goodall goes onto suggest that the presence of female rappers 'helps to combat the intensity of this sexism' (ibid), but too often these women have confronted barriers both within and without the industry which have been discouraging. This discouragement as Goodall suggests, has prevented women from fully expressing their social, political, emotional and sexual concerns within rap.

Rose states that the 'marginalisation, deletion and the mischaracterisation of women's role in black cultural production is routine practice' (2004:292). Nancy Guevara notes the 'exclusion and/or trivialisation of women's role in Hip-Hop' (1987:163), Angela Davis extends these criticisms by stating that this is 'an omission that must be attributed to the influence of sexism.' (1990:3). In her article 'Black women and Music: An Historical Legacy of Struggle' (1990), Davis argues that black women, in the documentation of African-American cultural developments, hold a marginal representation that does not adequately reflect women's participation. Furthermore, Davis suggests that there need be a close re-examination of black women's musical legacy as a way to further understand black women's consciousness. This re-examination, of which Davis speaks, seems near impossible within a genre such as Hip-Hop where there is such a marginalised view of black women and, lest we forget, black males.

First Wave

The importance of artists Salt 'n' Pepa, MC Lyte and Queen Latifah cannot be ignored especially within a genre that supposedly works within an extremely marginalised framework, 'To be a rapper in the 1980's assumed three immutable truths: that the performer be black, urban and male.' (2006:89). These female artists made their impact on the genre of Rap during the late nineteen eighties and early nineteen nineties with their highly influential, politicised and unapologetic lyrics regarding urban life in America. Goodall explains that:

> By exhibiting their verbal virtuosity as well as social and political conscience, pioneering female rappers, such as MC Lyte and Salt 'n' Pepa, have secured and steadily broadened the place of women in the industry. (1994:33).

Goodall's understanding of the role of female rappers is that, while the genre remains extremely male dominated there has been a female presence that has become as deeply entrenched within the genre or industry as comedic rap (i.e. Fresh Prince, Biz Markie). Therefore we cannot underestimate the presence or power of female rappers, however marginalised, misrepresented or underrepresented they may be.

Salt 'n' Pepa's 'Push it' and Queen Latifah's 'UNITY', discuss heterosexual relationships in a way that had not been explored by women within music before. Oware states:

> Women have been a part of Hip-Hop culture since its inception. Early female pioneers discussed similar issues to men; marginalization, oppression, and urban decay. They also rapped about heterosexual courtship from the perspective of women, domestic violence, and sexism, among other issues. (2009:787).

The role of women within Hip-Hop is extremely valid and present for Oware, the subject matter discussed within these female artists' music, presents these women as independent and autonomous in their songs. Feminist discourse has often marginalised (and often ignored) non-white women and questions of black female sexuality. However within these musics it could be suggested that black female sexuality is foregrounded and voiced in a way that it had not been up until that point, at least not within commercial popular music and culture. This is not to disregard the role Blues and Soul musicians played in representing black female sexuality and identity, however this paper is focused on hip-hop and rap only and the artists within these genres. Hip-Hop in this paper is also discussed as a 'new' representation of black female sexuality and identity as opposed to a reproduction of these earlier themes, although their influence is not unrecognised.

Rose suggests that in the beginning female rappers were 'at least indirectly responding to male rappers' sexist constructions of black women' (1994:147) she goes on to state that although at times female rappers are understood as responding to this male construction of black women, they are also responding to a variety of issues that relate to this including dominant notions of femininity, feminism and black female sexuality. She explains that, 'At the very least, black women rappers are in a dialogue with one another, black men, black women, and dominant American culture as they struggle to define themselves against a confining and treacherous social environment.' (ibid.:148)

Rose acknowledges multiple dialogues that were happening simultaneously and dismisses the simplistic view of female rappers as responding only to male rappers.

There are larger political and social agendas to be dealt with here. As this music is often thought of as reflecting African-American culture it is apparent that this sexism towards women is more deeply rooted in urban American culture and psyche. Their representation of themselves as women, and more specifically as black women added to the political and social meaning and awareness that hip hop had brought to issues of race, ethnicity, gender, sexuality and identity in particular amongst African American males and females. Hip Hop was the vehicle used by these early female rappers to liberate themselves and to find their own personal, social and sexual identities.

Second Wave

As stated in Section One, this early period of rap music was taken over in the early nineteen nineties by 'Gangsta-Rap', throughout this period there came a 'second wave' of female artists including Foxy Brown, Missy Elliot and perhaps most notably Lil' Kim. In nineteen ninety six, Lil' Kim released her debut album 'Hard Core'. The teasingly pornographic titled album was, as Hilson-Woldu describes 'a benchmark for women's presence in rap as it affirmed a brazenly discordant female voice.' (2006:89) and 'spat on the shoe of rap's male hegemony.' (ibid) Tricia Rose's work on gender within Hip-Hop, as mentioned in the introduction to this text, depicts the likes of MC Lyte and Queen Latifah as feminist or pro-woman. However, content analysis by Matthew Oware in 'Contradictory Messages in the Songs of Female Rappers, 1992-2000.' (2009:786-802) suggests that although these 'first wave' artists chose to empower woman, 'second wave' female rappers that came later on such as Lil' Kim and Foxy Brown 'featured many lyrics that 'self-objectify and self-exploit, seemingly employing a male gaze. Finally, and it is surprising to note, many of the female artists use derogatory and demeaning language when discussing other women.' (2009:790). This analysis is strikingly different compared with earlier artists such as Salt 'n' Pepa and Queen Latifah. Earlier artists are often praised within the media and by academics (see Rose, 1994) for tackling difficult issues regarding female sexuality and identity.

Oware suggests that much lyrical analysis or examination of music video (See Emerson 2002; Keyes 2004; Rose 1994) is focused on first wave rappers such as Queen Latifah and MC Lyte and carefully selects lyrics and videos that can be seen to promote the message of female empowerment. However, Oware suggests that thorough analysis of second wave artists such as Foxy Brown and Lil' Kim is neglected or glazed over in attempt to illustrate only messages of female empowerment or positivity. Oware suggests that 'bravado', 'boasting' and 'dissing' are often used by female rappers and are aimed at other women, objectifying and degrading them. Although there are often positive messages, there are too many exceptions that contradict these. The analysis states:

> Although female rap artists articulate a feminist approach in their narratives by employing empowering, autonomous, and independent lyrics, many of them also re-appropriate the sexist and misogynist tropes that present women as hyper-sexual beings who are contained and controlled, in this case, by other women. (2009:797)

We could suggest that these women are then reinforcing the structure of their own oppression and domination. By objectifying each other and degrading each other they are repeating the dominant ideology of women's social status as subordinate to men, which of course completely contradicts some of their more positive messages of female empowerment and independence.

Lil Kim is described as having 'decried hip-hop's misogynist attitudes' (Hilson-Woldu 2006:90) and has longed for 'a lot more respect for women' (The Source 1996:49). However, Oware's analysis of Kim's lyrics proves otherwise. The self-proclaimed 'queen bitch' of rap and her fellow 'sistas with attitude' (Keyes 2004) Foxy Brown and Da Brat are suggested as reproducing the same behaviours and language as their male counterparts 'partying and smoking blunts (marijuana) with their men; seducing, repressing, and sexually emasculating male characters; [and] dissin' their would be female or male competitors' (Keyes 2004:272). Although challenging male sexism, Oware's analysis proves that many of these second wave artists are, 'just like the guys' in their depictions of women. Oware suggests that, 'The message of female upliftment and empowerment becomes effaced by female self-exploitation and hyper-objectification.' (2009:789). The bravado, bragging and dissing is synonymous with male rappers and this appropriation of this masculine language and behaviour may pose more problems for women than realised; the reproduction of a hegemonic paradigm that continues to treat women as sexual objects which ironically, is the very thing that is being challenged by these female rappers.

Finally Oware suggests that the 'In the end, the positive and liberatory songs and lyrics of several female artists become effaced by the the lyrics and songs that are demeaning and degrading to women, especially Black women.' (Oware 2009:798). These female artists run the risk of disempowering themselves. These contradictory messages suggest that patriarchal hegemony is being reinforced even in areas where it is suggested as attempting to dispel of these notions.

So far, discussions have centred around nineteen nineties or nineteen eighties artists and performers, however the next section discusses modern performers and what we will call the 'third wave' of female artists, specifically Nicki Minaj in an attempt to gain an understanding of female rap artists within modern rap music.

Nicki Minaj: The Third Wave

This section will discuss female rapper Nicki Minaj and two of her musical tracks, lyrics and videos. Minaj has often been compared to other female rappers, in particular Lil' Kim, although the pair have had very public disputes due to Kim's claims that Minaj is replicating her persona and image. The purpose of this section is to analyse the representation of black female sexuality within her music and gain an understanding of how female rap artists are portrayed through their music and video images in the modern era. As Nicki Minaj is a new artist there is yet to be published any academic analysis of her music or image. Therefore, this section will use existing academic material to compare her music with; giving a new insight into an area that has so far produced no published texts.

Stupid Hoe's

Nicki Minaj released her first album *Pink Friday* in 2010 (Young Money, Cash Money). The album has sold nearly two million copies, produced a string of hit singles and led to Minaj being nominated for three Grammy awards the following year. Her second album 'Roman Reloaded' released in 2012 (ibid) also had great commercial success. Minaj has produced a series of videos for the singles of each album, this paper will discuss two of these singles lyrics and videos in particular; 'Stupid Hoe' (2010) and 'High School' (2013).

Firstly the song 'Stupid Hoe' appears to be an insult against what Minaj deems to be 'lesser' women. One of the first lyrics in the song reads, 'Bitch talking she the queen, when she looking like a lab rat, I'm Angelina you Jennifer, Come on bitch you see where Brad at.' (ibid) Emphasis is clearly placed on appearance or beauty, insinuating that a woman cannot speak highly of herself if she is not attractive. The reference to Angelina Jolie, Jennifer Anniston and Brad Pitt uses a celebrity situation to reference competition between women and to bring it to a shallow and appearance based assault at women Minaj deems less attractive than herself. The situation she discusses suggests that a man's choice in partner defines their attractiveness and in turn their worth.

Minaj uses the same 'bravado' and 'disses' to objectify and degrade women, as artists such as Lil' Kim have in the past. The words 'bitch' and 'hoe' are used to insult and degrade women. Within the song's lyrics Minaj refers to herself as, 'jump man', 'front man' and states that these 'stupid hoes' can 'suck her disnik' (slang word for penis). Minaj asserts her dominance over women by repeating the masculine language and behaviours of male rappers. She also states that, 'Pretty bitches only get in my posse' which again places a women's worth on her appearance. One would suggest this statement reinforces dominant ideology of female subordination and places attractiveness as the most important aspect of a women's being. Minaj asserts her dominance by controlling and dominating women, she wants to be viewed as 'the queen bitch', whom every other woman should feel inferior to. This theme, which is similar to artists such as Lil' Kim shows little empowering or uplifting messages to women and instead reduces women to sexual objects, void of intelligence or feelings.

Within the video for 'Stupid Hoe' Minaj's body is foreground in a way that is reminiscent of pornography. Hurley discusses how 'The sexual iconography of music video often draws heavily on that of pornography' (1994: p330). This 'sexual iconography' includes:

Long, thin, hairless, female legs. Breasts, mouths and buttocks. Bare, hairless male chests. Women suggestively caressing parts of their bodies. Women pouting and looking unhappy. Flowing hair. Leather, vinyl, chains, lingerie, high heels, stockings, mini skirts and dresses, bikinis. (ibid)

The majority of this iconography feature in the video, in particular the breasts, mouth and buttocks are focused upon very heavily. The camera shots of Nicki's bottom and breasts are extremely frequent. Certain scenes see Minaj dressed in sexualised outfits and dancing with her back to the camera with an emphasis on her posterior. Balaji states that 'The emphasis on the physical aspects of Black womanhood is amplified in music videos, where sex is often used to sell both the performer and the performer's image.' (2010:6). This is specifically the case in this video as the majority of the images are sexualised for, what would seem to be, viewer gratification. It also appears that the emphasis placed on certain body parts and the size of certain body parts is stereotypical of black female performers within male rap artists' videos, where these performers are discussed as being objectified and male artists are accused of being sexist or misogynistic.

There is no defining narrative to the video apart from overtly sexualised images and dancing which could suggest Minaj is self-objectifying herself for commercial success. However this self-objectification has repercussions for black female performers and audiences, Balaji suggests that the 'sexualised, stereotyped content has been replicated for mass consumption, often countervailing any attempts to present Black women in nonsexualised and nonobjectified ways' (2010:6). This leads us to question whether black women are able to control their representation on their terms, or are willingly participating in visual misogyny? This question is more difficult to analyse with regards to female rap artists as this would mean that they are either controlled by, or naïve to an industry that has the sole purpose of generating sales and wealth. Or that they themselves are willing to take part in this 'visual misogyny' to gain commercial success and economic benefits.

Railton and Watson suggest music video as being the forum for the disablement and reconstruction of the boundaries of race, gender and sexuality:

> For race is deployed within pop music videos to not only delimit or
> sanction sexual behaviour, but also sex and gender signify race in
> ways which tend to reproduce and shore up existing hierarchical
> power relations. (2005:52)

As discussed earlier on in this paper, black females are said to have
been marginalised and subjected to patriarchal hegemony in which they
are 'other' or subordinate due to two factors; their race and gender,
they are then what we will call the 'ultimate other' (Adams & Fuller
2006:943). However, the images in this video only reinforce these
ideologies and whilst female artists repeat masculine, patriarchal or
even misogynistic behaviours in the objectification or exploitation of
women, then these ideals become somewhat normalised or accepted as
appropriate.

The worry here is that this will have an effect on fans and audiences of
this music. This is not to suggest that audiences are passive subjects
that interpret all messages or information as correct or true, however
these images within rap are frequent and plenty and have potentially
become the 'norm'. Sut Jhally's documentary *Dreamworlds* (2006)
examines the narratives contemporary music videos tell about men and
women and encourages viewers to consider how these stories or
images shape individual and cultural attitudes about sexuality. The
documentary suggests that music video and popular culture more
generally filter the identities of young men and women through a
dangerously narrow set of myths about gender and sexuality.

The 'Stupid Hoe' is extremely sexually provocative and also
aggressively sexual, Minaj grits her teeth throughout the video which
makes her seem somewhat animalistic. This animal-like action is
repeated more obviously in another scene when Minaj is imprisoned
inside a cage like an animal. The cage is small in height meaning Minaj
has to remain on all fours, unable to stand up. At one point an image
of a Cheetah morphs into Minaj's face and not only is she dressed in
Cheetah print she has digitally enhanced yellow eyes. Jacobs suggests
that sexualised images of black women have become so prevalent and
commonplace that they now exist 'at the centre of a symbolic
constellation that links female sexuality, animals, and blacks.' (1988:27).
This animalistic depiction of Minaj is suggested by Bailey (1988) as
being a Western construction of black women as void of emotional or

intellectual worth: 'Black women in Western literature, painting and film are thus imagined either as (large) intuitive mother figures, or as the human embodiment of animal sexuality' (38). Within the video Minaj embodies this animal sexuality, it could be argued that the Cheetah is instead used as a symbol of empowerment or strength, however this message is lost by the caging and imprisonment of Minaj and instead she is reduced to a 'booty' shaking, hypersexual, animal that has little intellect and is controlled by sex.

'Jezebel' and Further Contradictions

The musical track 'High School' is a collaboration with fellow record label artist and owner Lil' Wayne. The pair has worked together on several tracks and Minaj has referred to Wayne as her 'mentor' on many occasions within the media and her song lyrics. Within the video for 'High School' Minaj plays the role of a 'gangster's wife/girlfriend' and Wayne is her love interest. The video starts with close up shots of Minaj's buttocks and breasts. Throughout the majority of the video Minaj is wearing a bikini or swimming costume of some kind, the video contains lots of 'sexual iconography' (Hurley 1994:330) including, lingerie, high heels, leather, breasts, mouth and buttocks. Minaj's role is that of a bored 'housewife' she appears to be a 'trophy wife' who spends her time lounging by the pool. Wayne's character is part of an illegal group that come to do business with Minaj's partner. When the pair meets there is an obvious attraction and although Minaj is involved in a relationship they begin a secret relationship and at the end of the video Minaj and Wayne run away together with her partners' money.

The lyrics that accompany the video and in particular the chorus sang by Minaj: 'I know you want it boy, I see you trying, just keep on pushing I'm a let you slide in....anyway, everywhere, baby it's your world, aint it.' (2013) put Lil' Wayne's character in control. This is 'his world' and she will do anything to satisfy him both physically and emotionally. There is also an element of female subordination and male control when Minaj suggests if he 'just keeps on pushing' she will let him have his way. As suggested by Oware in section two the contradictory messages female rappers are giving out 'appropriate the sexist and misogynist tropes that present women as hyper-sexual beings who are controlled and contained' (2009:797). Within the video

Minaj's character is firstly controlled by her partner with money, lavish homes and expensive living and secondly she is controlled and dominated by Lil' Wayne sexually.

Lil Wayne raps these lyrics during the video, 'She got a n***er at home and one on the side, her best friend is a dyke they f***ed around a few times' (ibid). Many of the later lyrics from Wayne are overtly sexual and the use of language is similar to that which one would find in pornographic footage. Minaj is described as being hypersexual and having multiple partners at one time, she also cheats on her partner. In this instance Minaj symbolise the 'Jezebel' (Adams & Fuller 2006:945) 'The Jezebel represents a loose, sexually aggressive woman. The Jezebel wants and accepts sexual activity in any form.' (ibid) This image and rational has been used historically from the slave trade period and perhaps still today to 'other' the black woman and to justify her objectification and control by white men, in this case the white corporate ownership of the music industries.

However Wayne is portrayed in a similar way, although he is understood as the heterosexual protagonist to Minaj's nubile and willing character he too is sexualised, often wearing only shorts, his body is arguably as foregrounded in the video as Minaj. These videos are here suggested as being equally harmful to black female sexuality as they are to black male sexuality. Lil' Wayne's presence in the video is that of a dominating, gangster who cheats and steals to make a living. These portrayals of black males in rap videos are arguably as racist and sexist as any other.

The use of the word 'n***er' by both artists is also extremely prominent and could be suggested as another form of self-objectification, exploitation or even a form of self-loathing. If we are to suggest in section one that the term black should be treated as suspicious, a term such as 'n***er' can certainly not be deemed acceptable by any standards. The counter argument to this is that these terms are used by 'black people, who felt marginalised by whites to unify and use the term to counter the symbolic domination and privileging of 'whiteness' over 'blackness' that had existed throughout history (Giddens 2006:248) However, to further advance minorities the use of these terms are now perhaps 'essentialist' (Spivac 1987:205) and give no thought to ethnicity or national identity. The term 'n***er' cannot possibly be needed now to further the cause of minorities and instead seems to only reinforce patriarchal hegemony in a capitalist society, which appears to be contradictory of the 'message' these artists perceive themselves as promoting.

Masculinised Authenticity

It could be argued that many female rappers gain their 'authenticity' or 'authorial status' from the male hierarchy within the genre, with whom they are associated with. For example Lil' Kim and her association with Notorious BIG/Bad Boy Records and Nicki Minaj with her connection to Lil' Wayne/Young Money/Cash Money Records. Both of these female artists were first launched within small parts of these male rappers songs or videos and have been known to appear in videos where they do not rap at all. They are given their authentic stamp by the males they are associated with rather than their talent, at least at first.

It could also be argued that authenticity and or 'authorship' is often gained by repeating masculine behaviours. Nicki Minaj in particular, often references Lil' Wayne within her music by referring to herself as 'the female Weezy' in the 'Stupid Hoe' video, which could suggest she is using his name and associated authenticity to authenticate herself as a performer. Authentic masculinity is so deeply entrenched within the genre of rap that female rappers have to emulate masculine behaviours and language to be taken seriously. Their talent as lyricists and musicians often goes unfairly unrecognised or even when it is given some form of acknowledgement it is never regarded as highly as male artists' music within the genre. These female artists do not appear to be granted the same 'authorial' status in Hip-Hop or Rap music despite a continued presence and success within the genre.

Nicki Minaj's relationship with Lil' Wayne, whether it be business or personal reinforces misogyny, she accepts his treatment of women within her and his own music and videos in a way that could be suggested as normalising these depictions of women as hypersexual and subordinate to men. Although it could be argued that there are positive aspects such as creative and economic success, one would suggest that the contradictory messages within these videos, lyrics and musics suggests that, 'The message of female upliftment and empowerment becomes effaced by female self-exploitation and hyper-objectification' (Oware, 2009:789). I would here suggest that misogyny has become an 'authentic indicator' within rap music and therefore it would be difficult, if not impossible, to eradicate its presence within the genre.

Conclusion

It has been the aim of this study to analyse the role of gender and sexuality within rap music. Within rap, it would be near possible to analyse these issues without including race, ethnicity and authenticity amongst the discussion as these are integral to the genre and these performers. It has been argued in this paper that 'authenticity' within rap is built upon masculine language and behaviours. There appears to be an emphasis placed on 'authentic blackness' with masculinity being the overriding 'authentic indicator'. One would suggest that the 'Gangsta Era' of the nineteen nineties brought with it misogyny which has now become normalised within commercial rap. This again is not to suggest that all rap music and performers are sexist and misogynistic in their portrayals of urban life in America. However this era transformed rap into the commercially successful global business that it is today and many of the themes within gangsta rap are now simply a part of commercial rap music and popular culture.

These performers rap about lavish homes and cars, money, possessions, sex, drugs, guns and violence and these messages are so present in the music that they nullify the more positive messages of racial equality, fair education or financial independence for women. Racial equality is often discussed by these rappers whilst simultaneously using derogatory terms or language which again demoralises the intended message and its possible power or influence.

Women and female rappers are suggested within this essay as subjecting themselves and other women to objectification and subordination within their music, lyrics and videos. This study acknowledges instances where female rap artists attempt to define their own sexuality or present new understanding of female sexuality; however the contradictory messages within their music often invalidate these more positive messages.

It is suggested in this study that the marginalisation of females in hip-hop and their representation within music video is reflective of their social status in the United States, 'Black women have been ideologically controlled by the images presented in the mass media.' (Balaji 2010:6) and as Collins (1991) notes, 'the nexus of negative stereotypical images applied to African-American women has been fundamental to Black women's oppression' (7). As suggested in this study Black women have been constructed in the West as physical rather than emotional or intellectual. These sexualised images speak of ownership and focuses our attention on the corporate structures responsible for the production, promotion and dissemination of these images and texts. However, this is not to suggest that these females' rappers are passive in their involvement and creative input. It is argued in this study that these female rappers appear to be 'endorsing' these attitudes towards women and more specifically Black women, in an attempt to assert their dominance within the genre and to gain commercial success.

As suggested in this study, the problem that female rappers face within the industry is that masculinity within the genre is what is deemed most authentic; the aggressive nature of the music and the culture it came from has been associated with 'maleness'. There has of course been a sustained female presence within the genre; however are we to think that any presence is better than none, even if it often reinforces dominant white patriarchal hegemony? I would suggest that it is not. From a musical genre that in its infancy acted as a rejection of its surroundings including; poverty, racial hatred, police brutality and violence. It appears as though this genre now glamourizes sex, violence, sexual violence against women, sexism, misogyny, drugs and crime in the aim of commercial success and economic prosperity. It is also apparent from this study that in the modern era artists such as Nicki Minaj are reinforcing this sexism and misogyny themselves, resulting in the 'othering' of black women and the 'normalising' of certain themes.

Finally, areas that seem to be lacking in research are within the latest 'wave' of female rappers such as Nicki Minaj but also Azealia Banks and Iggy Azalea. These female rappers are of course fairly new; therefore it is assumed that these analyses will come in the future. There also needs to be more analysis of 'guest appearances' from female artists within rap videos (such as Rihanna and Beyoncé) as this female interaction, as is the case with Minaj, appears to be reinforcing stereotypes and normalising negative attitudes towards women. As rap music continues to be one of the most lucrative musical genres in terms of economic success it could be suggested that we are unlikely to see a change in these attitudes, however with more academic attention in this area we can certainly move towards a better understanding of these behaviours and attempt to dismantle the hegemonic systems that allow for these attitudes to be presented to audiences as 'entertainment'.

Bibliography

Adams, T. M & Fuller, D. B. (2006) 'The Words Change But The Ideology Remains The Same: Misogynistic Lyrics in Rap Music'. *Popular Music* Vol. 36, No. 6 (June, 206).

Bailey, C. (1988) 'N***er/lover: The thin sheen of race in something wild'. *Screen* Vol. 29, No. 4 (Winter, 1988): 28-40.

Balaji, M. (2010) 'Vixen Resistin': Redefining Black Womanhood in Hip-Hop Music Videos'. *Journal of Black Studies* Vol. 41, N0.1 (September 2010): 5-20.

Borthwick, S & Moy, R. (2004) *Popular Music Genres: An Introduction.* Edinburgh: Edinburgh University Press.

Born, G and Hesmondhalgh, D. (eds.) (2000) *Western Music and its Others.* USA: University of California Press.

Collins, P. H. (1991) *Black Feminist Thought: Knowledge, consciousness, and the politics of empowerment.* New York: Routledge.

Davis, A. (1990) 'Black Women and Music: A Historical Legacy of Struggle'. In *Wild Women in the Whirlwind' Afro-American Culture and the Contemporary Literary Renaissance,* edited by J. M. Braxton & A. N. McLaughlin, 3-21. New Jersey: Rutgers University Press.

Emerson, R. (2002) "Where my girls at?': Negotiating Black womanhood in music videos'. *Gender and Society.* Vol. 16, No.1 (Feb, 2002): 115-135.

Frith, S. (1996) *Performing Rites; On the Value of Popular Music.* Cambridge: Polity.

Frith, S. (2007) *Taking Popular Music Seriously: Selected Essays.* Aldershot: Ashgate.

Giddens, A. (2006) *Sociology.* Cambridge: Polity.

Goodall, N. H. (1994) 'Depend on Myslef: T.L.C and the Evolution of Black Female Rap'. *The Journal of Negro History.* Vol. 79, No. 1 (Winter, 1994): 85-89.

Guevara, N. (1987) 'Women Writin', Rappin', Breakin.' In *The Year Left: An American Socialist Yearbook,* edited by M. Davis, 160-175. London: Verso.

Hatch, D and Millward, S. (1987) *From Blues to Rock; an analytical history of pop music.* Manchester University Press.

Hilson Woldu, G. (2006) 'Gender as anomaly: women in rap'. In *The Resisting Muse: Popular Music and Social Protest,* edited by I. Peddie, 90-102. Aldershot: Ashgate.

Hurley, J. M. (1994) 'Music Video and the Construction of Gendered Subjectivity (Or How Being a Music Video Junkie Turned Me into a Feminist)'. *Popular Music.* Vol. 13, No. 3 (October, 1994): 327-338.

Jacobs, L. (1988) The Censorship of Blonde Venus: Textual analysis and historical method. *Cinema Journal.* Vol. 27, No. 3 (Spring, 1988): 21-31.

Jarmen-Ivens. (2006) 'Queer(ing) Masculinities in Heterosexist Rap Music'. In *Queering the Popular Pitch.* Edited Whiteley, S & Rycenga, J. New York: Routledge.

Jeffries, M. P. (2011) *Thug Life: Race, Gender, and the Meaning of Hip-Hop.* US: University Of Chicago Press.

Jhally, S. (Director). (2006) *Dreamworlds III* [Documentary]. Northampton, MA: Media Education Foundation.

Keyes, C. (2004) 'Empowering self, making choices, creating spaces: Black female identity via rap music performance'. In *That's the joint! The hip-hop studies reader,* edited by M. Forman & M. A. Neal, 265-277. New York: Routledge.

Longhurst, B. (1995) *Popular Music & Society.* Cambridge: Polity.

Moore, A. (2002) 'Authenticity as Authentication'. *Popular Music.* Vol. 21, No. 2:.209- 223.

Oware, M. (2009) 'A 'Man's Woman'?' Contradictory Messages in the Songs of Female Rappers, 1992-2000)'. *Journal of Black Studies.* Vol. 39, No. 5 (May, 2009): 786-802.

Perkins, W. E. (1996) *Droppin' Science: Critical Essays on Rap Music and Hip Hop Culture.* Philadelphia: Temple University Press.

Price, E. G. (2006) *Hip Hop Culture.* ABC-CLIO. United States.

Queeley, A. (2003) *Hip Hop and the Aesthetics of Criminalization.* University of California Press.

Railton, D, & Watson, P. (2005) 'Naughty Girls and red blooded women: Representations of female heterosexuality in music video'. *Journal of Black Studies.* Vol. 41, No. 1 (September 2010): 5-20.

Ramsey, P. G. (2003) *Race Music: Black Cultures from Bebop to Hip-Hop.* University of California Press.

Rose, T. (1994) *Black Noise: Rap Music and Black Culture in Contemporary America. Music Culture.* Wesleyan University Press.

Rose, T. (2004) 'Never trust a big butt and a smile'. In *That's the joint! The hip-hop studies reader,* edited by M. Forman & M. A. Neal 291-306. New York: Routledge.

Scott, D. B. (2009) *The Ashgate Research Companion to Popular Musicology.* Aldershot: Ashgate.

Shepherd, J. (2003) *Continuum Encyclopedia of Popular Music of the World Volume 8, Part 3.* New York: The Continuum International Publishing Group.

Spivak, C. G. (1998) *Spivak In Other Worlds; Essays in Cultural Politics.* Oxford: Routledge.

Musical References

50 Cent (2003) *'In Da Club'* Shady/Aftermath/Interscope.

Jay-Z (2003) *'Black Album'* Roc-A-Fella, Def Jam.

Kanye West (2013) *'Black Skinhead'* Roc-A-Fella, Def Jam.

Nicki Minaj (2010) *'Stupid Hoe'* Young Money/Cash money/Universal Republic.

Nicki Minaj (2010) *'Pink Friday'* (Album) Young Money/Cash Money/Universal Republic.

Nicki Minaj (2012) *'Roman Reloaded'* Young Money/Cash Money/Universal Republic.

Nicki Minaj (2012) *'Pink Friday: Roman Reloaded'* (Album) Young Money/Cash Money/Universal Republic.

Nicki Minaj (2013) *'High School'* Young Money/Cash Money/Universal Republic.

Queen Latifah (1994) *'U.N.I.T.Y.'* Motown Records.

Salt 'n' Pepa (1987) *'Push It'* Next Plateau Records/London Records.

Music Video

Nicki Minaj (2010) 'Stupid Hoe' (Video Released: Jan 2012) Directed by Hype Williams.

Nicki Minaj (2013) 'High School' (Video Released: April: 2013) Directed by Benny Boom.

CHAPTER 6

Establishing the Sound of Star Wars: A Critical Analysis

Kevin Withe

The Star Wars universe over the years has expanded outside of the realms of the six currently existing films into numerous video games and animated series, yet, the soundtracks to them have always remained true to the sound that composer John Williams has so masterfully created. The video games in particular are able to interactively transport a person deep into the heart of the Star Wars Universe through the epic soundscape of the Star Wars sound. Despite Lucas often referring to his films as silent movies, Star Wars contains, by Williams's reckoning, '...more music per foot of film than anywhere else...' (Mullenger 1999) establishing a wealth of music that constantly draws the audience into its mystical world. It is by virtue of George Lucas's and John Williams's individual craft and overall 'genius' that Star Wars, particularly Episode IV: A New Hope (Lucas 1977), has become renowned as one of the pinnacle movies responsible for bringing the sound of the classical Hollywood score back to the cinema. However, what was it about the 'golden' era of Hollywood that inspired the revival in the first place, especially for a science fiction/ fantasy film set within Outer space? Once again John Williams has been assigned the task of recreating the Star Wars sound for the soundtrack of the up and coming, episodes VII-IX trilogy. But what is the Star Wars sound? It is something many people will instantly recognise upon hearing it but very few can explain. It also raises the issue of how does one determine what a sound or soundscape is?

The aim of this study is to critically analyse some of the key themes, concepts and sounds of the Star Wars Saga in order to obtain some insight into what the sound of Star Wars is and how Williams has managed to achieve this, potentially shedding some light as to what to expect when Episodes VII – IX are released. The aim is to also look into some of the aspects of film music in general and its role within cinema.

Literature Review

To understand the key concepts in analysing film music, an examination of the relevant literature was carried out. Two of the main authors connected with this study are Adorno & Eisler and Kalinak, who represent two opposing viewpoints. In the book *Composing for the Films*, Adorno & Eisler appear highly critical of film music, sustaining a rather pessimistic view and characterising film music as a problem that needs addressing, focusing on the 'technical and social potentialities and contradictions of music in relation to motion pictures' (Eisler and Adorno 1994:liii). They see the role of sound as an obstacle standing in the way of the visual imagery rather than an essential tool contributing to the overall experience. It is Adorno & Eisler that offer the most critique yet have arguably witnessed the least in terms of the development of film music. Film music has transformed over the years, as has its views cast upon it. The division between the concepts of high and low art have progressively dwindled, allowing film music to become growingly considered as an art form within itself.

Kalinak has adopted a more optimistic approach, examining how sound can benefit the cinematic experience, establishing setting, creating tension, ultimately taking upon the role as narrator, acknowledging its many functions. Three reoccurring themes that were brought up by Kalinak and Adorno & Eisler, also including authors, Larsen, Donnelly and Kassabian, are how film music works, semiotics and meaning in music. In an attempt to address how film music works, each of the aforementioned authors, with the exception of Adorno & Eisler, point towards a cultural based explanation, focusing on music as a universal language. Adorno & Eisler however claim that music, of any sort, holds only aesthetic value, a view that has been highly criticised over the years, in particularly by Kassabian in the book Hearing Film (2001:38-39).

Kassabian contests that before film music, music itself could only be talked of by trained musicians in terms of 'form, harmonic language, orchestration, etc' (Kassabian 2001:21) however now music can have meaning outside of this 'interiorized' context. Larsen breaks down meaning in music into two basic forms, structural resemblance and association with other music. The former is typically of perhaps a cartoon whereby the music sounds like or resembles the action onscreen; a form of musical onomatopoeia. The latter refers to association, perhaps towards a location for instance; a sitar heard in music may suggest links to India. To form their ideas and conclusions, many of these authors tend to use analytical methods, with the aid of musical examples or case studies.

Methodology

In order to establish and contextualise the 'sound' of Star Wars, an appropriate approach must be found. Gorbman proposes a number of ways in which film music can be analysed based on their goals, which are 'musical, fan or market, academic, cultural, and mainstream' (Gorbman, cited in Neumeyer and Buhler 2001:16). Of these, it is the academic, which examines 'music's position and function within a particular film' (Neumeyer and Buhler 2001:16), and the cultural approach, which 'places music within an historical account or a framework of culture criticism' (Ibid.:16), that may appear best suited to this study as Neumeyer and Buhler argue '...they best represent the activities of the film-music student and scholar' (Ibid.:17).

With such a broad history to cover, documentaries and online videos will be used in order to understand an overview of the key periods and influential figures related to forming the classical Hollywood. Once this has been achieved and successfully narrowed down, literally sources will be primarily used to ascertain the fundamental concepts and critiques behind finding meaning within film music, as well as further examining in more detail the historical processes which have occurred inspiring John Williams into scoring the Star Wars saga in the manner in which he did. This will account for the cultural elements suggested by Neumeyer and Buhler.

Analysing the music will be conducted primarily by visual and audio material, including the films themselves and their relative soundtracks. I will be listening and interpreting the music in relation to the visual context, as well as seeking comparisons to other pieces of music, to analyse and contextualise the 'sound' of Star Wars. It is my aim to examine numerous themes, either through importance within the context of the film, popularity amongst the audience or its use outside of the film, to search for elements contained within that may suggest reasons why Williams chose that particular manner to score the film.

In order to gain a closer insight into the mind of Williams, interviews from the man himself, found through either radio or television broadcasts, documentaries or internet based sources, will be used to establish a more definitive interpretation of the music. Lastly, internet source material will be examined, which may reflect more up to date aspects, such as material on the up and coming trilogy themselves.

Establishing the Hollywood Sound

Since the development of sound on film, music has become an integral part of the cinematic experience. In today's society it has become so ingrained into the ethos of moviegoers that its exclusion would appear to be somewhat of a spectacle. With audiences becoming so accustomed to the presence of film music it can often be difficult to truly appreciate the process and development that has preceded film scores as they exists today.

Arguably the success of the Star Wars Saga, as a film, stems from the successfulness of William's accompanying musical score. In order to understand why this has been the case it is important to consider and analyse the practises and devices Williams has implemented. This first section aims to look at how these practises have developed throughout history and examine influential figures that may have been an inspiration to Williams and will be referred back to when analysing the music of Star Wars.

Primarily it is imperative to understand why there is a need for film music. Without sound, cinema is merely a series of moving pictures, as they were so aptly named in its primordial stage. One of the first instances of a moving picture was the Lumiére Brothers' entitled L'Arrivée d'un Train À la Ciotat (Lumiére, A and Lumiére, L, 1896) which showed a train pulling into a station. So revolutionary was this, audiences would often brace as if the train was going to come out the screen and collide with them (Dixon and Foster 2008:7). To begin with these clips were relatively short, roughly only lasting no more than a minute, and were played in complete silence (FilmMusicHistory 2012a). However, as the technology advanced and the amount of film available increased, seconds developed into minutes and this extended silence became uncomfortable for audiences to endure (ibid.). A similar experience still exists today with Graphics Interchange Format, more commonly known as GIFs, which are short clips, found on the

Internet, of moving images lasting for a few seconds and are often looped. These GIFs are usually silent and after a while of viewing, the silence may become unpleasant.

In Western society a large majority of people have established a fear of silence, frequently perceiving it as a breakdown in communication when in another person's company, resulting in a sensation of awkwardness. It is so far uncertain as to the exact psychological answer as to why this is so, leading many to merely speculate on this. Claire Josa, an experienced trainer of Neurolinguistic Programming, meditation teacher and published author, believes that the reason people are 'scared' of silence is because they are scared of their own thoughts and that they use background noise to drown out them out (Josa 2013). It is suggested that hearing the sounds of the self for too long requires sounds of the 'not-self' (De Geest 1999). Throughout the 19th Century people expected some form of audio stimulation to accompany live shows, including dance, comedy and magic acts (Slobin 2008:vii) further indicating the desire to mask the silence.

To ensure the comfort of the audience, and to also assist in telling the stories that the longer films now included, live musicians were hired to play alongside the film to create background noise. The music aimed to propel the action of the film in a similar fashion as it did in 19th century opera (FilmMusicHistory 2012a). The biggest problem these musicians faced however was that they would not have known what music to play. The art of film music had yet to be discovered, in which case the experience would imaginably differ with each venue as each musician developed their own trial and error methods. Given that the most common venues for silent films in its initial stages, particularly in America, were vaudevilles or small theatres known as Nickelodeons, it is reasonable to assume that they would have mainly employed the use of a single musician, notably a pianist. It could also be suggested that some musicians may have attempted to play material that reflected the nature of the footage shown, others not so much. With little or no evidence existing of the music played in each venue, it remains to be speculative, however the adaptation and evolution of the cue sheet during the 1910's, including the French weekly 'Guide Musicale' and the 'Incidental Music for Edison Pictures' in the United States (Kalinak 2010:41), suggests that there was a demand for musical direction.

The cue sheet aimed to suggest existing musical pieces or 'ditties' to the musician as a reference to the style of music that should be played in each given scene. This would have created a more uniformed approach to film music, however the growing popularity and audience numbers throughout the 1910's meant that not only did cinema theatres grow larger, so too did the musical arrangements leading up to the accompaniment of a full orchestra (Butsch 2000:60-61). Therefore cue sheets could no longer suffice and instead full written scores were greatly desired (Larsen and Irons 2007). By the 1920s many theatres, such as the Loew's Theatre Jersey City, housed built in theatre pipe organs which could perform a wide range of sounds from percussion to sound effects. The expansion of cinema saw the transition between being deemed predominantly as a working class form of entertainment, to a higher form of art, appealing to the middle class; something the film industry was keen to develop and capitalise on (FilmMusicHistory 2012b; Butsch 2000:60-61).

With each theatre's film music composers writing their own scores and cue sheets, based on libraries of music that had developed, problems began to arise. The demand for new scores each week began to take its toll and most composers struggled to keep up with the demand for new music. So much so, that they began to 'murder' the classics of Beethoven, Mozart, Wagner and Tchaikovsky to produce enough material (Wierzbicki 2009:67). Also with each theatre performing different scores, the experience would still be drastically varied. A poorly composed accompaniment in just one theatre could spell disaster for the film. The studios needed a control on the music and in 1926 Don Juan (Crosland 1926) became the first full-length feature film to include pre-recorded sound (Sound on Cinema: The Music that Made the Movies - The Big Score, 2013). Through sound on film the need for musicians in every theatre dissolved, leaving hundreds, perhaps thousands, in turmoil at the brink of the impending recession. Nevertheless, Don Juan's composer Max Steiner would eventually be unearthed as one of the key figures that would become highly influential to John Williams.

Max Steiner sparked a revolution in film music, arguably cementing the foundations of the classic Hollywood film score. Since the introduction of sound on film, studios believed that music had to be sourced, by which the audience had to be able to identify where the music was coming from within the film, in order for them to except music on the soundtrack (Sound on Cinema: The Music that Made the Movies - The Big Score, 2013). As a result of this many of the early 'talkie' films only had accompanying music at the beginning and endings. Musicals on the other hand were saved by the fact that they could visually incorporate the band or music source into the film (ibid).

It was to be in 1933 where this method of film scoring changed with Steiner's work on the film King Kong (Cooper and Schoedsack 1933). Up until now, film music had been scored or cued to a particular sound. For instance a film portraying a scene out at sea would have music that suggesting a boat or the sea, usually backed on the basis of previous work (FilmMusicHistory 2012a). However, Steiner had the challenge of scoring a film about a '50 foot' gorilla, despite not actually appearing in the film as that tall (IMDb 2014). This had never been before and so Steiner had no library of music to refer to. Instead, having immigrated to the United States in 1914 from Vienna, Austria, Steiner used his European classical experience of the Romantic period to write a film score in a whole new way. Steiner masterfully:

> ...introduced the practice of precisely matching the music to the onscreen action – a technique exemplified in *Kong* when the Native chief strides forward toward the landing party, when Kong slams the *Elasmosaurus* in the rock in the cave scene, or when Kong pounds on the decimated subway car (because the technique was widely used in cartoons, it was known as 'Mickey-Mousing'). (Morton 2005:76)

King Kong was considered a huge risk, as not only was Steiner taking a leap into the unknown scoring an 'original' soundtrack but it was also entering the practice on non-diegetic music. With little dialogue, King Kong's soundtrack had to make Kong believable to audiences and break the boundary of the studio's belief that audiences would not accept unsourced music. Steiner had to create a way of developing music into a narrative, whereby the music tells the story. The way in which he succeeded in making Kong believable was through the use of the Leitmotif, something highly reminiscence of Wagnerian Operas of the 19th century. Giving Kong a 'theme' enabled him to manipulate and change the theme to suggest different moods or thoughts that were then reflected upon Kong himself (Sound on Cinema: The Music that Made the Movies - The Big Score, 2013). In this way audiences were able to empathise with the 'beast', feeling his love, anger and in one particular scene (where Kong lifts up the female's dress) his discovery of sex. It is quite easy to see perhaps, the reasons why King Kong came to be considered as arguably one of the 'classic' movies of all time. However, it is interesting to note that Larsen and Irons (2007:88), with reference to Kalinak, does propose an argument that Steiner had already perfected this Hollywood system in his first scoring of Cimarron (Ruggles 1931), yet it was King Kong that took the credit.

After Kong's success film studios wasted no time in capitalising on this new form of film music employing a host of European classical composers, one of which was to become another 'legend' of the trade, Erich Wolfgang Korngold. Unlike Steiner, Korngold unfortunately was not truly recognised as a 'great' until the 1970's (Steib 2013:381) however he did compose the soundtrack for timeless movies including The Sea Hawk (Curtiz 1940), Juarez (Dieterle 1939) and more notably King's Row (Wood 1942) and The Adventures of Robin Hood (Curtiz and Keighley 1938). The scores of the latter two films will be important to look at later on when analyzing John Williams' soundtrack to Star Wars. By the end of the 1940's the Hollywood sound had become well established, with Steiner, Korngold as well as composers Alfred Newman, Franz Waxman and Dimitri Tiomkin leading the way. However during the 1950's and 60's new forms of film music began to emerge including Jazz scores, notably established in the James Bond thriller Dr. No (Young 1962) and The Pink Panther (Edwards, 1963) and popular music scores, such as the Beatles' A Hard Day's Night (Lester 1964) and High Noon (Zinneman 1952).

By the 1970's the grand Hollywood classical soundtrack was overlooked with composers looking at cheaper alternatives, experimenting with synthesizers, particularly within the realms of Sci-fi (Rubin and Casper 2013:27). A perfect example of this is Eduard Artemev's soundtrack to Solaris (Tarkovsky 1972) and with its eerie sounding representation of space and the unknown.

However in 1977, despite this trend, director of Star Wars, George Lucas, wanted to go back in history and give his movie the classic sound of the 1930's epic soundtrack, employing John Williams who by which point already had successes with Fiddler on the Roof (Jewison 1971) and Jaws (Spielberg 1975) amongst others.

Kassabian states that 'since the late 1970's, one of the most important film score styles has been the heavy, Romantic symphonic score with thick instrumentation' (Kassabian 2001:92) and it can be argued that Williams' scores, amongst others, were hugely influential in bringing the sound of classical Hollywood back to the blockbuster movies, which is still in effect to this day.

The fact that film music, particularly blockbuster movies, has shifted back to those techniques and sounds developed in the 1930's, overshadowing more recent developments, shows the power and influences it holds. Eisler and Adorno (1994:45) argue that the history of film is irrelevant in its analysis, claiming that any development came through the clumsy attempts to pander to the 'taste' of the public, however, arguably this 'taste' was in fact a cultural development whereby, through initial trial and error, composers highlighted key aspects and functions that translated narratives through aural forms. This process of trial and error continued on past the classical Hollywood era until composers realised that it could not be beaten and have since adopted it back into its standard structure of scoring for film. This therefore makes the historical element relevant as it holds the key of understanding why the concepts have stuck.

Meaning in Music

As the previous section suggests, in the early stages, film music undertook a role of not only masking the potential silence but also providing an aural stimulus to the visual image that artistically brought the images to life. However, composers in the 1930's, such as Steiner and Korngold, went beyond this and developed their works into a tool for storytelling, taking on a more narrative role. Later composers have since gone on to build epic soundscapes drawing audiences into the illusion of cinema. This section will look into how this is done; how do you tell a story with music alone and capture the essence of an era or genre through sound? This section also aims to examine some of the key aspects and critiques of film music as a reference to understand and analyse Williams' scores and the Star Wars sound.

'When it comes to the analysis of the role of music, little help is at hand in the available literature' (Larsen and Irons 2007:36). Perhaps it is often too difficult to fully understand or describe what it actually does. On the surface we know that the film score establishes setting, fashions a mood and creates atmosphere, as well as helping us understand the plot and narrative developments amongst other functions (Kalinak 2010:1). Perhaps it is through the understanding of this that we accept its presence to begin with and even more so to demand it. Nevertheless, in order to attempt analysing its role there are certain concepts that can be examined; firstly through form and meaning.

To tell a story through music, arguably, there must be an element of meaning either within the brain or embedded into the scores, that audiences are able to access in order to understand its context. Theorists such as Bazelon, Adorno and Stravinsky claim that meaning in music only exists as a direct response of bad habits of the listener and that music only truly possesses aesthetic value (Kassaian 2001:16). However, based on this argument, they do not seem to account for the social elements towards meaning, favouring a more negative approach. Each culture across the globe has established their own musical language suggesting a relationship between cultural background and musical meaning. This would seem to support their theory of meaning coming from the response of the listener however it could be argued that meaning comes from society and culture, and that the subsequent music is the interpretation of this (Shepard 1991:11, 12). This would also indicate that the musical composers whether directly or indirectly, will interpret meaning into their work based on their social background. Historically, each artistic movement has been a result of an intellectual social evolution (Ibid.).

In terms of film music, this may suggest that the origin of musical meaning comes from the social background of where the film is made and its target audience. The trial and error approach to film music in its early stages suggests that it was the social collectiveness of the people that ultimately decided what worked and what did not; therefore it can be argued that the soundtrack to Star Wars and the sound of classical Hollywood, for instance, were developed and evolved from the American audience and culture.

As many absolutist theorists believe, meaning comes from symbols that refer to something outside of itself e.g. pictures refer to other physical objects, as do words, however problems arise when it comes to music. Shepard (1991) claims that their approaches are inadequate, favouring a more modern approach, separating music into a new category. Society seeks meaning through symbols, attaching them to situations whereby they can be used to reflect upon. '...Situations and symbols have a mutually interdependent, but not determinant, relationship crucial to the constantly changing dynamics of social process' (Shepard 1991:15).

This relationship has become immensely exploited in film music and debatably is the reason why it 'works'. It can be argued that by making a connection in a given scene between visual and aural stimuli, society as a collective attaches the same symbolism bonding the two together. For instance, in the famous shower scene from the film Psycho (Hitchcock 1960), as the killer attacks with the knife, the action is complimented with repeated high pitched shrieks from the violins. The two forms closely mimic each other suggesting the same meaning and as a society we have come to symbolise these two mediations with the perception of 'attack'. By establishing these subtle connections, and drawing upon experience, the audience expects the music to match or bond with the on screen action and it is this expectation that composers draw upon to either harmoniously aid the visuals or deceive the audience with conflicting symbolism.

In the movie The Shining (Kubrick 1980), the little boy, Danny, is happily playing darts in what appears as a fairly innocent scene, nevertheless the music heard is 'dark' and 'eerie'. This creates a conflict in the minds of the audience as they are being presented with two opposing symbols, causing confusion as to which to assume is correct, therefore veiling its true meaning. Essentially this brings about a sense of tension, not knowing what is about to happen. The scene continues and as the camera pans around Danny, the viewer sees the twin girl 'ghosts' standing there, revealing the true meaning as the visuals suddenly match the music. If, hypothetically, the music were to change to something that symbolised a happier sound as the camera pans, then once again the symbolic messages would clash creating tension and misleading the audience.

Russian film makers Eisenstein, Pudovkin and Alexandrov created a model, in the 1930s, claiming that film sound is merely used to parallel or counterpoint the image, suggesting that the image was the conveyor of meaning and the sound adjusted this meaning (Kalinak 2010:17).

However this model oversimplifies the matter and fails to recognise music's ability to carry meaning and symbolism. As Kalinak goes on to argue, this model cannot be applied in all instances, pointing out anomalies such as the torture scene in Reservoir Dogs whereby the visuals are based around the music.

Just as symbols can be used to define a situation, they can also be used to develop a 'sound' or soundscape. The human brain has an overzealous lust for categorizing, a process which helps it take in more information and organize it all easier. This explains why we feel it necessary to establish musical genres, constantly trying to find connections between different pieces of music. The brain naturally builds a semiotic model whereby particular situations are attached to symbols used to describe it. For example, most people when thinking of a beach setting may think of sand, buckets and spade, sun bathing etc. The same process applies with music.

Only a handful of people have actually visited outer space however certain types of music can be described as 'spacey'. By attaching characteristics to music that carry similar symbolic properties, we are able to establish connections between the two. Space is large and vast, almost incomprehensibly so, which is a characteristic that is usually portrayed with the use of powerful orchestral brass sections. Also Sprach Zarathrustra (Straus 1896) perfectly exemplifies this notion after its use for the opening of the film 2001: A Space Odyssey (Kubrick 1968) in which the visuals show the sun rising from behind a planet whilst in space. Since this piece, this symbolism between large brass sections and space has only grew stronger, a tool highly used in Star Wars which will be analysed in the next section.

Another characteristic of space is its mysteriousness of unknown worlds. Much of the early sci-fi movies employed a range of unfamiliar sounds, using a synstudyer, aiming to make this connection. These experimental sounds symbolised the predicted future of sound and impending innovation of space travel.

This practice of forming 'sounds' or 'soundscapes' has given audiences certain expectations prior to viewing a film. Audiences will often expect and stereotype a particular style of music depending on the genre or location. 'No music is completely new and original, it all reminds one in some way or another of other music. All music conveys culturally established connotations' (Larsen 2005:68). Going back to the scene in The Shining; knowing that the genre of the film is that of horror, when the music suggests something sinister, the prior expectation of something bad influences the decision between taking meaning from the visuals or the music. However it could be suggested that the consistent expectation of something bad happening only adds to the tension, as viewers are always waiting for it.

Once a soundscape has been established composers look for other techniques to help with the storytelling within this. One of the most common devices used, particularly by John Williams, is the Leitmotif. Originating from 19th Century Wagnerian operas the Leitmotif is an '...identifiable and recurring musical pattern' (Kalinak 2010:11) usually constructed through melody as either a motif or theme. These motifs are linked either to a person, place or environment or an emotion, with each occurrence of the theme aimed at reminding the audience of the first time they heard it or as a reference to that object it has become subject to (Larsen 2005:60).

The Star Wars saga is rife with Leitmotifs and themes from 'The Imperial March' to the 'Force Theme' and is arguably what makes the series so memorable however theorists Eisler and Adorno take on a slightly cynical view on the technique. They argue that the leitmotif may perhaps show a sign of 'laziness' from the composer, 'The ease with which they [leitmotifs] are recalled provides definite clues to the listener, and also are a practical help to the composer in his task of composition under pressure. He can quote where he otherwise would have to invent' (Eisler and Adorno 1994:4).This kind of approach towards film music has since become old fashioned and by signifying that the composer is male somewhat confirms this pre modern attitude. This negative approach seems to suggest a 'high art snobbery' attitude against that of low art, suggesting that composers are 'pandering' to the unsophisticated lower class audiences, and further goes on to argue that the Leitmotif serves no function in cinema (Ibid.). As Dickinson claims, the American approach to the Leitmotif fell between to gap of being neither 'exclusively populist nor entirely 'high art'...' (2003:3), which correlates to historical attempts to use film to bridge to gap as mentioned in the previous section. Eisler and Adorno claim that '...this assumption [of 'laziness'] is only illusionary' (Eisler and Adorno 1994:5) and that there is more depth to the

Leitmotif than initially assumed, notably outside of film music. They argue that 'Wagner conceived its purpose as the endowment of the dramatic events with metaphysical significance' (Ibid.) and its invention was to indicate a much deeper symbolic meaning. This correlates with Shepard's claim of finding meaning in music through forms of symbolism however it may be deemed that Williams's ability to develop the Leitmotif past the means of simply serving as signposts, which will be examined in the forthcoming section, contradicts their claim that the leitmotif serves no purpose in film.

So far, the historical aspects of film music have been established as well as what is expected from it in terms of meaning and soundscaping. The next section will look directly into, and analyse, the music of Star Wars, with reference to these elements, which will be important in order to determine what makes the Star Wars sound and what is to be expected of the next three episodes in the saga.

Analysing the Sound of Star Wars

Originally, Star Wars was only ever meant to be a one off, or at least that's how John Williams felt when scoring for A New Hope (Parker 2010). Director George Lucas sought out Williams' expertise in an attempt to recreate the essence of the 1930's classical Hollywood sound for his space opera. Whereas other sci-fi films were looking at atonal synth sounds, Lucas felt that these soundtracks felt too cold and wanted to exhibit the romanticism that classical Hollywood brought. Self admittedly unaware of the forthcoming success that Star Wars was about to endure, it can be suggested that Williams failed to comprehend the significance of the film, passing it off as another job to keep the 'bread on the table' (Star Wars Revisited 2013). With this Williams applied the use of Leitmotifs, common in Wagnerian opera, to score his music, which would perhaps support Adorno's view on Leitmotifs in reference to 'laziness'. However, as the Star Wars Saga expanded, so too did Williams' scores, highlighting at least three key themes; Space, War and Love. It is through these three concepts that this section will attempt to analyse.

Primarily, the storyline to Star Wars is about a war in space. How do you achieve the sound of this? As mentioned in the previous section, many composers have utilised the idea of using bold brass sections to emphasise the great vastness of outer space. Looking at the opening

Main Title theme heard at the opening to each of the six films, this theme, as with most opening sequences, aims to grab the audience's attention and instantly set the soundscape for the film. With this, the viewers are instantly hit with a 'blast' of brass, as the horn section bellows in with the opening fanfare motif, along with the flash of the Star Wars title and scrolling text onscreen. The 'blast' appears highly dramatic, potentially giving some viewers a small fright, as a result of the silence that precedes it following the all too familiar sound of the 20th Century Fox fanfare. As this sequence is repeated throughout each film it becomes part of the tradition, further accentuating the Star Wars ethos.

After the fanfare, the theme takes on a military-esque sound through the marching beat of the percussion highlighting the concept of war, before developing into a more graceful and romantic 'flying through space' sound as the string section smoothly takes over from the horns in the foreground whilst maintaining the boldness feel. Williams is able to not only capture the sound of space but also propose a further depth to the scene setting by introducing the symbolism of love and war within the context of the Title theme. It is interesting to note that the opening sequence does not seem to make any obvious reference to the force, one of the other important concepts of the saga, perhaps in an attempt to hold something back and allow the audience to discover this aspect at a later stage.

For many Star Wars fans, this opening theme, along with its orchestral texture and timbre, can be instantly recognised, forever ingraining itself into the memory the notion that 'this is Star Wars!' However, this theme is by no means original; instead it pays homage to one of Williams' greatest influences, Erich Wolfgang Korngold. The opening title theme bears remarkable similarities to Korngold's opening title theme to the film Kings Row (Wood 1942), both displaying qualities of Wagnerian heroic trumpet themes (Green 1993:100). It could be suggested that the connection to Korngold provides a sense of nostalgia, which may translate towards the story buried within Star Wars; providing a sense of 'A long time ago in a galaxy far, far away...' despite the technology within the film being 'futuristic'.

Arguably one of the most difficult challenges Williams faced in scoring for Star Wars was creating the sound of the force, a fictional unseen energy field in which those sensitive enough to it can use to gain 'magical powers'. Not only did Williams have to establish a sound to symbolically represent this, he also had to successfully sell it to the audience. It could be argued that part of the belief would also have to come from Lucas in his visual representation however the force is 'felt', much like an emotion, highlighting the need for a more emotional connection, established through music.

Musically, the force theme is based and starts around a minor key with a melody that appears to be struggling to reach the climax, suggesting a sad, negative feel, however, as the melody arrives at a climax the underlying chord appears major rather than an expected minor chord. Emotionally this musical struggle to resolution suggests going from something bad to something good; suggesting hope (Film Score Junkie, 2013a). In relation to the characters, the Jedi look to the force for help during an ordeal in a search for hope. It could be argued that it is through this symbolic connection that Williams is able to connect emotionally with the audience, they sense the struggle and the force theme acts as a ray of hope, as if the force is on their side.

The orchestration of the theme offers a mystical and mysterious feeling, emphasising the 'magical' connection with the force, as the melody is gracefully delivered by the woodwind section, before the grand brass section builds up and takes over. 'Most associated with the 'iconic' Binary Sunset scene in Episode IV: A New Hope, by which Luke Skywalker aimlessly looks out across the sunset contemplating his fate, the theme's melodic struggle appears to personify the tough challenges ahead. Buhler and Flinn et al. (2000:44) point out that the audience is able to understand the mythology of the force before it is actually explained by Ben Kenobi later on, as to what it is. It could be argued that earlier instances of this theme, such as when viewers first see Princess Leia placing Ben's message into the R2-D2 droid, provide suggestive clues as to the symbolic nature of the force. By developing the leitmotif in this way, the force theme is able to arguably go beyond the realms of 'signposting' and symbolise a concealed cosmic energy, not only affirming Eisler and Adorno's position of what the leitmotif can do, but also challenging their belief that it cannot be done in film.

Like many operas Star Wars has both its heroes and villains. In Episode V: Empire Strikes Back (Kershner 1980), the 'bad guy' Darth

Vader is given his own theme, The Imperial March, which is played each time himself or the Imperial fleet are seen, near or referred to, making a symbolic connection. As the title suggests the theme has a military march sound, depicting the sound of evil. '…the harmony Williams uses for the main melody are not your average chord progressions… The infusion of chords that *almost* sound like normal ones, and minor chords at that, gives the impression of a darkly abnormal, evil worldview' (Film Score Junkie 2013b). To add to this, the rhythmic triplet feel drives the march forward with a sense of almost unstoppable power. In contrast to the opening title theme, the minor-esque chords suggest a more sinister meaning however there is a risk of becoming too clichéd; major chords for heroes and minor for villains.

This may suggest why the Emperor's theme sounds even more disturbing as, surprisingly, the melody is predominately major, however the chords beneath are minor creating a menacing feel. The major element suggests something big and powerful however the minor chords reveal the evil behind it. In doing this, Williams is able to manipulate this theme, which becomes ideal for the prequel movies. Filmed long after the original Trilogy, the majority of audiences watching Episodes I, II and III may have already seen Episodes IV, V and VI and know who The Emperor/Palpatine is and recognize that he is evil. When he appears in The Phantom Menace disguised as a 'good guy' audiences are already aware of his eventual fate. Williams personifies this deception within the Augie's Great Muincipal Band music in the victory parade at the end of the film. Despite sounding 'happy' and celebratory for the heroes, the melody that the choir is singing is in fact reminiscent of the Emperor's theme sped up, applying the symbolic idea of 'hidden identity' and deception. The Emperor's theme is hidden, just like his true evil nature. This highlights one of the benefits of using Leitmotifs in order to establish character development. Themes can be manipulated and altered to suggest different emotions and actions, clearly exemplified with progression of Anakin Skywalker becoming Darth Vader.

Over the course of the prequel movies the Imperial March becomes increasingly prominent, starting off with a subtle hint at the end of Anakin's theme in the Phantom Menace, teasing the audience with a sense of dramatic irony in regards to Anakin's eventual fate, before working up to the fully established theme as he is unveiled as Darth Vader in Episode III: Revenge of the Sith (Lucas 2005). Williams admits that Anakin's theme was composed backwards, deconstructing Darth Vader's Imperial March theme and instigating a more innocent presence (Mullenger,1999).

Audiences are already familiar with the sound of the Imperial March and over the course of the prequel movies it becomes increasingly used, especially whenever Anakin thinks or does something with evil intentions. Williams throws in a clear reference to the march at the end of Anakin's theme heard on the soundtrack and at the end credits.

In scenes that refer to or suggest war, it could be argued that a high proportion of Williams' scoring has been influenced by Holst's planet's suite, particularly from the planet Mars, bringer of war. Both Star Wars and Mars share similar qualities in the brass sections, promoting the Star Wars feel; so much so that the two scores could debatably be interchangeable.

As with any war, there are usually battle scenes and the most notorious in Star Wars are the lightsaber duels. The duels found within the prequels and sequels are highly contrasting. In the original trilogy the fights are fairly static action scenes compared to that of those found in the newer prequel films. Episodes IV & V tend to rely on sound effects, including the humming of the lightsabers and the 'classic' breathy sound of Vader's mask, to create a 'nervous' tension. Lucas himself suggests that this was not only due to the fact that the characters fighting in the originals were a crippled half man half droid, an old Jedi and a young untrained boy, but also limitations of technology at the time meant creating the visual effects of a laser sword during an elaborate fight scene was not possible (Coin 2007).

Throughout the Prequels, the Jedi and Sith are mostly, if not all, fully trained and at their peak resulting in highly energetic and dynamic fight scenes. The music equally reflects this, ensuing in fast paced, highly dramatic scoring using leitmotifs and themes. It could be argued that many of the lightsaber duels in the prequels are fought in conjunction with other battle scenes happening simultaneously, with the music transcending across the scenes, however when directly focused on a particular duel there are instances whereby the music is withdrawn to highlight the sound effects of the lightsabers much like in the originals.

Perhaps it is likely that either Lucas or Williams wanted to keep this aspect in.

Elements of The Duel of the Fates theme, first heard in Episode I: A Phantom Menace (Lucas 1999) appears in almost every battle scene in the prequel movies, as it becomes the central overriding focus. Taking inspiration from 'Oh Fortuna' (Orff 1935), Williams incorporates a more choral element in an attempt to establish a ritualistic antique feel to the music. As the force is subtly referred to as an ancient religion in A New Hope, creating this symbolic connection between real life religion and the film's fictitious religion further brings the story to life to the audience and adds to embellishing the Star Wars sound.

The chants, sang in Sanskrit, provide an 'epic' quality or feeling to the battle scenes especially when heard as Darth Maul appears to confront Qui-Gon Jinn and Obi Wan in the Phantom Menace. In the scene prior to this moment, the Gungans are battling with the Droid army with dramatic military styled battle music to accompany it. However the action suddenly cuts to the heroes within the palace building preparing to move on and the music goes very quiet. This sets up for what the audience has been waiting for, the moment where the Sith finally reveal themselves and Darth Maul makes his entrance. As the heroes approach the door, they abruptly open to find Darth Maul standing there taking them all by surprise and leaving them shook up, until Qui-Gon announces 'We'll handle it'.

Although the battle between the two Jedi's and Darth Maul is well renowned it is the battle between Obi Wan and Anakin in Episode III: Revenge of the Sith, including the standoff between Yoda and The Emperor, that ultimately the prequel movies build up to. For such an important battle and plot in the story, Williams recalls a host of the existing themes to form the scoring for the Battle of the Heroes. The encounter between these characters is the one that ultimately ties the two trilogies together and arguably attempts to capture the entire essence of the sound of Star Wars within it; arguably inspiring other soundtracks including the scoring for the online multiplayer game Star Wars: The Old Republic (Bioware 2011).

Battle of the Heroes also incorporates the religious choral theme, allowing for the music to not only move between itself and the Duel of the Fates theme, but also to integrate the force theme in when references to the force are made, such as when Anakin and Obi Wan try to use the same force move against each other, highlighting similar styles of fighting. Its melody is highly similar to the Gregorian chant 'Dies Irae' often used as part of the Roman Catholic Requiem service. Perhaps it could be suggested that the link to the deceased may have been intentional and could imply the idea of a battle to the death. The use of this chant has been used, in some form or another, in numerous other films including the Lord of the Rings (Jackson 2001), Jurassic Park (Spielberg 1993), Groundhog Day (Ramis 1993), The Lion King (Allers and Minkoff 1994) and The Shining (Kubrick 1980), which all encounter elements of death.

Of course not all of Star Wars is about War and the Force. Love and romance does play a role despite the fact that it is forbidden for a Jedi to love. Across the Stars is deemed to be the first and only love theme within Star Wars however it could be argued that Leia's theme in the original trilogy develops the same effect. As mentioned in the previous section, Larsen states that Leitmotifs, or in this instance themes, are there to remind the audience of the moment that they first heard it and to begin with Leia's theme does just that. Viewers are reminded back to the moment they first see Leia recording Ben Kenobi's message. However it could be argued that as Leia's relationship between herself and Han Solo develops, the theme starts to evolve into symbolising their hidden love for each other, providing a glimpse into each of their inner thoughts and feelings. Leading up to the first kiss, the presence of Leia's theme becomes increasingly noticeable and as the kiss happens, the theme's Leitmotif melody comes in making a new symbolic connection. As C3PO enters the room and interrupts the kiss, the music is also interrupted further signifying the bond between romance and the theme.

The Across the Stars theme, mostly appearing in Episode II: Attack of the Clones (Lucas 2002), attempts to accentuate the romance between Anakin and Padmé. To begin with the theme has a gentle feel with lush sounding strings and woodwind parts, providing a melancholic romantic atmosphere signifying the pure and innocent love between the two characters. As the brass section enters suddenly the element of war appears changing the timbre of the piece. As the Leitmotif of the theme repeats, this time there seems to be a glimpse of tragedy emerging that the title suggests in its reference to the 'star-crossed lovers' of Romeo and Juliet (Shakespeare 1839). The two characters share a forbidden love, forced apart by conflict; the Republic vs the Separatists equating to the feud between Capulets and Montagues.

Unfortunately one of the main criticisms of this theme amongst fans of the franchise is the theme's resemblance to William's scoring to Hook (Spielberg 1991), supporting the notion of laziness proposed by Eisler and Adorno, however arguably it is the bold and deepness of the brass section parts that separates the two and gives the theme the Star Wars edge. The symbolic link between the fanfare styled horns and the ideology of war helps firmly place the romantic plot within the story into the ethos of the Star Wars universe.

Conclusion

Everything about the Star Wars saga and expanded universe appears to hold a sense of nostalgia, that the story depicts the tale of an old legend, a long time ago where gallant knights battled against evil tyranny. The revival of the classical Hollywood era emphasises a link to the past, perhaps linking the 'forgotten' art form and the Wagnerian Leitmotifs of the 19th Century, to the ancient mythical art of the Jedi order.

Some fans often hold a sense of nostalgia between the two trilogies, bringing up the well renowned debate of whether or not the Prequels were in fact appalling; failing to live up to the standard the original trilogy had set. In terms of music, however, this argument seems mute as many of the themes originated from the first movie in the first place and have arguably enjoyed successes of their own. The Duel of the Fates theme for instance is often played at the beginning of Premier League football matches as the symbolism and semiology of the epic battle 'to the death' can be transferred to apply new meaning as (Shepard 1991:15) describes.

It is likely that Episodes VII-IX will maintain the four main concepts of love, war, space and the force and so it is fair to assume that Williams will once again use the orchestration to adapt these elements into the context of the new storyline. The bold brass horns will most likely form a prominent component as they declare the wartime fanfares and the marching rhythms of the percussion will drive the music and storyline forward 'relentlessly'. The romanticism of the strings section will ostensibly aim to form the emotional connection with the audience, such as those heard in the love theme of Across the Stars.

Unlike the prequels, the sequel trilogy, as episodes VII-IX are often referred to as, are not likely to contain many of the existing themes as the characters they are attached to, are no longer around such as Darth Vader, The Emperor and Obi Wan. Even Luke Skywalker may not feature much of a role in the new films, although it is highly likely his theme will appear when he first appears in the movie. As a result of this Williams will have to create a new range of scores that will capture the Star Wars sound, although he will still have the force theme to refer to. Considering the main story plot will most certainly be based around rebuilding the Jedi order to some effect, an act that will involve searching out those who are sensitive to the force, it could be argued that this theme may be used frequently, along with the return of the religious choral features Williams employed to ascertain the nature of the ancient religion.

The soundscape that Williams has created for Star Wars has certainly managed to capture the imagination throughout the years and will no doubting continue for generations to come. The recasting of Williams to score for the next three films merely reaffirms his success and the next stage of the saga will most likely be hugely anticipated amongst the Star Wars fan community.

Bibliography

Allers, R and Minkoff, R. 1994. *The Lion King.* [film] USA: Walt Disney Pictures. (89 mins).

Bioware. 2011. *Star Wars: The Old Republic.* [online] PC. Austin: Electronic Arts Inc.

Buhler, J., Flinn, C. and Neumeyer, D. 2000. *Music and cinema.* Hanover, NH: University Press of New England.

Butsch, R. 2000. *The making of American audiences.* Cambridge: Cambridge University Press.

Coin. 2007. *Sword-Fighting in Star Wars Ep. I.* [video online] Available at: http://www.youtube.com/watch?v=rk1qghsNiok [Accessed: 25 Mar 2014].

Cooper, M and Schoedsack, E. 1933. *King Kong.* [film] USA: RKO Radio Pictures. (100 mins).

Crosland, A. 1926. *Don Juan.* [film] USA: Warner Bros. (87 mins).

Curtiz, M and Keighley, W. 1938. *The Adventures of Robin Hood.* [film] USA: Warner Bros. (102 mins).

Curtiz, M. 1940. *The Sea Hawk.* [film] USA: Warner Bros. (127 mins).

Dickinson, K. 2003. *Music, the film reader.* New York: Routledge.

Dieterle, W. 1939. *Juarez.* [film] USA: Warner Bros. (125 mins).

Dixon, W. W. and Foster, G. A. 2008. *A short history of film.* New Brunswick, N.J.: Rutgers University Press.

Donner, R. 1978. *Superman.* [film] USA: Dovemead Films. (143 mins).

Edwards, B. 1963. *The Pink Panther.* [film] USA: Mirisch G-E Productions. (115 mins).

Eisler, H. and Adorno, T. W. 1994. *Composing for the films.* London: Athlone Press.

Film Score Junkie. 2013a. *John Williams Themes, Part 1 of 6: The Force Theme | Film Music Notes.* [online] Available at: http://www.filmmusicnotes.com/john-williams-themes-part-1-the-force-theme/ [Accessed: 29 Mar 2014].

Film Score Junkie. 2013b. *John Williams Themes, Part 3 of 6: The Imperial March (Darth Vader's Theme) | Film Music Notes.* [online] Available at: http://www.filmmusicnotes.com/john-williams-themes-part-3-of-6-the-imperial-march-darth-vaders-theme/ [Accessed: 25 Mar 2014].

FilmMusicHistory. 2012a. *Film Music History S1 Ep2.* [video online] Available at: http://www.youtube.com/watch?v=p-ScPznZYlw [Accessed: 22 Feb 2014].

FilmMusicHistory. 2012b. *Film Music History S1 Ep3.* [video online] Available at: http://www.youtube.com/watch?v=Y1uZdIwjQcQ [Accessed: 22 Feb 2014].

Green, R. D. 1993. *Foundations in music bibliography.* New York: Haworth Press.

Hitchcock, A. 1960. *Psycho.* [film] USA: Shamley Productions. (109 mins).

IMDb. 2014. *King Kong (1933) - FAQ.* [online] Available at: http://www.imdb.com/title/tt0024216/faq [Accessed: 24 Feb 2014].

Jackson, P. 2001. *Lord of the Rings: The Fellowship of the Ring.* [Film] USA: New Line Cinema. (178 mins).

Jewison, N. 1971. *Fiddler on the Roof.* [film] USA: Mirisch Production Company. (181 mins).

Josa, C. 2013. *The Power Of Silence ~ Dumping New Year's Resolutions ~ A 3 Minute Magical Life-Changing Technique.* Soul-Sized Living. [podcast] 21st January. Available at: http://www.clarejosa.com/podcast/soul-sized-living-podcast-002-the-power-of-silence-dumping-new-years-resolutions-de-stressing-with-mindfulness/ [Accessed: 18 Feb 2014].

Kalinak, K. M. 2010. *Film music.* New York: Oxford University Press.

Kassabian, A. 2001. *Hearing film.* New York: Routledge.

Kershner, I. 1980. *Star Wars: Episode IV – Empire Strikes Back.* [film] USA: Lucas Film. (124 mins).

Kubrick, S. 1980. *The Shining.* [film] USA: Warner Bros. (144 mins).

Larsen, P. and Irons, J. 2007. *Film music.* London: Reaktion.

Lester, R. 1964. *A Hard Day's Night.* [film] UK: Walter Shenson Films. (87 mins).

Lucas, G. 1977. *Star Wars: Episode IV – A New Hope.* [film] USA: Lucas Film. (121 mins).

Lucas, G. 1999. *Star Wars: Episode I – The Phantom Menace.* [film] USA: Lucas Film. (136 mins).

Lucas, G. 2002. *Star Wars: Episode II – Attack of the Clones.* [film] USA: Lucas Film. (142 mins).

Lucas, G. 2005. *Star Wars: Episode III – Revenge of the Sith.* [film] USA: Lucas Film. (140 mins).

Lumiére, A and Lumiére, L. 1896. *L'Arrivée d'un Train Ã la Ciotat.* [film] France: Lumiére. (1 min).

Marquand, R. 1983. *Star Wars: Episode VI – Return of the Jedi.* [film] USA: Lucas Film. (134 mins)

Morton, R. 2005. *King Kong.* New York: Applause Theatre & Cinema Books.

Mullenger, L. 1999. *Star Wars Episode 1 - The Phantom Menace : Interview with John Williams April9 1999.* [online] Available at: http://www.musicweb-international.com/film/jwilliamsinterview.html [Accessed: 30 Mar 2014].

Neumeyer, D and Buhler, J. 2001. Analytical and Interpretive Approaches to Film Music (I): Analysing the Music. In: Donnelly, K.J. ed. *Film Music: Critical Approaches.* Edinburgh: Edinburgh University Press, pp. 16-38.

Orff, C. 1935. *Oh Fortuna.* Carmina Burana.

Parker, K. 2010. *A Conversation with the Masters: The Empire Strikes Back 30 Years Later* [Documentary] USA: Kevin M. Parker. (25 mins)

Ramis, H. 1993. *Groundhog Day.* [film] USA: Columbia Pictures. (101 mins)

Rubin, J. S. and Casper, S. E. 2013. *The Oxford encyclopedia of American cultural and intellectual history.* Oxford: Oxford University Press.

Ruggles, W. 1931. *Cimarron.* [film] USA: RKO Radio Pictures. (123 mins)

Shakespeare, W. 1839. *Romeo and Juliet.* London: Macmillan.

Shepherd, J. 1991. *Music as social text.* Cambridge, UK: Polity Press.

Slobin, M. 2008. Preview of Coming Attractions. *Global soundtracks.* Middletown, Conn.: Wesleyan University Press.

Sound on Cinema: The Music that Made the Movies - The Big Score. 2013. [TV programme] BBC, channel BBC FOUR, 7th February 2014.

Spielberg, S. 1975. *Jaws.* [film] USA: Universal Pictures. (124 mins)

Spielberg, S. 1982. *E.T. the Extra-Terrestrial.* [film] USA: Universal Pictures. (115 mins)

Spielberg, S. 1991. *Hook.* [film] USA: TriStar Pictures. (144 mins)

Spielberg, S. 1993. *Jurassic Park*. [film] USA: Universal Pictures. (127 mins)

Star Wars Revisited. 2013. [Radio Broadcast] BBC Radio 3, 4th October 2013.

Steib, M. 2013. *Reader's guide to music: History, Theory, Criticism*. 2nd ed. New York: Routledge.

Tarkovsky, A. 1972. *Solaris*. [film] Soviet Union: Unit Four. (167 mins)

Wierzbicki, J. 2009. *Film music: A History*. New York: Routledge.

Wood, S. 1942. *Kings Row*. [film] USA: Warner Bros. (127 mins)

Young, T. 1962. *Dr. No.*[film] UK: Eon Productions. (110 mins)

Zinneman, F. 1952. *High Noon*. [film] USA: Stanley Kramer Productions. (85 mins)

Analysing Creativity: The 'Author Function' in Popular Music

James Blackmore

In 1967, in his essay 'The Death of the Author', Roland Barthes argued against traditional literary criticism's practice of incorporating the intentions and biographical context of an author in an interpretation of a text, and instead argues that writing and creator are unrelated and that criticism need only deal with texts. In what is seen as a challenge to Barthes' assertion Michel Foucault published an essay in 1969 entitled 'What is an Author?' in which he addressed the question of the author in critical interpretation and developed the idea of 'author function' to explain the author as a classifying principle within a particular discursive formation (Burke 1998).

Foucault asks 'what is a work?' followed by two further questions: an author's name and how does the name function, which enables him to put to one side the issue of the work's meaning and its connection to the authors individuality. Macarthur says, 'He is not interested in what an author is but rather in how it functions.' (2010:57) Macarthur gives an example using the name Webern (an Austrian classical composer and conductor 1883 - 1945):

> Webern is a reference to someone who has produced that body of work. It is not a reference to his moods feelings or his physical characteristics it performs an indicative function referring to the 'work' not the person… in this sense the author is dead or does not exist as a real person in relation to the text: the text cancels out any idea of the authors individuality … which leads to the questions about the work and what we mean by the 'work'. (2010:57)

Seeing the author as a phenomenon that transcends the writing subject, Foucault finds that there are authorial functions that have remained despite the disappearance of the modern author. He calls this the 'author-function', a concept which he sets out to map the relationship between an author and the literary text attributed to him. He wants to examine how the text points to an author-figure that exists beyond the text and is of a different kind than the actual writer. Foucault asserts that even if a particular individual is 'accepted' as an author, without a theory of the 'work', it is not clear what writings are to be included in his work of art therefore his privileged status, in being removed, is merely shifted to the text itself. By showing how an author's name does not have the same relation to an individual that a proper name does (it may not refer to an identifiable individual at all), Foucault reveals the author's name as a form of classification that exists beyond the writer and his writing. This author-function, 'characteristic of the mode of existence, circulation, and functioning of certain discourses within a society' (2000:179), now becomes Foucault's focus. He identifies four characteristics of the author-function, the first being 'Author-function must be linked to whatever institutions of judgment, legal or ethical, exists in a society with respect to discourse.' (2000:179)

From this idea of locating authorship in someone held responsible for writing or speech came also the idea of ownership of works, and the idea of copyright rules associated with ownership. In discussing the application of Foucault's Author-function category, popular music is certainly linked to Foucault's first category which helps tease out and locate authorship-function and Coldplay is a prime example:

On 7th May 2008 Coldplay released 'Viva La Vida', their first single to go to no1 in the UK singles chart as well as the Billboard hot 100. It was nominated for a Grammy award however after its release a virtually unheard of group from Brooklyn called Creaky Boards claimed that Coldplay had copied their song called 'Songs I Didn't Write'. Creaky Boards were so upset that they argued their case on YouTube. Andrew Hoepfner, Creaky Boards' singer and songwriter, claimed that the melody of his song was used by Coldplay and Creaky Boards' song was played first. He demonstrated this by comparing Coldplay's iTunes commercial in 2008 with a video of his own group's performance at the CMG Music Festival NYC October 2007. This gained Creaky Boards huge publicity and they achieved overnight fame before retracting their allegations and claiming that both songs shared a common source in a video game, 'The Legend of Zelda'. Interestingly there is no record of the makers of the video game contesting either song. Then on 4th December 2008 guitarist Joe Satriani accused Coldplay of plagiarizing 'Viva La Vida' from one of his songs 'If I could fly' (2004). Fifty seconds into 'If I could fly' Satriani plays an eight second melody line which is similar to the refrain on Coldplay's 'Viva La Vida'. Satriani went to court seeking all profits from 'Viva La

Vida' and although the case remained sealed, in Sept 2009 legal sources said a financial settlement between the two parties may have been reached (Bosso 2009).

At virtually the same time as Satriani, Yusuf Islam, formerly Cat Stevens, also identified similarities with his 'Foreigner Suite' published in 1973 . However his allegations were dropped as Bently, Davis and Ginsburg report him saying, 'I don't think they did it on purpose... I'd love to sit down and have a cup of tea with them and let them know it's okay however sad' (2010:271). Interestingly enough they also say that in 2005 Chris Martin from Coldplay admitted to Rolling Stone magazine, 'We're definitely good, but I don't think you can say we're that original. I regard us as being incredibly good plagiarists' (2010:272) This certainly supports Foucault's first characteristic of author function.

Foucault's second author-function also helps us to analyse what appears to be attribution of a discourse to a certain individual or in this case a band (The Prodigy) which Lodge reports is the result of 'a complex operation which constructs a certain rational being which we call 'author'' (2000:179) The single 'Smack My Bitch Up' released in November 1997 by The Prodigy is a case in point. Prior to its release, Liam Howlett (Prodigy) was presented with three remixes of the title song, one by Jonny L, one by DJ Hype and one by Slacker. Howlett chose the DJ Hype remix to be released on the single. The complex operation which constructs a certain rational is demonstrated by the following analysis of the track. The vocals are all sampled and altered from the Ultramagnetic MCs song 'Give the Drummer Some'. The original lyrics, performed by rapper Kool Keith, are: 'Switch up change my pitch up' / 'Smack my bitch up, like a pimp...'. Kool Keith had previously been sampled by the Prodigy in the track 'Out of Space'. The female vocals in 'Smack My Bitch Up' were performed by Shahin Badar. Badar's vocals and harmonies are based on 'Nana (The Dreaming)' performed by Sheila Chandra. The track also contains samples from 'Funky Man' by Kool & the Gang, 'In Memory Of' by Randy Weston, 'Bulls on Parade' by Rage Against the Machine and 'House of Rising Funk' by Afrique (Pavloff 2009). This demonstrates in Foucault terms, how the text points to an author-figure that exists beyond the text and is of a different kind than the actual writer.

Thirdly, Foucault (in Lodge) says that, 'Author-function does not refer to a real individual, since it often consists of several, simultaneous subjects; this is shown to be true whether in fiction or in technical or scientific writing.' (2000:180) Fourthly, Foucault says that 'The author function arises out of the difference, and separation, between the 'author function' and the writer signified in the text. This is most easily seen in narrative fiction, but is true of any form of discourse. The text always bears signs that refer to the author, or create the 'author function.' (2000:180). Or. as Lodge says, 'it results from various cultural constructions, in which we choose certain attributes of an individual as 'authorial' attributes, and dismiss others' (2000:556). How can Foucault's 'author function' theory then be applied to popular music? Foucault went further than Barthes by explaining the power dynamics supporting the author but he also agrees with Barthes that one day the author, or the 'author function' for him, will disappear. Could this be the case with music sampling? Stephen Heath refers to narrative fiction when he says, 'Sampling allows for the death of the author and the author function to take effect once we enter late capitalism, because 'writing' is no longer seen as something truly original, but as a complex act of re-sampling and reinterpreting material previously introduced, which is obviously not innovative but expected in new media' (1977:142). But does this not apply to popular music? Perhaps his vision has not materialised to date because the struggles over the ownership of literature continue in every sense.

Lodge tells us that Foucault also introduces the idea of 'transdiscursive' authorship meaning not simply an author of a book, but the author of a theory, tradition or discipline, transcending or of overarching concern to multiple discourses, for example Sigmund Freud and Karl Marx as a subset of this kind of author, whom he calls 'founders of discursivity' (2000:183) there are similarities between the various modes of cultural production although the definitions given above seem more applicable to the visual arts than to popular music. In the context of popular music, to understand authorship as a one-to-one relation between the author and his/her work often comes across as too simplistic, since there are no specific guidelines for making popular music in the first place, and since the musical backgrounds of popular music artists vary a great deal (Homer & Swiss 1999). Another essential point here is the fact that popular music is usually produced by the joint effort of a group, not by individuals (Brackett 2000). The making of popular music could in this sense be compared to the making of cinema: both art forms; cinema and popular music; are typically authored by several people who together share authorial responsibility for the work in progress (Gracyk 1996). That is to say, popular music, like film, is usually made collectively. That does not mean, however, that belief in single authorship might not still exist. Yet Michel Foucault's author-function, which allows a text to have an 'author' without referring to any specific person, is an important concept and may well be starting to gain much more credence in the 21st century as in attempting to define and apply 'the author function', it is worth considering another typical aspect of authorship in popular music, its mediated nature. Wall states that, 'Today's popular music is seldom received in a non-mediated form, since it is produced for and through various technological media' (2003:108). The mediated nature of author images does not then refer only to a means of technological transmission or to the intermediary practices of all the people who intervene in the making, distributing and consuming of popular music, but also to social relationships (of power and influence) that Negus says '...occur between and across these activities' (1996:65). As a result, the constructed author images communicate only a limited range of specific meanings, and thus, present a specified, while at the same time constructed, image of a particular artist.

Michel Foucault's author-function, which allows a text to have an 'author' without referring to any specific person, is in addition to the use of music technological innovations which has led to the emergence of totally new ways of music making, including the practices of DJing and sampling. This helps us to analyse the author function of Daft Punk, who remain anonymous behind electronically programmed helmets and electronically programmed music and also Jori Hulkkonen, who has also released records under such aliases as Zyntherius, Eternal Boyman, Bobby Forrester and Jii Hoo, who both serve as examples of artists with diffused public images. Faceless imagery, logos, and pseudonyms are typically used in manufacturing the public personas of such artists as representatives of electronic (dance) music. Despite the masked and distant author images, many of these artists seek to retain control over their careers, visual imagery and music, making the phenomena of diffused authorship and parallel authorial voices serve to bolster the poststructuralist agenda, which questions the author's status as the guarantor of meaning, and emphasises the reception of musical texts as an active, socially determined process. Further the question could be asked of electronic dance music in that it has an overarching span over pop music, having created many sub genres, could it be classed as an example of Foucault's idea of 'transdiscursive' authorship?

In popular music culture, the author is placed front and center. It is the author who is typically seen as the point of origin of musical texts and who is believed to be responsible for songs' emotional charge. Author images also work as a means of classification, in as much as they group together certain texts, thereby distinguishing them from other texts. Through a dis-tinctive public image, the artist's star persona is presented as a unique and original figure to aid in establishing an artist's public identity. Artists such as Springsteen, Bjork and Prince meet the criteria for auteur, and their music is seen as the artist's personal storytelling. Even when they participate in collaborative music making, it is usually assumed that such artists have chosen those with whom they wish to collaborate, such that the final outcome is believed to present the artistic vision of the auteur in charge. However Lodge says, 'Foucault's author function does not refer to a real individual, since it often consists of several, simultaneous subjects; this is shown to be true whether in fiction or in technical or scientific writing' (2000:180). Later he says, 'Rather, it results from various cultural constructions, in which we choose certain attributes of an individual as 'authorial' attributes, and dismiss others' (2000:556).

Foucault's assertion helps us dissect the misplaced notion of single authorship which is evident in the case of Coldplay's Chris Martin. Martin is highlighted in the media as the authorial source of Coldplay's songs, whilst the input of the rest of the band is disregarded. Laura Ahonen reports, 'Although hailed as the band's front figure and driving force Martin sees the band's functioning as a democratic team to be more important than squabbles over writing credits and royalties' (2007:126). Coldplay have no set way to compose, all compositions are credited to group and Coldplay use the term 'we' at interview. Also by sharing the writing credits, the band signals the fact that its members have contributed equally in the making of albums. Even though Martin is as focal point in photos/ onstage, the band often swap roles and use their dressed down appearance to try and reduce Martin's star status. Yet despite the band's efforts to present themselves as co-equals, the lead singer, Chris Martin, has been profiled as front man and lyricist of all Coldplay songs (Ahonen 2007).

Foucault's fourth category of Author Function arises out of the difference, and separation, between the 'author function' and the writer signified in the text. This helps us analyse the boundaries that once separated the role of musical author from that of the listener, or the amateur musician from the professional. In the case of DJs and sampling artists, authorship is no longer a question of whether the artist is the originating source of each sample and sound. Authorship is therefore viewed in terms of the artist's skill at choosing and manipulating the borrowed material. This creative use of 'borrowed' material may also indicate their knowledge of popular music history and its social references to the listener, which evidences the difference and separation that Foucault suggests. In addition the developments in music technology and the Internet have necessitated changes and expansions in the criteria by which musical authorship is defined. Although it has become more common to regard musical authorship as a collective and social process, the concept of single authorship persists, as they help us to formulate the fundamental concepts with which we comprehend popular culture in general (Ahonen 2007).

Against this, Lodge reports that Foucault sees 'the author-function, instead of simply attributing discourse to a certain individual, is the result of 'a complex operation which constructs a certain rational being which we call 'author'' (2000:180) Foucault builds on this as he sees the author as a limiting agent upon the 'free circulation, free manipulation, the free composition, decomposition, and recomposition of fiction', which he implies is seen by others as a 'great peril' (2000:186) Perhaps we are moving towards his vision in the twenty first century as demonstrated by The Prodigy who discovered that two fake albums

'Inflicted' and 'The Castbreeder' were set up by a webmaster of an unofficial Prodigy site. The tracks have been identified as obvious hoaxes by many real Prodigy fans. The 'Inflicted' album was a hoax set up by Tobi Wood during the 'countdown' to The Fat Of The Land release. They were authenticated with barcodes, record label logos, an XL catalogue number and a copyright note. The music featured inside though was amateur and clearly not Prodigy (Jussi Lahtinen 2014). The Prodigy took no legal action possibly due to the fact that none of The Prodigy band sings on the older genuine Prodigy tracks. Many of the vocals were performed by other artists and Liam Howlett only used vocal samples for 'Music Reach', 'No Good' and 'Out Of Space'. Lahtinen also proposes that the Music for the Jilted Generation album intro is from the horror movie The Lawnmower Man, (but this is disputed as others say that it is from the 'Naked Lunch' movie. Which means The Prodigy are exemplifying Foucault's theory (as reported in Taylor and Winquist) of '....the free composition, decomposition, and recomposition of fiction?' (1998:216). Does therefore the application of Foucault's theory of 'author function' highlight popular music's 'great peril' in this, the twenty-first century? As Jarmusch says,

> Nothing is original. Steal from anywhere that resonates with inspiration or feeds your imagination...If you do this, your work (and theft) will be authentic...and don't bother concealing your thievery – celebrate it. (2004)

Bibliography

Ahonen, L. (2007) *Mediated music makers Constructing author images in popular music* [online]. Available at https://helds.helsinki.fi/bitstream/handle/10138/19458/mediated.pdf?sequence=2t [Accessed 5th April 2014].

Bently, L., Davis, J. & Ginsburg, J. (eds) (2010) *Copyright and Piracy: An Interdisciplinary Critique.* Cambridge University Press.

Bosso, Joe (2009) *Coldplay and Joe Satriani settle lawsuit* [online]. Available at: http://www.musicradar.com/news/guitars/coldplay-and-joe-satriani-settle-lawsuit-220134. [Accessed 4th April 2014]

Brackett, D. (2000) *Interpreting Popular Music.* Berkeley, Los Angeles & London: University of California Press

Creaky Boards (2008) *creaky boards + coldplay + itunes fiasco* [online]. Available at: https://www.youtube.com/watch?v=eUhFLiw6h6s. [Accessed 4th April 2014].

Burke, S. (1998) *The Death and Return of the Author. Criticism and Subjectivity in Barthes, Foucault and Derrida.* 2nd edition. Edinburgh: Edinburgh University Press.

Gracyk, T. (1996) *Rhythm and Noise. Aesthetics of Rock*. London: Duke University Press.

Heath, S. (ed) (1977) *Roland Barthes 'The Death of the Author' (1968)*. New York: Hill &Wang.

Homer, B. & Swiss, T. (eds) (1999) *Key Terms in Popular Music and Culture*. Malden & Oxford: Blackwell.

Jarmusch, J. (2004) *Jim Jarmusch > Quotes* [online]. Available at: https://www.goodreads.com/author/quotes/314980.Jim_Jarmusch. [Accessed 6th April 2014]

Jussi Lahtinn (2014) *Interesting The Prodigy facts* [online]. Available at: http://theprodigy.info/facts/#sort. [Accessed 5th April 2014]

Lodge, D. (ed) (2000) *Modern Criticism and Theory: A Reader*. New York: Longman

Macarthur, S. (2010) *Towards a Twenty-First-Century Feminist Politics of Music*. England: Ashgate.

Negus, Keith (1996) *Music Genres and Corporate Cultures*. London & New York: Routledge.

Jim Pavloff (2009) *Making of 'The Prodigy - Smack My Bitch Up' in Ableton by Jim Pavloff* [online]. Available at: https://www.youtube.com/watch?v=eU5Dn-WaEll. [Accessed 5th April 2014]

Taylor, V and Winquist, E. (eds) (1998) *Postmodernism: Critical Concepts*, Volume 3. London: Routledge.

Wall, T. (2003) *Studying Popular Music Culture*. London & New York: Arnold.

Globalisation and Popular Music: Should we be Celebrating Globalisation?

Rebecca Birchall

Globalisation is a term open to much conjecture, often utilised as a blanket term, whilst there exist various different definitions. In this case, it seems to be most accurately described and understood by observing what it implies, rather than through an absolute definition of the term itself. The advent of communication technologies, television, radio and specifically the introduction of the internet, has allowed for globalisation to become substantially more efficient in the production and dissemination of information and texts reflective of different cultures. Its negative connotations have generally overpowered any positive light shed on the matter due to associated terms such as 'cultural imperialism' because the word 'imperialism' implies that there is an imposition of one culture onto another and holds a particular disregard for the personal and the individual. However, it is not a question of weighting the pros against cons but a matter of understanding through what means it comes to be enforced and whether or not it is a phenomenon to be embraced. This essay will primarily discuss the impact of globalisation through the concentration of ownership in global media. It will also explore cultural hybridisation and the meaning and reasons behind it.

McChesney (1999) highlights the effect of deregulation and the implications it holds for transnational media conglomerates in the West, specifically in the United States. These alterations in government law regulations benefit private companies urging the monopolisation of the media sector. Post-deregulation, now independent from government control, these companies are responsible for communicating information globally. Therefore, in theory, the lack of government control on mass commercial media should urge a thriving, politically-involved society. However, in reality, an opposing effect occurs, previously democratic mediums such as journalism and radio have now become part of media empires resulting in a society that is less democratic. Adorno (1991:83) suggests that 'on the radio, the authority of society that stands behind every speaker immediately addresses its listeners unchallenged'. The effects of monopolisation are thus mirrored in the filtering of this information, sifting out political material and converting it into a sensationalist form of entertainment in the hopes of financially profiting whilst simultaneously satisfying the status quo, this could be seen as the commodification of information. To achieve this, these large media conglomerates aim to increase the potential of maximising profit often occurring through synergy and in some cases by becoming as vertically integrated as possible if it is deemed more productive or profitable.

One result of synergy is discussed by Edwards (2012:1) who suggests that the notion of 'multi-platform storytelling' is a principal example of corporate synergy in media conglomeration. Multi-platform storytelling describes how texts are distributed 'in a coordinated way' by these media corporations 'often comprised of production units trying to generate transmedia content across film, games, TV, the Web, and mobile phones'. This refers back to and highlights the relationship that globalisation has with new communication technologies. By expanding the means of which companies can distribute, it encourages a ubiquity of these cultural products and increases the chance of global access.

The hybridisation of some aspects of culture is another method of globally engaging different cultures. This can be seen in the film industry, where synergy and multi-platform storytelling also occurs. An example of this is evident in hybridised feature length films that have gained commercial global success. Suárez-Orozco and Qin-Hilliard (2004:131) describe how Taiwanese-born film director Ang Lee, directed the American film 'Crouching Tiger, Hidden Dragon' by including values and characteristics borrowed from Eastern culture intertwined with that of Western culture, primarily to engage both Eastern and Western audiences. Lee termed this hybridisation as a 'combination platter'. This is a prime example of a characteristic of globalisation and could be viewed as Western corporations embracing other cultures in order to defuse their financial competition with Eastern film industries. If products contain a hybridisation of cultures, they will hold a certain appeal to members of such cultures, making each increasingly aware of the other.

On the other hand, Suárez-Orozco and Qin-Hilliard (2004:130) also state that 'Hybridity has often been discussed as a strategy of the dispossessed as they struggle to resist or reshape the flow of Western media into their culture'. This can be seen in Yothu Yindi's 1991 song 'Treaty', an example of hybridisation between aboriginal music and Western popular music, as a method of raising political awareness and preserving aboriginal culture. Corn and Langton (2009:137) explain that, 'In a world where globalisation and mass poverty forces the attrition of more and more language and distinct regional cultures with each passing year these exceptional achievements are to be cherished.' However, it could be argued that the 'success' of such musics would not exist without the driving forces of globalisation. To promote the aboriginal political issues written into the song 'Treaty' it was necessary to adopt Western musical characteristics and 'dilute' their culture in order to highlight the issues at hand. Whilst this notion seems unfair and unequal, hybridisation is not something that is forced onto cultures especially not in Yothu Yindi's case. Mandawuy Yunipinju of Yothu Yindi explained that:

> My struggle was to preserve my culture, and the way i wanted to do that was to write a song with all the modern Western elements but also with lines and lyrics that described what I was thinking in the traditional way. (Corn and Langton. 2009:30)

Therefore, in one sense, globalisation is commended and could on the surface, be seen to contain an equal cultural exchange, yet in another it could be viewed as the cause of the problem. Biddle and Knight (2007) discuss how some Afropop succumbs to this hybridisation in order to gain commercial success in the West. They cite Senegalese artist Youssou N'Dour as one particular musician whose music gradually became increasingly westernised in order to capture a mainstream Western audience. They write, '...despite Youssou N'Dour's attempt to crack the mainstream Western pop market, his remains a marginal product in the West'. Although 'World music' has broken into the West (this is known because it is the West who named it so), it is, like any other non-mainstream genre such as folk or heavy metal existing only in the periphery. To argue that their music has become increasingly westernised, is to imply that it has become increasingly standardised. Globalisation, in one sense, urges one to think of the commodification of culture as part of a culture industry. German academic Theodor Adorno (1991) argued that culture had been developed into another commodity under the capitalist system, thus coining the term 'Culture Industry' to describe the mass of cultural products manufactured to appeal to large audiences (Andrae 2005). In order to appeal to large audiences, Adorno (1941) argues that popular music has become increasingly standardised and that a piece can be composed to a set of rules, so much so that there are song writing books to inform on how to compose a hit song. Therefore, the mainstream popular music of the West is no longer representative of the nationality or traditions of artists, but of the West as a whole, through acts linked to globalisation.

In conclusion, globalisation could be viewed as something to be embraced; additionally it also holds reason to be combatted or opposed. The concentration of global media ownership is in fact detrimental to the democracy of society and although it promotes global consciousness, there is a certain inauthenticity regarding the reliability of globalised information and products. In this respect, globalisation is imbalanced economically and culturally, benefitting only the media conglomerates and large companies, highlighting its disregard for the individual. Moreover, it has been acknowledged that the commodification of the individual's culture and way of life is damaging in some ways, yet the aforementioned explanations and examples given regarding hybridisation, explore a more balanced means of globalisation. Whilst globalisation can be seen to homogenise culture and in some ways damage it, certain aspects of globalisation like hybridisation can create a platform for artists like Mandawuy Yunipinju to aid them in political quests to preserve their own culture. It was discussed that cultural hybridity can 'dilute' culture yet Biddle and Knight (2007) focus on the point that it should not be assumed that Afropop is the popular music of Africa, overall, globalisation plays a significant role in how the world operates, exists as a seemingly irreversible process and with the advent of more and more technologies it can only be seen as a further opportunity for globalisation.

Bibliography

Adorno, Theodor. 1941. *On Popular Music*. Studies in Philosophy and social sciences, no. 9.

Adorno, Theodor. 1991. *The Culture Industry: Selected Essays on Mass Culture*. London: Routledge

Andrae, Thomas. 2005. 'Adorno on Film and Mass Culture: The Culture Industry Reconsidered'. http://www.ejumpcut.org/archive/onlinessays/JC20folder/AdornoMassCult.html, accessed 12th January 2014.

Biddle, Ian and Vanessa Knight. 2007. *Music, National Identity and the Politics of Location*. Hampshire: Ashgate Publishing.

Corn, Aaron and Marcia Langton. 2009. *Reflections & Voices: Exploring the Music of Yothu Yindi with Mandawuy Yunipinju*. Sydney: Sydney University Press.

Edwards, Leigh H. 2012. 'Transmedia Storytelling, Corporate Synergy and Audience Expression'. *Global Media Journal* 12/20.

McChesney, Robert. 1999. *Rich Media, Poor Democracy*. New York: New Press.

Robertson, Ronald. 1992. *Globalisation: Social Theory and Global Culture*. London: Sage Publications.

Rogers, Richard A. 2006. 'From Cultural Exchange to Transculturation: A Review and Reconceptualization of Cultural Appropriation'. *Communication Theory* 16/4: 474-503.

Suárez-Orozco, Marcelo M. and Desirée Qin-Hilliard. 2004. *Globalization: Culture and Education In the New Millennium*. Los Angeles: University Of California Press.

CHAPTER 9

The Heroic Outsider: An Analysis of Virtuosity

Jack Tully

From the rise of civilization with the development of agriculture, to a unification through a worship of the arts and elevation of philosophy and the sublime, an enduring connection between human beings has always existed; a shared consciousness and fundamental way of thinking, communicating and the idea of a need to belong.

> We wage wars, believe in religions, bury our dead and get embarrassed about sex. We watch television, drive cars and eat ice cream. We have had such a devastating impact upon the ecosystems of our planet that we appear to be in danger of destroying everything on which our lives depend. One of the problems of being a human is that it is rather hard to look at humans with an unprejudiced eye. (Blackmore 1999:1)

As Susan Blackmore states, we humans are indeed strange creatures; we unconsciously and innately imitate others, apportion prestige and social status to those in a position greater than ourselves and mythologize through an endless cycle of pastiche and replication. The construction of an individual that is obsessed, passionate and devoted to their art has long fascinated us; the ability to transcend art into the metaphysical is what differentiates us from the 'virtuoso'. From the Latin, *Virtus*, translated as one who is skilled, masculine and excellent; the virtuoso is an individual capable of ascending to a genius categorisation; we consumers are mere mortals who appreciate fine art under the assumption that we could never replicate what has been done, we could only dream of being able to fulfil the process between production and completion.

The study of this study is that the archetypal construction of a musical virtuoso – the lone genius, the romantic hero that is capable of escaping the constraints of the band or orchestra, is archaic – it no longer exists as the gradual emergence of new technologies have created new paradigms. Subsequently, technology in the manner that the musician of today utilises it is comparable with the Cubism movement; the human figure is dehumanised and '[...] non-exceptional to reality' (Appignanesi 1995:17), in consequence, this study is as much to do with identity as it is about formulating skill, beauty and truth. The virtuoso has the aptitude to both pleasure and shame through the chaos they embrace, yet for many, the image of the virtuoso is rooted in its nineteenth century origins: the anthropocentric figure detached from mankind, veiled in a shroud of mystery with an aura of untouchable triumph.

In Section One, *Virtuosity and the Human Condition*, I will trace the ontological development of virtuosity in the arts through an analysis of the role in which it has occupied in western civilization since the Renaissance. I will discuss the traditional perspective taken by the virtuoso; the idea that the limitations of the body are something that must be overcome in order to accomplish astonishing feats; the body in this sense can be seen as a filter or a channel through which the virtuoso can become a possessor of spirits, capable of entering the liminal world and returning enlightened through a contact with the sublime. I will finally put forth the notion that it is intrinsic in our nature to worship a genius as it enables us to contextualise the human condition; referring to the writings of Michel Foucault and the parallels between madness and the genius.

In Section Two, *Virtuosity and Technology*, I will detail the ways in which technologies have rendered the quasi-mythologized construction of the virtuoso as redundant; through this exploration I will deconstruct the points made in Section One. Thus, the focus of this Section is to discuss the ambiguity of the technological age of advancement and how the apparent democratisation of music has affected the audience's perception of the virtuoso musician.

Section Three, entitled *Virtuosity and the Death of Postmodernism*, will argue that the internet has changed the epoch of how we live unbeknownst to academics and scholars who still maintain we live in a bourgeois, postmodern society. I will argue that there is a new emerging cultural paradigm: 'metamodernism', through which virtuosity can exist via oscillation between modern and postmodern ideals. Through this oscillation, I will state that a new form of virtuosity can potentially manifest.

Through writing this study, my intention is to incur debate, stimulate an appreciation and understanding of the complexities surrounding popular music discourse, and ultimately to provide a crucial guidance to the study of virtuosity. I hope this exploration will enhance studies in postmodernism and through theorising virtuosity in a metamodern landscape – I hope to make this impact more perceptible.

Methodology

The inchoation of this study lay in my interest in virtuosity as both a concept and a metanarrative; a synchronisation of the senses that is rooted in its ideological apportion of both performance and 'liveness' as well its archaic affirmation of the technically skilled, elevated demi-God figure. Is there still a position in contemporary society that the virtuoso can occupy? Have the technological developments of the last century shaped the postmodern simulacrum of the genius? And if we are moving towards a new cultural paradigm, is there a still a role for the virtuoso in popular music discourse? These are the questions I hope to answer through an analysis based on scholarly research; including books and journal articles, alongside my own speculation and intuition as a Popular Music undergraduate.

Working with such a broad topic that encompassed an array of art forms and critical theories meant that generating original research was an extensive, time-consuming task; therefore a large period of time was spent researching before beginning to write the study. As such, key sources that defined the project also helped stimulate my own creative thought and thus shaped my writing style and the construction of the study. Friedrich Nietzsche's philosophical novel *Thus Spoke Zarathustra* (Nietzsche 1974) was an important text; a text I feel encapsulated the development of nineteenth century critical thinking – an important period of time for the development of the virtuoso musician. A fictitious novel; the inter-connected themes of reactionary thought and philosophical concern is written in an expressive, poetic style – ensuring Nietzsche's meaning is articulated through his expert use of language. The European pessimism of Nietzsche was a direct influence on the theories of French philosopher and social theorist, Michel Foucault; his first book *Madness and Civilization: A History of Insanity in the Age of Reason* (Foucault 1964), a key source in my first two sections. Foucault's nihilistic response to how society of the Middle Ages treated those that were deemed 'mad' related to my own sentiments regarding the virtuoso musician in the postmodern landscape and provided a stimulating narrative to the idea of 'genius' as 'madness'. Like Nietzsche, the language used by Foucault is expertly crafted and utilised in a coherent, persuasive manner, allowing me to fully understand the theories in discussion.

Francisco Monteiro's study of virtuosity in the journal article, 'Virtuosity: Some (quasi-phenomenological) thoughts' (Monteiro 2007), was another useful source; his views on the body being something that the virtuoso must master in order to produce prodigious works of art is something I develop further in Section One – as I incorporate Shaman ideology alongside this concept. Monteiro writes in a sophisticated, engaging style; the subject matter of which provided a useful link with Nietzsche's work and the concept of ascending.

Jean Baudrillard's philosophical treatise *Simulacra and Simulation* (Baudrillard, 1994) was another quintessential component of my research, particularly in Section Two: *Virtuosity and Technology*; in contrast to Foucault's structuralist discourse, Baudrillard's postmodern text allowed me to deconstruct the points made in Section One regarding the archetypal construction of a virtuoso and see how the operation of signs and symbols in society smothers our existence – effectively creating a 'hyperreal' to which there is no origin to culture, only the ephemerality of said signs and symbols. A complimentary text to Baudrillard's discussion was J. G Ballard's novel, *Crash* (Ballard, 1973), a cult, fictitious postmodern novel that deals with the surreal notion of technological fetishism; a concept I also explored in detail in Section Two.

An Analysis of the Position and Status of Sound Ratio in Contemporary Society (Moy 2000) was another useful book; the accessible writing style of Ron Moy combined with a clear explanation of theoretical issues ensured the information received was understood and engaged with; likewise Philip Tagg's *Music's Meanings: A Modern Musicology for Non-Musos* (Tagg 2012) forced me to reflect on my own use of language; the musicological discourse of Tagg's work – both coherent and complex in its nature.

Finally, as 'post-postmodernism', or 'metamodernism', is a new and disputed term amongst academics, the literature available was sparse; as such the research for Section Three relied heavily on online journals and academic papers; the studies of Timotheus Vermeulen and Robin van den Akken being particularly useful. In *Notes on Metamodernism* (Vermeulen and Van den Akken 2010) Vermeulen, and Van den Akken proclaim postmodernity is over – it has been for some time- as we shift towards a new cultural paradigm that oscillates between modern and postmodern ideals. Nevertheless, both writers have reliable credentials; Vermeulen is a teacher in Cultural Studies and Theory at Radboud University, Nijmegen in the Netherlands, whilst Robin Van den Akken is a Doctoral candidate in the Department of Philosophy at the Erasmus University in Rotterdam, the Netherlands. Through questioning whether virtuosity can exist in such a paradigm, I hope to give a new slant on what is essentially an insecure area of research; through a thorough engagement with this new epoch.

Virtuosity and the Human Condition

Since print culture, the conglomeration of written texts in the form of a visual representation of language, it has been inherent in our nature to require an author – an individual that is elevated above all others; contrary to Ancient and Classical traditions, in which philosophers such as Homer problematized the term; the author in this circumstance being used as a singular name for a collective consumption of work. The move from oral tradition into the marketable production of language increased the commerciality of art, transforming the literary prose of the likes of Shakespeare through allowing the audience access to his words; words which could be seen as '[...] windows through which we see a glimpse of him' (Carlyle 1986:18). In reference to the construction of the romantic virtuoso musician, Philip Tagg observed how the nineteenth century bourgeois subjectivity of mass-production influenced the affluence of sheet music; a tangible quality that ensured acts such as Tieck, Wackenroder and Hegel became recognizable authors – almost as identifiable as 'stars' of the late twentieth century. (Tagg 2012:126-132) The romantic period encouraged the 'cult of personality' – the lone mythologized genius and increased the aura of individuality within art, as evidenced in the developing stance of the author and the nature of the painter. Meyer Howard Abrams noted how the prose of the eighteenth century poet shifted from what was once imitation to '[...] the poet's natural genius, creative imagination and emotional spontaneity' (Abrams 1953:17), whilst Montouri and

Purser suggest the development of the self-referential anthropocentric figure is exemplified in the self-portraiture of the nineteenth century. (Montouri and Purser 1995:35-69) Before painting pictures of what one conceived to be 'reality' had become anachronistic, primarily because of the invention of photography, artists like Van Gogh, Goya and Cézanne opted to paint themselves. Van Gogh painted as many as thirty-seven self-portraits between 1886 and 1889; omnipresent and at the epicentre of the viewer's eye, the purposeful gaze of the subject is often inescapable for the viewer. The act of artistic creation was itself the specific symbol that many were feeling or desiring during the Renaissance period, as such, the self-portraits of the nineteenth century could be identified as an extension of this period – the ideas resonating from the period of enlightenment in which art was seen as a resistance against the collective, a shift away from a utilitarian approach and a move towards an expressive aesthetic, as the pursuit of beauty and truth were seen as important.

The concept of individualism was reflective of the socioeconomic change in the nineteenth century; the diminishing power of the church through the challenge of Darwinism, coinciding with new technologies, scientific discoveries and advancements, paralleling the emergence of the 'virtuoso musician.' Friedrich Nietzsche's *Thus Spoke Zarathustra* in particular can be seen as an important text; Zarathustra, the archetypal modern protagonist, challenges man to reach their highest potential, stating that man is simply a bridge to the 'übermensch', translated into English as 'the superman', the proclamation that the body is something that must be conquered; one must descend in order to ascend once more and surpass the limitations of our own anatomy (Nietzsche 1974). In *Music in the Western Civilization*, Piero Weiss and Richard Taruskin state that it was during this time that the term 'virtuoso' had been refined from someone who was 'a highly accomplished musician' to an individual '[...] whose technical accomplishments were so pronounced as to dazzle the public' (Weiss and Taruskin 2007:430). This sentiment is backed by Francisco Monteiro, who stated that whether the performer plays fast or slow is of little importance, what is important is that 'the audience has to be astonished' (Monteiro 2007:317).

As such, the synergetic marriage of 'liveness' and performance was established in the etymology of defining the 'virtuoso musician', as

Adrian Stokes noted in his observations regarding the effect of sound in the choreography of ballet: 'Music placed alongside movement transforms it' (Cited in O'Pray 1995:197). To witness a live performance is to enter a potential realm of chaos, as '[...] there seems to be something about the performance relationship which is fundamentally volatile, given to interruption and undecidability' (Toynbee 2000:60), the unpredictability of which excites us; the potential between performer and audience the epitome of art in its purest form, 'The admiration of skill is not just intellectual; skill [...] can cause jaws to drop, hair to stand upon the back of the neck, and eyes to flood with tears. The demonstration of skill is one of the most deeply moving and pleasurable aspects of art' (Dutton 2009:53).

The synchronisation of motion and sound is satisfying; as an audience, we admire its achievement; sometimes responding in ecstasy or through experiencing jouissance – but ultimately, we are made aware of the potential of humanity through the medium of art. Tagg discusses the importance of sound and visual synergy in his work when he talks about 'Gestural Interconversion' – which he defines as '[...] a two way process that relies on anaphonic connections between music and phenomena, perceived in relation to music' (Tagg 2012:502). This translates as a semiotic concept, suggesting that music can express '[...] common denominators, both kinetic and tactile' (ibid.: 507) of external or internal phenomena, '[...] by synaesthetically connecting appropriate gesture with the music, 'allowing us to '[...] concretise the sort of spaces, objects, textures and movements represented in sounds' (ibid). Nevertheless, the grandiose gestures of the virtuoso; the astonishing feats and the mesmerising skills, were difficult to contextualise - particularly so for nineteenth century audiences who witnessed the emergence of Paganini and Liszt first hand; as a consequence, mythologies were created to explain the unexplainable.

Violinist, Nicolo Paganini, regarded as '[...] the first great virtuoso and superstar within modern memory' (Davies 1985:6) was accused of having supernatural powers due to his intonation and bowing techniques; possessing an unparalleled repertoire of skill capable of dazzling audiences. Similarly, in an analysis of a Franz Liszt performance, Robert Schumann stated:

> The demon began to flex his muscles. He first played along with them (the audience) as if to feel them out, and then gave them something more substantial until, with his magic, he had ensnared each and every one and could move them this way, or that, as he chose. (Schumann 1965:157)

Thus, the nineteenth century modes of reception had a direct consequence on how we understand virtuosity today; the virtuoso becoming synonymous with the supernatural, possession and control. Although the image of the Devil as a musician pre-dates this concept, the idea that one must undertake a 'Faustian sacrifice' to harness such talents is widespread through popular music discourse; in the twentieth century, such mythologies are evidenced in the legends of blues musicians such as Robert Johnson and excessive rock bands of the 1970s like Led Zeppelin. The archetypal characteristics of a musician that is obsessed, devoted and passionate; with perhaps physical advantages, dexterity or supernatural gifts also lends itself with the twentieth century mythological construction of a 'guitar hero'. Jimmy Page was even labelled, the 'Paganini of the Seventies' (Welch 1970:10) in *Melody Maker* due to the apparent similarities between the pair.

The recurring cultural motif of the 'pact with the Devil' as an explanation for the origins of 'supernatural' ability is representative of the disembodied aura of the virtuoso; the idea that one must channel their passion and creativity into an existential empyrean and thus, overcome the constraints of the body. The shamanic quality of the virtuoso; someone who may be bisexual, authoritative, an emotional adolescent or schizophrenic, is hereby similar to the characteristics adopted by a performer of Japanese 'Noh' theatre; the mask of the performer becomes symbolic of the battle waged between the conscious and the unconscious mind.

Thus far, this section has traced the ontological development of virtuosity in the arts since the Renaissance and discussed the traditional perspective taken by the virtuoso; including the ideology that the body's potential can be surpassed; yet before I detail the ways in which technologies have rendered the quasi-mythologized construction of the virtuoso as redundant in Section Two, I must pose the question: why do we worship a virtuoso in the first place? The construction of a virtuoso and our need for an elevated individual can be observed through a study of Michel Foucault's study of madness.

The dedication to one's art through an act of performance parallels the concept of madness; the possibility of which is '[...] therefore implicit in the very phenomenon of passion' (Foucault 1964:88). There is a trend of insanity within the high arts; several prominent historical figures – including Van Gogh, Nietzsche and Sir Isaac Newton, have posthumously been diagnosed with ailments such as schizophrenia and bi-polar disorder whilst Hershman and Lieb argue that a '[...] manic depressive has a better chance of winning the title genius than someone of equal talent and training who does not have the disorder' (Hershman and Lieb 1988:12). Likewise, 'Evidence for genius, madness link comes from the fact that close relatives of creative people have higher rates of schizophrenia, and vice versa (psychotics have more creative relatives)' (Simonton 2005). Although I would never claim to be an expert regarding neuroscience or psychoanalysis; I find the correlation between insanity and virtuoso ability to be a fascinating subject of discussion. The creative restlessness demonstrated in the prolificness of a genius artist; for example David Bowie during 1971-1973, in which he released four albums, including *Hunky Dory* (1971) and *The Rise and Fall of Ziggy Stardust and the Spiders from Mars* (1972); suggests that mania can elicit indefatigability. Bowie's own fear of hereditary on-setting madness could be considered to be a catalyst for his own shamanic forays into schizophrenic theatricality; thus the unstable nature of the shaman is reflected in the archetypal restless virtuoso. As Takiguchi states:

> They tend to be born in poor and illiterate families, undergoing lonely and often difficult childhoods because of ill health, poverty and display of mystical powers [...] Having overcome these traumatic experiences, shamans open the path to the gods. (Takiguchi 1990:3-4)

Situated on the opposite side of the spectrum; the tragedy of madness can also produce short bursts of genius; as evidenced in the brief yet everlasting creative output of artists like Jimi Hendrix, Syd Barrett and Kurt Cobain. In this sense, the ephemeral nature of the virtuoso is comparable to a Greek tragic hero; the hamartia of the virtuoso humanises them - we empathise their fall, placing them on a pedestal after death. As Zarathustra proclaimed:

> One must have chaos still in oneself to be able to give birth to a dancing star. (Nietzsche 1974:9)

Thus the virtuoso embraces chaos; and we vicariously observe.

Before the construction of institutions and marginalisation of those deemed 'mad' in the seventeenth century, the mad of the Renaissance were respected; in the plays of William Shakespeare for example, 'The Fool' spoke in soliloquies and prose, occupying a wisdom and knowledge of the world that other characters did not possess – speaking outside the constraints of the narrative and thus, breaking the fourth wall. In tarot cards, The Fool is considered, '[...] the major arcane to become at last the fully initiated, perfectly balanced figure, the World' (Weatherly 1986:112).

The marginalisation of those that were deemed 'mad' – the transportation onto ships, allowing people from nearby towns and cities to observe them before they left, is similar to how we have traditionally responded to the virtuoso musician; they sacrifice as we observe from a distance; conjuring images of the ephemeral carnival-esque notion of the soloist as a public figure that steps away from the rhythm section, '[...] we hear his statements as public announcements, with an element of show. We see the virtuoso fingerings and are stimulated by their riskiness [...] we are as childishly sadistic as the crowd at a circus' (Eisenberg 2005:100). When considering the link between virtuosity and madness, one must criticise the hypocritical stance undertaken by society; a society that defines itself on the achievements and elevation of 'mad men'.

This leads to the impetus of whether suffering is innate in the construction of a genius, or whether mythologies surrounding the 'historical virtuoso' pre-determine the path aspiring musicians take. In hindsight, one can note how a formative experience in any individual's life can be attributed as a pre-cursor to future events; thus becoming a part of the archetypal 'tragic arc'. Suffering and sacrifice have long helped construct a contextual analysis of the human condition; from Biblical narratives to fables and allegories; the virtuoso performs great feats that astonish us, yet it can be sacrificial and detrimental to their health and sanity. Monteiro claims that mastering the body itself is '[...] composed in an intentional and devilish way, intended to be torture, to be conquered by the performer' (Monteiro 2007:318). This is similar to the view shared by Theodor Adorno:

> Virtuosos make the paradoxical essence of art, the possibility of the impossible, appear. Virtuosos are the martyrs of artworks; in many of their achievements [...] something sadistic has been sedimated, some traces of the torture required to carry it out. (Adorno 2004:359)

The change in cultural paradigms creates new aesthetics, critical approaches and binary polarisations; the synergy of time and space is hereby crucial to our understanding of and engagement with artworks. As our relationship with the mad changed throughout history, it is important to refer back to the notion of print culture transforming the artist; appealing to our seemingly natural desire for an author of a text, as this itself has changed through time with the acceleration of technological development and the birth of electronic culture; symbolising how the ear has been replaced by the eye as the dominant sensory organ in western civilization. In Section Two: *Virtuosity and Technology*, I will stress how this is evident in the postmodern landscape, as the precession of the simulacra has become more substantial than the real and the metanarrative of the virtuoso musician has reduced in persuasiveness.

Virtuosity and Technology

As previously indicated, the oscillation of one cultural movement to another shifts toward new critical analysis, aesthetics and approaches; as such the importance of time and space is crucial to an understanding of the position occupied by the virtuoso musician in society. Although one could argue that a genius musician like Jimi Hendrix for example, would contribute and challenge the hegemonic order of guitar playing in any era; the homogenous relationship he shared and embraced with 1960s counter-culture suggests that it was vital he emerged at the time he did. As Philip Tagg expresses:

> For musical communication to work, transmitter and receiver need access to the same basic store of signs, by which I mean a common vocabulary of musical sounds and norms. If the two parties don't share a common store of signs, codal incompetence will arise, at either the transmitting or receiving end of the message, or at both ends. (Tagg 2012:179)

The relationship that exists between artist and audience must be complimentary; thus allowing the audience to situate and contextualise the unconscious, symbolic and the imaginative construct – else music ventures into experimental territory or becomes a disturbance, intrusion and irritation of the senses. An artist such as Pablo Picasso, for example, may have been committed to the institutions I discussed in *Virtuosity and the Human Condition* had he painted in an experimental Cubist style in earlier centuries. The model of the time and space compression is satirised to great effect in Robert Zemeckis' Science-Fiction film, *Back to the Future* (1985). When protagonist Marty McFly, played by Michael J. Fox, travels back to the 1950s and plays 'Johnny B. Goode' (1959) in a 1980s, 'Van Halen style' – complete with finger-tapping and legato runs (techniques that could be considered virtuoso) the audience reacts to this performance with shock and silence; indicating that they don't understand - and are not prepared to receive, this style of music. Thus, as mentioned in the introduction to this study, the emergence of new technologies creates new paradigms; as such the approach towards new practices can affect the expectations and assumptions of the receiver (the audience).

> Mechanical reproduction frees art from its dependence on ritual and gives it a more socio political dimension. New technologies transform art practices. Photography acts upon painting; the film camera and the radio drama influences acting styles; and the sound recording affects music and singing styles. (Moy 2000:33)

As Moy alludes, the undeniable synergetic relationship that exists between technology and artistic expression has altered the traditional construction of the virtuoso musician. Computer sequence software (such as Ableton, Pro Tools and Logic) along with samplers, have shaped the postmodern composition of popular music.; just as Cubism affected how one could perceive reality; tools are used to overcome our limitations and blur reality – creating binary oppositions of cultivated or natural talent and method and imagination; reducing the division between musicians and non-musicians in the field. In Section One, I stressed the importance of the body; how witnessing virtuosity is to be in the presence of the sublime; an exuberant and astonishing performance – a potential shamanic display of control and power that can lead an audience to ecstasy or jouissance. As such, virtuosity, in the traditional sense, is a hegemony that is egalitarian in its rationing of visual and auditory importance; yet I argue that the role virtuosity occupies in a technologically advanced society links to the disproportionate conservation of such rationing; as demonstrated in how the eye has overtaken the ear as the dominant sensory organ in western culture.

Through history there has been a battle seemingly waged between sound and vision as to which holds the revered status as the 'dominant sensory organ.' This is discussed in 'Treatise on Musical Objects', as post-war French theorist and founder of *Musique Concrete* Pierre Schaeffer noted how Pythagoras would teach his disciples concealed behind a curtain, obscured from sight, with only the sound of his voice reaching the ears of his disciples (Schaeffer 2004:76-77). The teaching methods deployed by Pythagoras are a demonstration of how the ear gathers information that the eye cannot; sounds can be picked up, interpreted and transmitted acousmatically whereas, 'To look is an act of choice' (Berger 1972:8). To be hidden from sight is to be obscure, meanings can be distorted and interpretations can alter; in the art world this is no exception, as the Surrealist movement of the early 1920s exemplifies. 'The Son of Man' (1964), by Belgian surrealist Rene Magritte is a self-portrait, showing Magritte in an overcoat and hat; his face is mostly concealed behind a green apple; the simple addition of which alters the image - as a result, the meaning is ambiguous and left to personal interpretation. In a radio interview with Jean Neysens in 1965, Magritte reflected on the piece:

> There is interest in that which is hidden and which the visible does not show us. This interest can take the form of quite an intense feeling, a sort of conflict, one might say, between the visible that is hidden and the visible that is present. (Magritte and Torczyner 1977:172)

As the sensory preference of humans slowly shifted in the West, what was once obscure, hidden and distorted became visible. Writing in 1973, Canadian composer and theorist R. Murray Schafer discussed how in western civilization, this development had meant the ear had given way to the eye '[...] as the most important gatherer of information' (Schafer 2004:31). Schafer further acknowledged how the development in human sight is demonstrated in how our interpretation of God has changed.

> It was not until the Renaissance that God had become portraiture. Previously, He had been conceived as a sound or vibration. (ibid)

This sentiment is reinforced by Hanns Eisler and Theodor Adorno in their essay, 'The Politics of Hearing':

> The human ear has not adapted itself to the bourgeois rational, and ultimately, high industrialized order as readily as the eye, which has been accustomed to conceiving reality as made up of separate things. (Eisler and Adorno 2004:74)

Some theorists suggest we have become a society fascinated by visual stimuli because over time our relationship with sound has been abused by hegemonic forces and authoritative institutions and as a result the perception of the virtuoso musician as a performer has suffered. Schafer stated how in pre-industrial European towns and cities, the church was apportioned power that enabled it to make loud noise, whereas street musicians and others would be punished for much less. (Schafer 1977) Likewise, Philip Tagg notes how the loudest noise in society today, emitted by helicopters and cars, is absolved – yet a gang of young people in the street are not because '[...] their din causes disruption of the socio-acoustic order in ways that jets and helicopters do not' (Tagg 2012:435-436). This is now an afterthought in postmodern culture, as Moy remonstrates, this discourse has seeped into our use of language; we talk of going to 'see' a film rather than the accurate terminology of 'consuming ' or 'experiencing' the synchresis of sound and motion - such is the power of language (Moy 2008:8).

It can be argued that technology itself was built for the eye; the utilisation of which can be seen as the final deconstruction of the body; this concept being an expansion upon Nietzsche's philosophy and teachings regarding the 'übermensch' - as the body is seen as a medium through which electricity can pass (rather than spirits like the liminal shaman); thus technology becomes an extension of the user. (Nietzsche 1974; McLuhan 1964) If virtuosity can be seen as an internal battle of the body's constraints, followed by a release of otherworldly talent; a process of communicating with the sublime and traversing into liminal worlds for enlightenment, then it is clear that technologies have allowed this manifestation to become easier. In the postmodern scheme of destabilising 'Grand Narratives', virtuosity can be seen as a result of nurture rather than natural or even supernatural conception; although the transformation from skilled musician to virtuoso performer is still acquired like a shaman, through '[...] training, initiation and practice' (Schechner 2002:198). This sentiment is shared by a number of academics and writers; Christopher Lake regarded natural talent as, '[...] talents that happen to us rather than have come to us rather than talents that have come to be as a result of something we have done', yet concluded, '[...] there is likely no such thing, empirically, if not conceptually, as a pure case of natural talent and a pure case of non-natural talent' (Lake 2003:109). Likewise, Vernon Alfred Howard compared mastering a musical instrument to '[...] typing or practicing one's backhand' (Howard 2008:10), whilst Malcolm Gladwell stated it is possible that anyone can become a genius or a virtuoso if they dedicate ten thousand hours of practice to a particular skill set (Gladwell 2008).

Technology has the ability to transform competently skilled musicians into virtuoso players, and virtuoso players into iconic figures that have the potential to shape a culture. Sonorially, a comparison made between *Where the Streets have no Name* (1987) with and without the usage of reverb and delay effects is testament to this statement, as David Guggenheim's *It Might Get Loud* (2008) allows The Edge from U2 to demonstrate how his usage of technology enables him to incorporate the idea of 'sonic architecture' in his work – ideas that are built from the simplest chord progressions. Although a proficient guitar player, The Edge is not as technically proficient (in the 'traditional' sense I constructed in Section One) as virtuoso guitarists such as Steve Vai, Yngwie Malmsteen or Joe Satriani, his style of playing; one that prioritises textures, layering and the idea of sonic architecture over displaying technical prowess is instantly recognisable; the amalgamation of sounds encapsulating the spirit and sound of U2. Through elevating the artist or composer to a genius status, the role of technology is marginalised as digital manipulation has the capacity to inform the creative process, alter meanings and artistically heighten the emotional content of an expressive performance. It is difficult to imagine Jimi Hendrix's *Machine Gun* (1970) to have the same cultural impact without the Wah and Octavia pedals he used to symbolically express anger, fear and the horrors of the Vietnam War; although one would imagine the decrease in effect would be significant. In these two examples, Jimi Hendrix and The Edge utilise effects and technology for the benefit of their music. Nevertheless it is the technology that defines the meaning and gives it substance.

Despite the moments of jouissance musicians can accomplish through a manipulation of effects, music itself would be evanescent without the technology that allows us to hear it again. In an essay entitled, *The Studio as Compositional Tool*, Brian Eno wrote:

> Music, until about 1900, was an event that was perceived in a particular situation, and that disappeared when it finished [...] The effect of recording is that it takes music out of the time dimension and puts it into the space dimension. (Eno 2004:127)

Even if one believed it to be 'all about the music', the purpose of playing music loses its appeal if it is evanescent. Although it has been established that technology can influence the production and consumption of music, this is no different to the paint of the artist, the knife of the sculptor or the camera of the director; it is necessary conduit to communicate through the medium of art. With new technologies at their disposal, the composer or arranger can take the empirical stance of a painter; the computer sequence software the canvas onto which they layer sound.

> You're working directly with sound, and there's no transmission loss between you and the sound –you handle it. It puts the computer on the identical position of the painter – he's working directly onto a substance, and he always retains the options to chop and change, to paint a bit out, add a piece etc. (2004:129)

Thus the human remains in control of the process; technology can be considered as another instrument which is to be learnt, another skill to be honed in order to achieve the sounds the omnipotent virtuoso desires.

Returning to the construction of the virtuoso and applying the work of Jean Baudrillard; one could argue technologies have shaped the postmodern simulacrum of virtuosity, '[...] of a real without origin or reality: a hyperreal' (Baudrillard 1994:1). Baudrillard's hyperreal concept of an exaggerated reality could be applied to how musicians today are overly reliant on technologies; no longer are guitarists practicing scales, songs and exercises; things are made easier as a result of new technology; multi-tracking creates the illusion multiple musicians or players in a scenario where there actually may only be one person. Despite the advantages in technology there is also the idea of a loss of feel and emotion in music if those playing music have nothing to say in the first place. With the excessive use and reliance on technology, there is always the risk of technology fetishism; a potential by-product of postmodern life, which is satirised in J. G. Ballard's novel *Crash* (Ballard 1973) – an extreme metaphor for the psychopathologies and dangers of technological fetishism.

Before moving onto the final section of this study, *Virtuosity and The Death of Postmodernism*, it is vital to consider how technological fetishism can be seen as a conduit of the postmodern condition – it can elicit madness through an obsession, passion and devotion that mirrors the nineteenth century archetypal virtuoso construction of an unstable, romantic hero. Status on stage or through improvisational skill has been replaced by the studio, knowledge of equipment and hardware; challenging archetypal notions of authorial presence. Through the unfolding paradigms of the twentieth century; the rise of visual stimuli alongside the precession of signs and symbols, the utilisation of music inspired an environment in which audiences are told what to think and how to feel – resulting in isolation and arguably a loss of 'feel' in musical creation.

This section provides evidence that the simulacra has overtaken the real just like the eye has overtaken the ear; music without an origin – an unprecedented perfection beyond the capabilities of human endeavour, ascending further from the body's constraints than Nietzsche could possibly have comprehended. Nevertheless, one could argue art itself could be conceived as a human technology; therefore it is to be diverted and utilised in whatever way seems effective for us. In Section Three, I will discuss how a shift in the cultural paradigm that is postmodernism can emit a return of the bourgeois romantic notion of the virtuoso musician.

Virtuosity and the Death of Postmodernism

In Section One: *Virtuosity and the Human Condition*, I reflected upon the archetypal construction of the virtuoso musician; how the epistemology is rooted in nineteenth century criticism, and how 'genius' can elicit 'madness' in a performer, as evidenced in the link between insanity and the creation of high art. Section Two: *Virtuosity and Technology* hereby deconstructed the metanarrative of the anthropocentric figure; focusing upon the postmodern simulacrum of the virtuoso musician. Instead of genius as a sublime master of spirits, evidence suggests that the genius is rather influenced by electronic equipment and the utilisation of technology itself. In this final section, *Virtuosity and the Death of Postmodernism*, I will detail how the possibility of a shifting cultural paradigm can stimulate a resurgence in the desire for a virtuoso musician, and how an oscillation in modern and postmodern ideals can hereby result in genius as legacy.

Despite hegemonic forces and hierarchies of power stressing the importance of collaboration and collective works in postmodern culture, a new school of thought suggests that we are moving into a new cultural paradigm, beyond the cynical fragmentation of the postmodern landscape, into a 'metamodern' or 'post-postmodern' reality; as such the role of the virtuoso musician can still be seen as crucial in popular music discourse. The internet has changed the epoch of how we live and as a result we are in a permanent state of inertia; we look back as often as we look to the future. Richard Jones conceptualises this condition with the phrase, 'Neo-Romanticism', (Jones 2013) as cultural theorists Timotheus Vermeulen and Robin Van den Akken digress; artists are looking back at the Romantic not because they want to laugh or cry, but because looking back allows us to '[...] perceive anew a future that was lost from sight' (Vermeulen and Van den Akken 2010:12); through this process manifests an endless possibility of multiple points of entry; the possibility of music that longs for a past that eluded it yet yearns for a future of pragmatic control – a postmodern sense of irony and lament alongside a modernist self-consciousness, optimism and ambition of overreaching transformations in western society.

> One should be careful not to think of this oscillation as a balance however; rather, it is a pendulum swinging between the modern and the postmodern. (2010:6)

The oscillation between modern and postmodern ideals opens up the possibility of a return to Romanticism; encouraging a renaissance in the rise of the bourgeois individual and the 'cult of personality' in which manifests the virtuoso archetype. Before speculating the role that virtuosity could occupy in a metamodern society, it is important to contextualise postmodernism, so that a binary opposition can be established. As metamodernism was introduced by Vermeulen and Van den Akken as a philosophical and aesthetical reaction; a proclamation to the collapse of postmodernity – so too did postmodernism arise in a similar fashion; a claim that modernism, the period of western civilization which had festered since the Enlightenment, ceased to exist. From the Latin 'modo', meaning 'just now', and spanning several eras in human existence, including the Gothic and Renaissance period, Appignanesi states: 'Modernism in the infrastructural productive sense, begins in the 1890s and 1900s' (Appignanesi 1995:11), a period which experienced mass technological change as a result of the Industrial Revolution. The invention of the telegraph in 1837 meant that global communication between human beings could be instantaneous; the increased usage and development of communicative technology in the post-industrial age of the twentieth century resulting in '[...] the tearing down of all spatial barriers' (Harvey 1989:205). As virtuosity thrived in a modern culture, documented throughout *Virtuosity and the Human Condition*; the birth of print culture resulting in the commodification of sheet music, the growing status of the 'author' of a text – alongside the rise of the bourgeois individual; the overarching illusions are broken down in a postmodern landscape. Metanarratives are less persuasive and the romantic hero is deconstructed; mythologies remain just that and are swept away as we lament its passing.

Postmodernism is in a perpetual state of change and adaptation – a process that is liberatory; '[...] symptomatic of our escape from the claustrophobic embrace of fixed systems belief' (Barry 2009:81). It combines and recombines – as I noted in the introduction to the study, '[...] human creativity is a process of variation and recombination' (Blackmore 1999:15), we are a culture that replicates – a natural trait that can be traced back to infancy. In infancy, we discover ourselves through reflection; the mirror image giving the young child '[...] a false persuasion of Self'- the mis-recognition and mis-interpretation resulting in the condition of an '[...] ideal ego for the rest of our lives' (Appignanesi 1995:90). This theory is derived from the psychoanalytical work of Jacques Lacan in the 1940s, in which he states that we are confined to this world of mirrors as 'Signifiers' (Lacan 2001:502-509), which in turn distort our interpretation of how we see others; as such it can be argued that we live vicariously through those that are held in high esteem in the arts - those who take risks and may be considered a genius or an auteur – someone who is a manifestation of all the variations of the ego. Metamodernism can thus be understood as a process that is striving to return to the spiritual enlightenment of a bygone era; a return to childhood naiveté in order to escape the nihilism of postmodern existence.

According to some theorists, metamodernism is already prevalent in a number of artforms – James MacDowall notes that the 'quirky cinema' of directors such as Wes Anderson and Michel Gondry can be seen as an attempt to restore a childhood naiveté to the audience – a contrast to the cynical, postmodern cinema of the 1990s (MacDowall 2010). Nevertheless, the return to childhood innocence is not possible, according to Moy:

> As so much adult time and energy seems to me to be an attempt to return to the mythical state of childhood jouissance [...] I am convinced that we have, collectively, lost this facility via the narrative radio form. (Moy 2000:55)

Returning to the ideology of metamodernism and how virtuosity can operate under its cultural formation, it is interesting to note the etymology of the term 'meta' – a derivation from Plato's 'metaxy'- a term used to describe two poles of human existence; the real and the transcendent, the substantial and the metaphysical – 'with', 'between' and 'beyond' (Rossbach 1999; Vermeulen and Van den Akken 2010:2). With this impression, it could be stated that improvisation, in its '[...] willingness to be open to the sounds produced by others' (Meelberg 2012) is a demonstration of how virtuosity can exist in a metamodern society. The implementation of sound in an improvised environment has long been considered a virtuoso trait; 'Improvisation was an intrinsic part of the euroclassical tradition. Bach, Handel, Mozart and Beethoven were not only famous composers but also improvisers' (Tagg 2012:96). Beethoven's improvisational skill was so well documented, one of Europe's most renowned and refined pianists Daniel Steibelt, was humiliated when he competed against him in an improvisation contest, vowing to never return to Vienna for as long as Beethoven lived there (Suchet 2014), Meelberg continues:

> It is an oscillation between two opposing poles [...] It is impossible to unite these two stances, but musicians sincerely try to do so anyway, by entering into a state of self-deceit during the performance. (ibid)

Improvisation, is thus a practice that works 'with', 'between' and 'beyond' the existence that it operates – here the importance of the body is demonstrated once more of how the human element still crucial to producing virtuous work. The shamanic displays of power and importance of liveness and the body suggest that metamodernism – like virtuosity, is egalitarian in its rationing of visual and auditory senses, signifying a potential rebalance in the sensory organ spectrum. The authenticity of the supposed battle between the senses is questionable, regardless of the emergence of the metamodernism; particularly when one considers how closely linked they are as to be inseparable. I digress, the combination of sound and vision offers more to us together than apart.

> Musically speaking, the sender musician throws his hypergesture [a complex combination of physical and musical gestures] to the sender's hypergesture. What does this mean? It means that the sender's gestural surface is projected to the receiver's one. (Mazzola and Cherlin 2009:94)

The synchronisation of sound and movement is one again seen as vital; hereby entering the realms of gender and sexuality, masculinity and pleasure. Laura Marks states that the relationship between improvising musicians can even be considered erotic:

> [...] the ability to move between control and relinquishing, between being giver and receiver. It's the ability to have your sense of self, your self-control, taken away and restored – and to do the same for another person. [...] [It is the ability] to trust someone or something to take you through this process; and to be trusted to do the same for others. (Marks 2002: xvi)

Nevertheless, metamodernism is not the only paradigm to be offered to us beyond postmodernism. In 2006, Alan Kirby proclaimed 'pseudo-modernism' – although he defined it as '[...] no more than a technology motivated shift to the cultural centre of something which has always existed' (Kirby 2006). The idea of the image as the signifier; the importance of signs and symbols, is represented in communication – Kirby denotes how someone would read in postmodernism, whereas 'One phones, clicks, presses, surfs chooses, moves, downloads' (ibid) in a paradigm beyond postmodernity.

While it is clear that the internet has changed the way we live, it could be argued that it has also changed the cultural paradigm, unbeknownst to academics and scholars who still maintain we live in a bourgeois, postmodern society. From the research gathered; evidence of metamodernism in artworks such as film and residing in musical improvisation – an oscillation between the ideals of the modern and the postmodern are possible. Despite the deconstruction of 'Grand Narratives', the fragmentation and self-reflexivity of postmodern culture may be coming to an end.

Conclusion

An honourable term, at the epicentre of artworks through the history of human excellence, I feel virtuosity is deserving of our attention. Nevertheless, as I made clear from the introduction of the study, I set out to emphasise how a musical construct – the mythologisation and validation of the virtuoso musician – is archaic; it is an outdated model due to the subsequent implementation of technology and the acceleration of electronic development in the postmodern age. I sought to deconstruct the archetypal metanarrative of the anthropocentric, omnipotent figure; entrenched in nineteenth century epistemes, in the hope of demonstrating how there is still a role for a genius or virtuoso musician in a society that may be shifting towards a new paradigm.

As stated in the Methodology section of this study, there were a number of questions posed that I hoped to answer through conducting thorough researching. I questioned whether there was still a position in contemporary society that the virtuoso musician can occupy; from the research gathered in Section Two, it became clear that in a postmodern society, the virtuoso can still occupy a reasonable level of control over the creative production of popular music as technology, for the moment, still requires human incorporation.

Despite the deconstruction of 'Grand Narratives', the fragmentation and self-reflexivity of postmodern culture may be coming to an end. Section Three: *Virtuosity and The Death of Postmodernism* attempted to come up with some answers, positioning the role that virtuosity would take in what is essentially fertile ground. However, as it is a recent development in academic theory, further research is needed on the encroaching paradigm that is metamodernism. I hope contemporary theorists will analyse my own research in the subject and make a greater contribution to academic scholarship, in what is a much under-represented field.

A further task for future study will be an attempt to answer the question as to why some people are more inclined to prodigious talents, challenging Gladwell's ten thousand hour practice theory. The repetition and robotic nature of practicing for so long, the virtuoso would be no different to the machinery which some question has marginalised them in a postmodern epoch- however, this is beyond the remit of my study.

The fascination of reflection; self-reflection and the vicarious observations of those we apportion prestige and status, is evident throughout this study. The self-portraiture of the nineteenth century offered a representation of the artist's inner desire for authorial status and acclaim – the importance of performance in both a modern and potential metamodern culture emphasised the hypostudy of Section Two – in which I stated the eye had taken over the ear as the dominant sensory organ. Although I cannot claim originality for this discussion, I hope the incorporation of this within my own research of virtuosity will make a small contribution to academic scholarship.

The idea of reflection and self-containment also links with what I call an 'awakening' of the sense through being in the presence of a virtuoso performance; a phenomena I still feel is possible, as the improvisation section of Section Three indicates. This awakening is comparable to birth, in the sense that to witness virtuosity is to be fully awakened into the potential of humanity. In utero, sound – a panoramic sensory organ, acts as an emissary between the ephemeral world of the mother's womb and the outside world. Through the birthing process, we are awakened to the possibility of the fully realised synchronisation of the senses. To witness virtuosity is to vicariously transcend into the metaphysical – reborn into the jouissance of childhood naiveté.

Finally, to question the feasibility of a return to romanticism:

> The only cure for postmodernism is the incurable illness of romanticism. (Appignanesi 1995:173)

Thus, any future that restates Romanticism will mark an inevitable future in which virtuosity can manifest.

Bibliography

Abrams, M. H (1953). 'The Mirror and the Lamp: Romantic Theory and the Critical Condition.' In. *Theories of Authorship.* edited by John Caughie. Reprint (1986). London: Routledge.

Adorno, T.W (2004). *Aesthetic Theory.* Reprint. ed. London: Continuum International Publishing Group.

Appignanesi, R. (1995). *Postmodernism For Beginners.*UK: Icon Books Ltd.

Back To The Future (1985). [film]. Directed by Robert Zemeckis. USA. Universal Pictures (116 mins)

Ballard, J. G (1973). *Crash.* UK. Jonathan Cape Ltd.

Barry, Peter. 2009. *Beginning Theory: An introduction to literary and cultural theory.* 3rd ed. Manchester and New York: Manchester University Press.

Baudrillard, J (1994). *Simulacra & Simulation.* Reprint ed. USA: University of Michigan.

Berger, J (1972). *The Ways of Seeing.* 1st ed. London: Penguin Publishing

Blackmore, S (1999). *The Meme Machine.* UK: Oxford University Press

Carlyle, T (1827). 'The State of German Literature.' In *Theories of Authorship,* edited by John Caughie. Reprint (1986). Routledge: London.

Davies, S (1985). *Hammer of the Gods: Led Zeppelin Unauthorized.* London: Pan Books.

Dempsey, J. (2004) 'Adaptation: Beyond Postmodern.' Cinema Review [online] http://cinema-review.com/films/000006/ Accessed 2nd March 2014.

Dutton, D. (2009). *'The' Art Instinct: Beauty, Pleasure, and Human Evolution.* 1st ed. New York: Oxford University Press.

Eisenberg, E. (2005). *The Recording Angel: Music, Records and Culture From Aristotle To Zappa.* Reprint. 2nd ed. USA: Yale University Press.

Eisler, H and Adorno,T.W (1947). 'The Politics of Hearing'. In *Audio Cultures: Readings in Modern Music.,* edited by C. Cox and D. Warner, 73-75 (2004). Continuum.

Eno, B (1983). 'The Studio as Compositional Tool.' In *Audio Cultures: Readings in Modern Music.*, edited by C. Cox and D. Warner, 127-130 (2004). Continuum.

Foucault, M (1964). *Madness and Civilization: A History of Insanity in the Age of Reason.* New York: Vintage Books.

Gladwell, M (2008). *Outliers: The Story of Success.* UK: Penguin.

Harvey, D (1989). *The Condition of Postmodernity: An Enquiry into the Origins of Cultural Change.* Cambridge: Blackwell Publishers.

Hershman, D. J and Lieb, J (1988). *The Key To Genius: Manic Depression and The Creative Life.* Buffalo: Prometheus Books.

Howard, V.A (2008). *Charm and Speed: Virtuosity in the Performing Arts.* 1st ed. USA. Peter Lang Publishing.

It Might Get Loud. (2008). Documentary Directed by David Guggenheim. Austin, Texas: Thomas Tull Production Company.

Jones, R (2013). 'Neo-Romantacism.' [online] http://metaxy-art.com/metaxy-and-new-romanticism/ Accessed 6th April 2014.

Kirby, A (2006). The Death of Postmodernism and Beyond. http://philosophynow.org/issues/58/The_Death_of_Postmodernism_And_Beyond Accessed 3rd March 2014.

Lacan, J (2001). *Ecrits: A Selection.* New Edition. UK: Routledge.

Lake, C. (2003). *Equality and Responsibility.* 1st ed. New York. Oxford University Press.

MacDowall, J. (2010). 'Notes on Quirky Cinema.' *Movie: A Journal of Film* Criticism [online] http://www2.warwick.ac.uk/fac/arts/film/movie/contents/notes_on_quirky.pdf. Accessed 7 April 2014.

Magritte, R (1964). *The Son of Man.* [Painting]. Private Collection.

Magritte, R and Torczyner, H (1977). *Magritte: Ideas and Images.* Illustrated ed. University of Michigan: H.N. Abrams.

Marks, L (2002). *Touch: Sensuous Theory and Multisensory Media.* Minneapolis: University of Minnesota Press.

McLuhan, M (1964). *Understanding Media: The Extensions of Man.* Canada: McGraw-Hill.

Meelberg, V (2012). 'Playing Touchy-Feely' http://www.metamodernism.com/2012/09/25/playing-touchy-feely-musical-improvisation-as-metamodern-performance/ Accessed 11th February 2014.

Mazzola, G and Cherlin, P.B (2009). *Flow, Gesture, and Spaces in Free Jazz: Towards a Theory of Collaboration.* Berlin: Springer.

Monteiro, F (2007) Virtuosity: Some (quasi-phenomenological) thoughts. *International Symposium on Performance Science.* [online]. P315-320. Available at <http://www.legacyweb.rcm.ac.uk/cache/fl0020256.pdf> Accessed 12th February 2014.

Montouri, A and Purser, R.E (1995). 'Deconstructing the Lone Genius Myth: Toward a Contextual View of Creativity'. *Journal of Humanistic Psychology.* Vol.35, No.3: 69-112.

Moy, R (2000). *An Analysis of the Position of Sound Ratio in Contemporary Society.* USA: The Edwin Meller Press.

Nietzsche, F (1974). *Thus Spoke Zarathustra* (translated by Hollingdale, R. J) USA: Penguin Classics.

O'Pray, M (1995). 'Eisenstein and Stokes on Disney: Film Animation and Omnipotence.' In Pilling, J. Ed. (1997) *A Reader In Animations Studies*, 195-201. Sydney: John Libbey.

Rossbach, S (1999). *Gnostic Wars: The Cold War in the Context of a History of Western Spirituality.* Scotland: Edinburgh University Press.

Schaeffer, P (1966). 'Acousmatics.' In Cox, C and Warner, D. Eds. (2004) *Audio Cultures: Readings in Modern Music*, 76-81. Continuum.

Schafer, R.M (1973). 'The Music of the Environment'. In Cox, C and Warner, D. Eds. (2004) *Audio Cultures: Readings in Modern Music*, 29-39. Continuum.

Schafer, R.M (1977). *The Tuning of the World.*Bancroft, Ontoraio: Arcana Editions.

Schechner, Richard (2002). *Performance Studies: An Introduction.* Ed.reprint. London: Routledge.

Schumann, R. (1965). *Schumann on Music: A Selection Of His Writings.* 1st ed. Dover: Dover Publishing.

Simonton,D. K (2005). 'Are Genius and Madness Related? Contemporary answers to an ancient question.' *Psychiatric Times*, Vol 22.No.7.

Suchet, J (2014). 'Daniel Steibelt (1765-1823): Humiliated by Beethven.' Available at http://www.classicfm.com/composers/beethoven/guides/daniel-steibelt/ Accessed 20th April 2014.

Tagg, P (2012). *Music's Meanings: A Modern Musicology For Non-Musos.* UK: The Mass Media Scholar's Press (MMMSP).

Takiguchi, N (1990). 'Liminal Experiences of Miyako Shamans: Reading a Shaman's Diary. *Asian Folklore Studies.* Nanzan University. Vol, 49: 1-39.

Toynbee, Jason (2000). *Making Popular Music: Musicians, Creativity and Institutions.* London: Arnold.

Vermeulen, T and Van den Akken, R (2010). 'Notes on Metamodernism.' *Journal of Aesthetics and Culture.* Vol.2:1-14.

Weatherly, Joan. (1986). 'Yeats, The Tarot & T he Fool.' *College Literature.* Vol. 13 No. 1:112-121.

Weiss, P. and Taruskin, R. (2007). *Music In The Western World: A History In Documents.* 2nd ed. California: Wadsworth Publishing.

Music Sources

Chuck Berry (1959) 'Johnny B. Goode.' Chess Records

David Bowie (1971) *Hunky Dory.* RCA

David Bowie (1972) *The Rise and Fall of Ziggy Stardust and the Spiders from Mars.*RCA

Jimi Hendrix (1970) *Machine Gun.* Polydor

U2 (1987) *Where The Streets Have No Name.* Island